DATE DUE			

THE GOLDEN HORDES

Louis Turner and John Ash

THE GOLDEN HORDES

International Tourism and the Pleasure Periphery

ST. MARTIN'S PRESS   NEW YORK

Copyright © 1976 by Louis Turner and John Ash
All rights reserved. For information, write:
St. Martin's Press, Inc., 175 Fifth Ave.,
New York, N.Y. 10010.
Manufactured in the United States of America
Library of Congress Catalog Card Number: 76-25498
ISBN — 312-33740-X
Library of Congress Cataloging in Publication Data

Turner, Louis, 1942-
    The golden hordes.

    Bibliography: p.
    Includes index.
    1. Tourist trade.   2. Travelers.   I. Ash, John,
joint author.   II. Title.
G155.A1T87   1976   301.5′7   76-25498

Contents

Illustrations

Acknowledgements

In the preparation of a book like this, we have obviously been helped by people in a number of different ways. Amongst the following are people who have helped us by listening, editing, typing, indexing, illustrating, informing, humouring, encouraging or actively seeking facts on our behalf. We are grateful for your help and hope you enjoy the end-product.

Richard Arthur, Mike Ashfield, Norman Brunskill, A. J. Burkart, Jean and Win Carr, Stephen Danos, Rigas Doganis, Laurent Enckel, Marilyn Evans, Mike Fliderbaum, Jutta Greaves, Simon Green, Margaret Greenhaulgh, John Harounoff, the Haslemere Group, Herb Hiller, Shirley Hobson, Richard Holland, Jafar Jafari, Cliff Jones, Len Koven, Alex Latham, Harry Matthews, Professor Medlik, Paul Neville, Elfreda Powell, Patrick Rivers, Patsy Robinson, Henri-Jacques Ruff, Michael Sissons, Reinhild Traitler, Lynette Turner, Nabiha Watson, Moll Balfe, Robin Hanbury-Tenison, Trevor Blackwell.

We should also like to thank Hart-Davis, Macgibbon for their kind permission to quote from Anthony Haden-Guest's *Down the Programmed Rabbit Hole* (1972).

Introduction

Names like Waikiki, Nice, Majorca, Acapulco, Bali and Marrakech roll across the page evoking images of sun, pleasure and escape. In a world dominated by bureaucracies and machines, we are offered these destinations as retreats to a childlike world in which the sun always shines, and we can gratify all our desires.

Tourism is no trivial phenomenon. It is a visible result of the fourth of the great waves of technology which have changed the social geography of the world since 1800. First the railways opened up the continents, carrying the food and materials which made possible the great nineteenth-century industrial cities. Then came steamships which served as the sinews allowing the Empire builders to stretch across the globe to take what they wanted from their colonies. The car started to decentralise nations by sapping the vitality of the cities through the development of extended suburbs. Finally we have the aeroplane which, when linked with rising affluence, has led to a whole new tribe – the Mass Tourists. The barbarians of our Age of Leisure. The Golden Horde.

It is perfectly legitimate to compare tourists with barbarian tribes. Both involve the mass migration of peoples who collide with cultures far removed from their own. There is, however, one major difference. The old Golden Horde (a Tatar Empire led by Genghis Khan's successors) was a nomadic, non-monetary people which threatened the settled urban civilisations of Europe. Today the pattern is reversed. Tourists come from the industrialised centres but, this time, it is they who are fanning out through the world, swamping apparently less dynamic societies, including the few pre-industrial ones which still remain. In the past, it was the great commercial centres of the world like Constantinople and Vienna which were threatened. Today, it is the Nomads of Affluence, coming from the new Constantinoples – cities like New York, London, Hamburg or Tokyo – who are creating a newly dependent, social and geographic realm: The Pleasure Periphery.

This periphery has a number of dimensions, but is best conceived geographically as the tourist belt which surrounds the great industrialised zones of the world. Normally it lies some two to four hours' flying distance from the big urban centres; sometimes to the west and east, but generally toward the equator and the sun.

Thus the North American periphery includes Caribbean playgrounds like Nassau, San Juan, Montego Bay and Port-au-Prince; Mexican resorts like Acapulco, Tijuana and Mexicali; then, far out in the Pacific, those specks in the ocean, the Hawaiian Islands. North Europeans make primarily for the Mediterranean searching for older resorts like Monte Carlo, Nice and Cannes on the Riviera; newer destinations like Palma, Torremolinos and Benidorm in Spain; or historic North Italian cities like Venice and Florence. The Japanese are still too young an industrialised power (and too geographically isolated) to have created such a well-defined periphery in the Far East but, even here, they are enthusiastically roving west toward Hawaii, and south toward the Philippines, Taiwan, Hong Kong, Indonesia's Bali and Thailand's Bangkok.

These Pleasure Peripheries are never static, possessing a dynamism of their own, which depends on the extension of the range of planes, and the increase of leisure and affluence in general. The pioneer tourists are ever moving outward looking for new destinations which have not yet been swamped by mass tourism. Those who went to Honolulu five years ago, fly further into the Pacific to Tahiti or Fiji. Those who are tired of the crowds in Majorca now go to Greece, North Africa or the Indian Ocean. Japanese who were once satisfied with Hong Kong now turn up in Europe. So, while each individual periphery is expanding independently, they are now, for the first time, starting to merge into one giant, global Pleasure Periphery, where the rich of the world relax and intermingle.

The force behind this phenomenon is tourism, one of those great twentieth-century paradoxes – the Leisure Industries. As such, it is large. In 1974, there were approximately 209 million international tourists, which is roughly equivalent to the entire population of the United States, or four times the population of France. Between them, they spent some $29 billion,* which is about 6 per cent of total world trade. Until the crisis of October 1973 both the numbers of tourists and the amount they spent had been rising at around 10 per cent per annum for the last two decades. The most notable success story has been Spain which recieved 7.4 million tourists in 1961, against 34.6 million in 1973, and before the energy crisis the authorities were preparing for some 50 million by the end of the decade. Since the

* Billion means 'thousand million' throughout.

Spanish population is a mere 34 million, some social impact is inevitable.[1]

Despite these kind of numbers, international tourism is still a minority activity. In large parts of the world, it is rare for people to have holidays away from home, let alone to travel abroad. Ninety-five per cent of the world's population did not cross an international border in 1971, and only 1 per cent have ever flown in a plane. Even within the richest nations, foreign holidays are still an exception – only 15 per cent of the British planned a foreign holiday in 1973; while only 5 per cent of the United States' population has passports, and only 3·2 per cent left the North American continent in 1972. In poorer parts of the world, the proportions are still lower. For instance, 85 per cent of the Portuguese population still has no holiday of any sort; neither do 75 per cent of the lowest income groups in Madrid; only 3 per cent of the Madrileños take foreign holidays, despite the fact that Spain itself is the prime tourist destination of the world. It is little wonder, then, that industry experts believe that tourism's growth potential is almost limitless.[2]

This élite can be relatively closely defined by age, income and social status. The younger generation tends to travel somewhat more than its elders; people in managerial and professional jobs tend to be internationally mobile; so do people whose jobs give them long paid holidays. The key factor, however, is obviously income. There seems to be a minimum income below which any form of holiday is out of the question. Author George Young cites evidence suggesting the threshold comes for a British family when it earns around £1,200 per annum; in the USA this will be around $10,000. He further suggests that for every £1 in extra income, tourist expenditure will rise somewhere between £1·5 and £1·9, though the French figure seems to be £3·2.[3]

What we are in fact seeing is the transformation of 'Play' into one of the stronger roles in our culture. This has not always been the case. In the past leisure has been seen primarily as 'time remaining at one's disposal after work'.[4] Even into the 1950s, the majority of people still saw leisure as 'time', rather than as an 'activity'. The general feeling thus still reflected the Protestant Ethic, which placed non-work activities in a limbo by conferring all its legitimacy on work.

Gradually, rising affluence and greater time away from work have changed this situation and led to an increase in active leisure-time pursuits. The passive spectators of urbanised society are using their greater mobility to take up activities which the large cities make difficult, like fishing, sports, mountain climbing or, at the lower level of extra activity, getting into their cars and going sightseeing. Purely passive activities like watching television are considered somewhat demeaning. Active pursuits are what one is increasingly judged by. We are starting to be judged on our leisure persona, rather than our work role.

Tourism thus works at two levels. At a deep level, a foreign holiday is an institution giving meaning to non-work; it is something positive and understandable one can do with one's spare time. It also gives an impression of activity, even if one spends it supine on some beach. Through the sun tan, participants even gain an outward sign of their initiative.

At the same time, it is a product developed by an industry which views non-work as merely another marketing opportunity. Leisure industries like tourism ensure that workers remain motivated to stay within the system. Although people want more leisure, they work harder than they would ideally choose, to save the money necessary to allow them to spend their leisure time in sufficient style. By making leisure relatively expensive, the tourist industry helps keep the industrial machine rolling smoothly along.

The tourists themselves are not a particularly homogeneous group. There are car workers from Detroit and Coventry, hippies, intellectuals, sports enthusiasts, pilgrims, would-be permanent migrants, big-game hunters, Third World élites, and so on. The members of each of these groups have separate needs, and the unifying factor is not their motives or attitudes (which can range from the totally crass to the highly sympathetic), but the existence of a coherent industry which strives to recognise, stimulate and serve the travel needs of all of them.

Thus, we have scheduled airlines (like Pan Am, Lufthansa and Qantas), charter airlines (Laker, Donaldson, Condor), hotel chains (Hilton, Sheraton, Holiday Inn), tour operators (Neckermann, Dr Tigges, American Express, Thomsons), car hire firms (Avis, Hertz), cruise operators (P & O, Cunard, Holland America), bus companies (Greyhound, Wallace Arnold), and a host of smaller companies involved with such fringe activities as making skis, building marinas, chartering yachts, or air-freighting fresh vegetables to tourist hotels.

It is this apparently amorphous industry which has developed the Pleasure Periphery, which individual travellers were opening up in the eighteenth and nineteenth centuries. It is these firms which are reinforcing people's instinctive desire to get away from the pollution and alienation of our industrialised, urbanised societies – at the same time providing the means by which these dreams can be fulfilled.

None of this would matter much, if it were not for the response of the governments of the Pleasure Periphery. Make no mistake about it, they desperately want tourists and that precious foreign exchange. Many of them can see no other industry open to them which has anywhere near the same promise. So they go to practically any length to attract the airlines, hotel chains and tour operators. They set up Ministries of Tourism; they build airports and subsidise hotel building; they launch 'Be Nice' campaigns in which they instruct their citizens that tourists are of vital importance and must be treated as friends – not as a group of rich, idle, white voyeurs who are, in the classic complaint, 'Over rich, over sexed, and over here'.

It is this blindly enthusiastic response which makes the industry politically unhealthy. Most Third World countries have only recently gained their political independence from the old imperial powers. Yet tourism is an industry they want so badly that they are welcoming back their old masters with open arms. In so doing, they are falling into a trap. This industry admittedly has none of older industries' pollution from chimneys, mines or wells, but tourism is just as much a major economic activity. When its managers discuss potential investments, they are just as calculating as the great mining and oil companies of past decades, from whose grip many Third World countries are still trying to escape. In some more subtle way, tourism may be even more destructive.

At one level then, the international tourist industry is effectively redrawing the geography of the world; already one can see the start of a slow drift of North American and North European industry down toward the southern tourist belt, thus indicating that the industrial northern regions are now doomed to slow, inexorable decline, depopulation and eventual demise. On a second level, one can argue that the creation of the Pleasure Periphery is a step of vast political importance, fully the equal of the imperialist expansion of the nineteenth century; however, whereas the old imperialists over-ran the Third World with force, their successors use economic logic – which is far more dangerous in the long run. On a final level though, one can simply argue that international tourism is like King Midas in reverse; a device for the systematic destruction of everything that is beautiful in the world.

SECTION ONE: HISTORY

1 The Pre-history of Mass Tourism

THE EXOTIC AND THE SIMPLE

La Chair est triste hélas! et j'ai lu tous les livres.
Fuir! là-bas fuir! . . .
Je partirai! Steamer balançant ta mâture,
Lèves l'ancre pour une exotique nature!
                        Mallarmé, *Brise Marine*[1]

Tourism and touristic attitudes are closely allied to the pursuit of the 'exotic' and its obverse, the cultivation of the simple. Both are highly artificial – necessarily the products of a long-established urban culture of wide extent. In such a culture people will become interested in the 'barbarians' and 'monsters' to be found beyond the borders of what they consider to be the civilised world. What might have been terrifying and monstrous to a more archaic society will now produce a pleasurable excitement – precisely because it is outside normal experience. If the means of transporting large numbers of people, safely and cheaply, over long distances are lacking then the 'exotic' will be imported. Thousands of wild beasts were imported to die in Roman amphitheatres – the rarer and stranger the better; less dramatic examples would be the blackamoors and chinoiserie of eighteenth-century Europe, or the nineteenth-century and *fin-de-siècle* obsession with oriental and primitive *objets d'art*. This attitude requires an imperialist culture with a unified and dominant style that has been expanding aggressively – either absorbing or stamping out alien cultures. As the known world becomes more standardised sheer variety and difference become highly prized in the metropolitan centres. The 'booty brought home by the empire builders'[2] provides ample material for this enthusiasm, but the process of discovery and experimentation with alien styles can lead to their destruction. The 'exotic' forms once taken up by the metropolitan culture tend to lose their original meaning and vitality. If art, religion and the world of leisure have developed complex hybrid forms there will be a reaction against these. Those with leisure, sophistication and social advantages can afford the luxury of turning away from this complexity to some ideal of 'the simple life', 'the noble savage' or 'the Paradise Isle' of modern travel brochures. They may even attempt to act out these myths by 'playing pastoral', 'dropping out', or, if the transport technology is available, by travelling to 'get away from it all' – to attain some approximation of Eden or Arcadia for a few weeks.

UNIFORMITY AND COMPLEXITY

There is always something new from Africa.
Pliny

Thus tourism, as we understand it, is the product of a 'final phase'. It requires both large, claustrophobic cities and the means to escape from them. For this reason it is probably inaccurate to talk of Greek tourism as such before the conquests of Alexander in the fourth century BC, and the subsequent development of the Hellenistic urban system (as Sigaux does in his *History of Tourism*). The Greeks were unquestionably great travellers. Their colonies were spread between Spain and the north coast of the Black Sea, but communications from Marsilia (Marseilles) to the Bosporan colonies (the Crimea) were not for purposes of pleasure. Travel was a risky business – you were quite likely to be the victim of shipwreck, piracy or highway robbery (should there be a highway). Individuals such as Herodotus travelled widely and exhibited in their observations of foreign places typically 'sightseeing', credulous, tourist attitudes. Such travellers were exceptional, however. Small-scale pleasure tours, let alone visits to Egypt or Mesopotamia, were not customary even for the very wealthy.

There was, of course, much travel within the Greek world to oracles and festivals in the great religious centres, e.g. Eleusis, Delphi, Olympia and Epidauros. People travelled from widely scattered cities to take part in games and competitions at such centres, or to consult oracles. Inevitably facilities to cater for large influxes of visitors developed around the purely ceremonial buildings. Epidauros could even be said to foreshadow the health-resort since it centred on an *asclepeion* (a shrine for the worship of Asclepeios, the god of medicine) and was thus a place to 'take the cure'. The number of such places increased in the later Greek world and their religious significance diminished. During the archaic and classical periods, however, visits to these centres retained their sacred character, and they were in no sense attempts to escape from social realities.

Gatherings at centres of mythic and ritualistic significance reinforced the Greeks' sense of their own identity: the world outside was inhabited by 'barbarians' (in the Aristotelian definition of anyone non-Greek).

There was, in any case, no need to 'escape' from the classical cities of Greece and Asia Minor. By modern standards or even by Hellenistic and Roman standards the greatest were only splendid towns, beautifully placed in the surrounding landscape. The conquests of Alexander created a new Greek world – dominated by such expanding cosmopolitan cities as Antioch,* Alexandria† and Pergamum,‡ and ruled by semi-divine despots. Throughout the eastern Mediterranean and the Near East, Greek culture became the dominant, imperial culture. The commerce-of the East in materials, ideas and styles flowed into its metropolises. These cities, uniform in style and laid out according to geometrically regular plans, rapidly became overpopulated and prone to mob violence and political disturbances. From now on holiday habits were shaped by the urge to escape uniformity and complexity.

In the last two centuries BC some of the prerequisites for the development of tourism existed in the eastern Mediterranean; but during this period technology did not advance significantly. Practical scientific knowledge was applied largely to the construction of robotic statues and elaborate fountains, and not to the mechanics of industry or transport. Despite this travel did increase greatly in the eastern Mediterranean which was prosperous and united culturally if not politically. Merchants, mercenaries, philosophers, athletes, poets, actors, dancers and musicians moved fairly freely between Pergamum, Antioch, Alexandria, Rhodes and Seleucia. These were people whose profession or calling naturally inclined them to travel – whether to new venues or to seek new patrons, and they cannot truly be termed tourists. Travel to the ancient religious centres of Greece and Ionia continued with people now travelling from the more distant cities of the Hellenistic world – in Syria, Egypt and Mesopotamia. It is probable that such visits took on an increasingly touristic character as religious belief declined. Yet travel purely for pleasure – without strong spiritual or materialistic motivation – was still uncommon, requiring a lively spirit of adventure. The intrinsic hardships of travel,

* In Syria, Capital of the Seleucid Empire.
† In Egypt, Capital of the Ptolemaic Kingdom.
‡ In Asia Minor, Capital of the Attalid Kingdom.

combined with the continual internal warfare among the various Greek kingdoms, prevented lengthy pleasure trips from becoming an accepted mode of leisure.

In consequence the great cities developed pleasure resorts on their immediate peripheries. Antioch had Daphne, famous for its springs and its oracle of Apollo, and Alexandria had Canopus, on a branch of the Nile. Daphne's oracle lent it some trace of 'high moral tone' but the only *raison d'être* of Canopus was pleasure. Both these resorts achieved something approaching international renown and they were to have lengthy histories. Alexandria became the symbol of elegant living, and remained so for the Romans. Under the Ptolemies it reached the height of luxury and excess. Ptolemy Philadelphus, for example, staged a procession that seems to have lasted all day and cost the equivalent of five million pounds; a royal yacht contained a whole sequence of banqueting rooms, audience chambers, sleeping chambers and was surmounted by a temple of Aphrodite. Owing to the abundance of cheap Egyptian labour and the existence of a prosperous merchant class, non-creative leisure was available to a large part of the population. A canal gave easy access to the delights of Canopus, and boating parties, often complete with singers and musicians, were enormously popular. The rich would also have villas on the shore of lake Mareotis. Such escapes from the stresses and ennui of the urban life were very necessary to the Alexandrians. Their city was overcrowded and oddly claustrophobic – being wholly Greek in style – placed in an alien landscape. There was considerable racial tension between Greeks, Jews and Egyptians who each had their separate 'quarters'. As the ruling dynasty became degenerate and ineffectual these tensions broke out into riots and mob violence.

Thus, the pleasure resort becomes highly developed in a decadent situation. Hellenism had over-extended itself. There was still intense intellectual activity in science, philosophy and art – but literature, at least, was no longer cast in the 'heroic' forms of classical Athens; it was not so much cathartic as escapist. The poets of Alexandria, who were almost totally ignorant of the agricultural hinterland of Egypt, turned to idealising the lives of Greek rustics. It is only possible to idealise poverty and simplicity from the vantage point of excessive wealth and sophistication. This is escapist literature *par excellence* and as a continuing tradition it exercises an important influence on attitudes to leisure throughout the Roman period and even on the development of modern tourist attitudes.

The Roman urban system was a continuation and extension of the Hellenistic system, inheriting both its splendours and its elements of decadence. At its height Rome had a population of around one and a half million – many of them crowded together in appalling high-rise tenements. It had all the appropriate civic appurtenances (forums, thermae, circuses, etc.) and it also had such banal drawbacks as a traffic problem, some kinds of heavy vehicle being banned from the city centre. Its arts and entertainments were derived directly from the models of the Greek East – although the extravagant cruelty that became endemic to Roman entertainments was quite alien to the Greeks. The enormous resources of the Empire carried the pursuit of the exotic and the extreme to new heights: gladiatorial displays, wild beast shows, mock sea battles (with real deaths) and a whole series of bizarre and sanguinary pageants concerned with the execution of criminals and other *noxii*. Literary models were Greek, with tragedy tending towards the morbidly violent and comedy tending towards mechanical farce. Poetry was profoundly indebted to Alexandrian erotic and pastoral verse (for example, Virgil's *Georgics*). The leisure habits of the rich were based increasingly on the elegant Alexandrian models; it was customary even for the most ignorant to have Greek slaves capable of reciting the 'classics'. It follows that Roman holiday habits would closely resemble those of Alexandria, especially as the Romans had much the same motivations for escape from their metropolis.

The wealthy and the literary men would retire whenever they could from the *occupatio* of Rome to the *otium* of villas in the hills in the regions of Tibur (Tivoli), Tusculum and Praeneste. These were especially useful to public men since they were within easy reach of the city and something of a commuter system seems to have developed. The *villa rustica* might be genuinely rustic like Horace's 'dear Sabine farm' where he gloried in the virtues of the 'simple life'. Others might be highly elaborate with artificial lakes, canals, porticoes, colonnades, baths and collections of Greek statues. Hadrian's villa at Tibur was the size of a small town and incorporated special features such as a 'Canopic waterway' to remind him of his travels. Any sizeable city in the Empire, from Trier to Antioch, developed an outer ring of well-appointed villas; indeed the most substantial existing remains of Antioch are its surrounding villa resorts.

More important from our point of view is the development of a full-scale resort complex at some considerable distance from Rome (well in excess of 100 miles). This was the Campanian littoral, on the northern shore of the Bay of Naples. A string of resorts extended from Cumae through Misenum, Baiae, Puteoli to '*otiosa Neapolis*', a place so relaxed in atmosphere that even senators forsook their formal togas. Of these by far the most popular and notorious was Baiae. For the modern American poetess H.D., Baiae evoked the image of: 'some lovely perilous thing / orchids piled in a great sheath . . .', but for many contemporary Roman commentators it stood for something quite different. It is characteristic of the peripheral resorts of the Greco-Roman cities that, although they grew out of the desire to escape, to pursue a simpler life of fishing, boating, and bathing, they soon became extensions of metropolitan excess without even the restraint of civic responsibilities. Like Canopus, Baiae became a favourite target of criticism for its luxury and moral laxity. Propertius described it as 'corrupt' and feared its deleterious effects on Cynthia when she was there without him. Seneca found it so insupportable that he left after only a day, commenting that:

> Certain encounters are contrary to purity of behaviour and the wise man would do well to avoid them. Let him therefore not go to Baiae, the home of vice. Inside its walls, licence is triumphant.

He was especially horrified by *singing* boating parties (Canopus-style) and 'immoderate displays of swimming', for it was in the Campanian resorts that something closely resembling the bikini first made its appearance. Seneca, of course, was crying in the wilderness and Baiae remained popular until the fall of the Western Empire in the fifth century AD. Three centuries after him Symmachus echoed his disapproval with the words, 'Indulgence begins at Formae'. The last Emperor of the West, Romulus Augustulus, ended his days as a pensioner of the barbarian Odoacer in a decaying Campanian villa.

The development of the Campanian littoral bears a striking resemblance to the development of the French Riviera as a summer resort in our century. Like the Riviera resorts Baiae began as a winter resort. It was not until Augustus improved the unhealthy condition of the nearby Avernine and Lucrine lakes that it was frequented in summer. After this the resort was busy throughout the year and began to expand enormously; the 'boom' was given a further boost by the building of the Via Domitiana which connected it to the Via Appia and thence directly to Rome. The smartest season was the spring, probably because travel over such a distance in the hottest months was still extremely uncomfortable, even with imperial road improvement. Those who could afford it would buy a series of *diversoria* (resting places) along the roads from Rome to Baiae. Any farmer with land adjacent to the Via Appia or the Via Domitiana could profit by opening an inn or *taberna*, but these never gained respectable status, and it was preferable to spend the night at your own *diversorium* or at the villa of a friend. The very rich might well own several Campanian villas. These would be replete with thermae, peristyles, nymphaeums and even heated swimming pools. Elaborate gardens and groves were planted, often at enormous expense, since the coast was arid and rocky. The real connoisseurs would water the roots of their cypresses and plane trees with wine; the plane tree, appropriately enough, being the symbol of uncreative leisure. An extraordinary fixation with fishponds developed among villa owners. Freshwater fish were utterly unfashionable and vast expense and ingenuity was devoted to the creation of fishponds fed by sea water. There are even records of unsatisfactory slaves being fed to their owners' lampreys and more exotically carnivorous fish. It was in such surroundings that the Romans gave the idea of 'conspicuous consumption' its most literal expression, having the delicacies of their tables brought halfway across the world and then neglecting to digest them.

The entire coastline from Cumae to Naples became so built up that villas were built out over the sea; these of course had the added advantage of enabling you to fish without getting out of bed. In these conditions property values rocketed. The rich indulged in speculation and made handsome profits from letting their land holdings to tenants. Martial complained in verse of the expense of holidaying in Baiae:

> Oh give me back the gloomy baths of yore;
> Why bathe in luxury and sup no more.

Although the Campanian resort complex must have maintained higher aesthetic standards than its modern equivalents, not everything was in the best of 'classical' taste. Petronius' description of Trimalchio's vulgar opulence in *The Satyricon* is undoubtedly based closely on existing examples. It should be remembered also that many of the works of art adorning the villas of the Roman aristocracy and *nouveaux riches* derived from the ruthless artistic pillaging of the Greek East.

Horace's criticisms of Baiae are rather more acute than Seneca's moral pomposities and show a genuine awareness of some of the harmful consequences of intensive resort development:

> 'No bay in the world outshines lovely Baiae.' If so the rich man has said, lake and sea suffer from the eager owner's fancy. . . .[3]

He was well aware that the arrival of the rich in an area did not necessarily bring benefit to all. In his *Second Book of Odes* he rebukes the rich man whose only thought is to extend the magnificence of his Baian villa; not only does he trespass on the sea, but he invades his tenants' lands without a thought for their well-being: 'Man and wife are driven forth bearing in their arms their household gods and ragged children. . . .' This is a situation which, sadly, we will meet again in the development of the modern Pleasure Periphery. Horace's comments reduce the credibility of Statius' eulogy of a similar villa:

> What was that site, that land before it had the fortune to fall into your hands. . . . The owner has established his dominion. He has shaped and conquered the rocks and the land has submitted gladly.

We may reasonably doubt the 'glad submission' of the land. The peculiar vices of pleasure resort development are not found again, on a comparable scale, until this century and it is, perhaps, sobering to think that they first appeared during what is generally accepted as *the* classic era of decadence. Finally, the modernity of the Campanian Riviera is highlighted by the discovery at Puteoli of engraved pieces of glass portraying its sea-front; these must have been sold to Roman holiday-makers as souvenirs.

If the Campanian littoral foreshadows modern Riviera development Rome also had something resembling the European Grand Tour of the sixteenth to eighteenth centuries, that is, a cultural tourism devoted largely to visiting places of historical and literary interest. Travel was considered an essential part of a young man's education and those who could afford it commonly sent their sons to Athens or Rhodes, both eminent academic centres. Although Horace's father was far from wealthy he sent his son to Athens. There was also a University of Marsilia but for obvious reasons the West was considered less educative than the East. The Greek cities were the source of civilisation and also of social refinement. Great snob value was attached to a good knowledge of the Greek language and its literature. For themselves the Greeks never ceased to consider Latin barbarous.

A student with wealthy parents, studying at Athens or Rhodes, would have ample opportunity to see Greece and Asia Minor. Athens itself was the object of great veneration and respect and Rhodes, quite apart from its academic qualifications, had a unique tourist attraction in the shape of its fallen colossus. In mainland Greece the principal sights apart from Athens were, predictably, Epidauros, Delphi and Olympia, where the tourist would hire a *periegetes* or guide. Among the Aegean islands Chios, Lesbos and Samos were considered particularly worthy of visiting. Beyond them lay Iona and Aeolia (Greek Asia Minor) with their delightful climate and landscape and their profusion of historic cities – Ephesus, Sardis, Smyrna, Colophon, Miletus, Pergamum. All these cities had some particular distinction and Iona, with Lesbos, was the birthplace of Greek lyric poetry. Here Sappho, Alcaeus and Anacreon had lived and before them Homer. All Romans with any pretensions to culture dreamt of visiting these places at least once.

Egypt had even more to offer. Alexandria was in regular communication with Rome by sea, the voyage taking some twelve days. It was still considered the 'crown of cities' and it remained a great centre of learning. It also had spectacular tourist sights, notably the Pharos (a great lighthouse that was numbered among the Seven Wonders of the World), the tomb of Alexander the Great and the massive temple complex known as the Serapeum. Nearby were the delights of Canopus. From here the tourist would sail up the Nile to Memphis, the traditional capital of Lower Egypt. Here the sacred bull of Apis was brought out of its sanctuary to frisk around an open court, according to Strabo, 'particularly for the benefit of tourists'. Close at hand were the pyramids, then as now the subject of endless speculation. In Upper Egypt the tourist would visit Thebes where he could see the temples of Karnak and Luxor. The principal object of his visit, however, would be the Colossus of Memnon, in fact one of the two statues of Amenophis III and the only remaining part of his funerary temple. The colossus constituted the best kind of tourist attraction since it 'performed' reliably. Each morning the fractured statue would emit a 'melodious twang', supposedly to greet the dawn, a rare example of man and nature combining to create a touristic pseudo-event. The feet and legs of the statue are covered with antique tourist graffiti, 45 in Latin and 63 in Greek. Some of these are simple 'wish you were here' inscriptions but others are more ambitious, for example, four execrable verse compositions in Aeolian Greek executed by Balbilla, a lady-in-waiting to the Empress Sabina. Another is signed somewhat optimistically, 'Done by Asclepiodotus, poet and imperial procurator'.[4]

These graffiti are revealing. They were written largely by provincial administrators or soldiers on leave, in other words people whose professions brought them close to the sights. Some emperors, notably Hadrian, travelled widely and took every opportunity to see the sights, but this was only a secondary function of their travelling, the principal reason would be political or administrative. The Younger Pliny wrote that 'works of art or nature motivate men to travel and cause them to visit such places as Greece, Asia Minor and Egypt', but it was not customary for individuals to make a complete circuit of these places. They visited them when the opportunity arose, in the intervals of education, commerce, military and administrative service. A Roman Grand Tour of the eastern Mediterranean would have constituted a much more daunting prospect than the conventionalised English eighteenth-century trip to Italy via France. The 'Pax Romana' had made travel much easier but it had not entirely eliminated piracy or brigandage. The road system was designed chiefly to assist army movements and still left much to be desired from the tourist's point of view.

The man who travelled widely, purely for the purposes of seeing and learning, was rare, although such did exist. Plutarch, for example, cites a certain Cleombrotus of Lacedaemonia. Strabo travelled in something of the same spirit as Herodotus. He claimed to have travelled from the Euxine to Ethiopia and from Armenia to Etruria, and did so to study geography, social customs and antiquities. Extensive touring was considered not quite respectable; both Horace and Seneca viewed travelling abroad as a symptom of the restlessness of the age.[5] According to Seneca, always a good touchstone of conservative opinion:

Men travelled widely to different sorts of places seeking different distractions because they are fickle, tired of soft living, and always seek after something which eludes them.

2 The Grand Tour

The idea of loot is pretty fundamental to the tourist experience . . .
Mary McCarthy, *Birds of America*

Grand tourism has its origins in the relationship of *parvenu* to aristocrat. Its development follows a shift in the focus of culture and of
economic and political power. The wealthy and educated, of states
whose position of dominance in the world is comparatively new, visit
countries that have passed their peak of prestige and creativity but
are still venerated for historic and cultural reasons. Thus Romans
visited Greece and the eastern Mediterranean; the English, from the
sixteenth century onwards, visited Italy; and in this century Americans 'do' Europe. The new world pays its respects to the old.

The relationship is ambiguous since the rise of the new world is
directly or indirectly dependent on the decline of the old world. The
grand tourist respects the learning, antiquities and social refinements
of the old world. He is also usually confident of the superior virtues
of the more efficient and vigorous ways of his home country. He
respects the natives of the old world but also despises them for their
supposed 'decadence', their 'effeminacy' of manners and excessive
subtlety. Thus the Romans, who were so profoundly indebted to the
superior culture of the Hellenistic east, sometimes regarded the
Greeks as mere wily, degenerate orientals, capable of any kind of
treachery and perfidy.

If the Greeks were demoralised this was, to a large extent, the
direct result of Roman policies. The gradual Roman encroachment
on the eastern Mediterranean in the last two centuries BC progressively deprived the Greeks of effectual political power and came near
to destroying the thriving Hellenistic economy. The rich provinces of
Asia Minor were bled by extortionate taxation and the vast art
treasures of such cities as Pergamum and Ephesus treated as booty.
Whole areas were seriously depopulated to meet the growing Roman
demand for slave labour. But the single most notorious atrocity
committed by the Romans against the Greeks was the brutal destruction of Corinth in 146 BC. During the course of the sack the Romans
were careful to spare all outstanding works of art that could be

moved. These were collected, packed and shipped back to Rome.
Such acts, along with the earlier Roman conquest of Greek Italy,
prepared the ground for Roman cultural tourism. From its beginnings
tourism is a kind of secondary invasion, secondary to outright
military invasion or economic penetration.

The reappearance of tourism in Europe follows the Italian Renaissance and the development of a full-scale urban system. The rise of
the Italian city states in the later Middle Ages again involves an
ambiguous relationship with the Greek East, now ruled by the
Byzantine Empire, the direct descendant of the eastern Roman
Empire. The civilisation of Venice was, to begin with, entirely
Byzantine, yet its rise depended on ruthless economic and political
exploitation of the Empire's increasing weakness. By the end of the
fifteenth century Italy itself became the object of attentions that were
as much predatory as appreciative. At this time Italy was Europe's
economic and cultural leader, but was totally disunited politically.
It was therefore an easy prey, 'an artichoke to be eaten leaf by leaf',
or in V. H. H. Green's words, 'the richest country in Europe, the most
rewarding to loot and the easiest on which to park an army'. The
conflicting ambitions of France, the Holy Roman Empire and Spain
met on its soil. Wars were fought on Italian soil irrespective of Italian
interests. Italy's political humiliation was such that Machiavelli
ended his treatise *The Prince* with an impassioned plea for a national
leader to rid the land of 'barbarian tyranny'.

These wars played an important part in the dissemination of the
Renaissance and the subsequent development of the Grand Tour.
Although the Italian expeditions of the French kings Charles VIII
and Francis I (in 1494 and 1515 respectively) were expensive failures
they aroused in the monarchs a passion for things Italian. The expeditions 'showed the French the elegant and luxurious life of the
Italian nobility and middle class. They saw a civilisation outstanding
for the brilliance of its social life, its taste for luxury, its passion for
pleasure and its cult of beauty.'[1] While in Naples Charles VIII
collected statues, jewels, painters, sculptors, goldsmiths and silver-
smiths, musicians and carpenters. Francis I became the patron of
Leonardo da Vinci, Benvenuto Cellini and Andrea del Sarto. Italian
craftsmen were set to work on the châteaux of Blois, Amboise,
Chenonceaux and Fontainebleau. Inspired by the Italianate stucco
decorations of Fontainebleau young French noblemen began to visit
Italy in large numbers. The poets Joachim du Bellay, Jean Lemaire

des Belges and Jean Marot all visited Rome; du Bellay became the
chief advocate of the adoption of classical forms in French poetry.
Flemish and German painters had also begun to visit Venice,
notably Dürer, Massys, Mabuse and Van Leyden. The philosopher
Erasmus visited Turin, Florence, Bologna, Venice, Padua and Rome.
In 1580 the great French essayist Montaigne travelled to Italy chiefly
for health reasons but also for the sheer pleasure of travelling. On
arriving in Rome he was deeply moved, declaring, 'I knew the
Capitol long before I knew the Louvre', sentiments echoed by
Goethe two centuries later. Thus by the close of the sixteenth century
Italy was already the focus of European tourism. It was fast becoming the 'old world'. The Italian Wars had helped to perpetuate its
political disunity, and its wealth was declining. Europe's economy
was in the process of changing radically: the principal trade routes
were shifting away from the Mediterranean to the north and west.
The process of Italy's decline had begun and with it, its long history
as a tourist destination.

ENGLAND AND ITALY

Although in decline materially Italy was still the intellectual capital
of Europe. For the aristocracy and intelligentsia of north-west
Europe it represented both the classical heritage and all the latest
ideas and inventions. The fascination with 'the Italian' rapidly spread
from France to England where it is vividly reflected in contemporary
drama. In the sixteenth century England was emerging from late-
medieval isolation to take its place in post-Renaissance Europe. In
the popular imagination the foreign was identified almost exclusively
with the Italian. In the hands of such dramatists as Marlowe, Webster, Middleton and Ford this is extended to mean all that is exotic,
perverse and bizarre. In Marlowe's *Edward II* (first printed in 1594)
Italy is indirectly given credit for one of the most horrible murders in
English history; the king's murderer boasts:

> I learned in Naples how to poison flowers;
> To strangle with a lawn thrust down the throat.

Webster's *White Devil* and *The Duchess of Malfi*, Middleton's

Women Beware Women and Ford's *'Tis Pity She's A Whore* were all
written in the early seventeenth century and all have Italian settings.
Collectively they present an extraordinary vision of a land chiefly
populated by mad dukes, lascivious cardinals, incestuous lovers and
great courtesans – with murderers and villains *ad libitum*. Italy is a
land of hyper-elegant depravity, pervaded by an atmosphere of
baroque *fleurs du mal* with Machiavelli as its presiding genius. It is
hardly surprising in these circumstances that 'the Englishman
Italianate' was generally considered 'the devil incarnate'. The old
world had been firmly typecast as a symbol of something which
always both attracts and repels – that is, decadence.

The 'foreign' often remains stereotyped long after it has ceased to
be truly unfamiliar. During the years in which these plays were written
a growing number of young noblemen were being sent abroad to
complete their educations in France and Italy. In Shakespeare's
Merchant of Venice Portia pours scorn on the Englishman who
'bought his doublet in Italy, his roundhose in France, his bonnet in
Germany and his behaviour everywhere'. Seventeenth-century drama
also shows the influence of the Italian forms, chiefly the masque. This
is a hybrid form in which music and dance play major roles and it
requires a sophisticated audience, since it first developed in the
epicene courts of Renaissance Italy. Such an audience did not exist
in England until the aristocracy came into direct contact with the new
modes of Italy and France. Bedazzled English noblemen first observed
the masque and the ballet on visits to the French court of Catherine
de Medici.

The first actual reference to the Grand Tour in English does not
appear until 1679 when Richard Lassels' *An Italian Voyage* was published, but when Sir Philip Sidney embarked on his tour in 1572 he was
already conscious of those who had gone before him, 'A great number
of us never thought in ourselves why we went but a certain tickling
humour to do as others had done'. Sidney was the perfect Elizabethan
courtier, an aristocrat, a soldier and a distinguished writer of poetry
and prose. As he was to take up government service a European tour
was considered essential to his career. He visited Paris, Vienna,
Venice and Padua, then the intellectual capitals of Europe. It was
assumed that he would collect any political information that he could
and pass it on to the Elizabethan secret service. His 'tickling humour'
was highly contagious. Henry Wotton, another aristocrat and poet,
began an extensive tour in 1589. He travelled with the assistance of

government subsidies for, like Sidney, he was both a tourist and an amateur secret agent. From Vienna he wrote, 'The secretest debates about the Empire I have good means to learn by the gentlemen with whom I live'. From Florence he wrote, 'If any matter of weight stir in Florence it shall not fail in five or six days to be with your Honour'. Rome was still unsafe for Protestants at this stage and Wotton made his entrance flamboyantly disguised as a German Catholic 'with a mighty blue feather in a black hat'.

Even from such skeletal accounts it is plain that for Sidney and Wotton the Grand Tour was no mere sightseeing trip. Like the young Romans in Greece they travelled to complete their educations. One of Lassels' chief recommendations for undertaking 'The Grand Tour of France and the Giro of Italy', is that they improve one's understanding of Livy and Caesar. In the early years of the seventeenth century the new Paris of Henry IV served as a kind of finishing school for the young English aristocrat, offering social refinements as well as academic subjects. A tour would normally take several years, allowing the young man time to enrol in courses at the great universities of Padua and Bologna. The tour was considered especially useful as the prelude to a diplomatic career and Henry Wotton, for example, was to become English ambassador in Venice. The Grand Tourist was not interested in the picturesque whether manifested in scenery or the habits and customs of the peasantry. There was no attempt to escape social class. The nobleman travelled as a 'member of an international élite whose aim it was to safeguard and perpetuate the interests of the ruling class'.[2] Any real contact with the lower orders was likely to be both accidental and undesirable. For example Fynes Morrison, one of the few strictly non-aristocratic Grand Tourists of the seventeenth century, was accosted while riding through Rome by a man who shouted, 'What, do you ride to heaven and we poor wretches go on foot without shoes to visit these holy churches?' Any modern tourist in a Third World country is likely to meet with a similar reaction if he moves about unaccompanied, outside the tourist enclaves. This merely verbal affront was not the worst of Morrison's experiences; on his way home through France he was attacked and robbed by a gang of unemployed soldiers.

In his essay *Of Travel* Francis Bacon speaks of the importance of meeting 'eminent persons in all kinds', and the tourist would take letters of introduction with him to ensure this. Contact with the middle and lower classes would thus be minimal, perhaps even less than in the tourist's home country. Bacon's essay is probably the best summary of this official view of the Grand Tour though its author never travelled further than Paris. He gives an exhaustive list of 'things to be seen', among them courts of princes and courts of justice, churches and monasteries, walls and fortifications, havens and harbours, antiquities and ruins, libraries, colleges, disputations and lectures, shipping and navies, armouries, arsenals, magazines, exchanges, bourses, warehouses, exercises of horsemanship and finally 'capital executions and such shows . . .'. It was also considered only proper to learn the languages of all the countries that might be visited; in Bacon's words the young man who goes abroad ignorant of French, German and Italian 'goeth to school and not to travel'. To assist him in his strenuous intellectual exercises he is further advised to travel in the company of 'some tutor or grave servant'.

There were, of course, eccentric Jacobean tourists, most notably Thomas Coryate whose accounts of his travels, *Coryate's Crudities* (1611), was to prove highly influential. He considered travel to be 'of all the world's pleasures the sweetest and most delightful', a conviction which survived a rough Channel crossing during which he speaks of 'varnishing the exterior parts of the ship with the excremental ebullitions of my tumultous stomach . . .'. He found Germany full of 'lewd and murderous villains', at Fontainebleau he admired the codpieces of the Swiss Guards, describing them as 'a significant symbol of the most laborious employments which lie upon them in peace'. In Venice he was shown around by the ambassador Henry Wotton and carried out objective researches into the lives of the 'noble courtesans', and yet, he claims, 'was nothing contaminated therewith nor corrupted in manner'. In Italy he also encountered for the first time, forks, fans and umbrellas. Indeed, he is credited as the first person to introduce the fork into England. It had originally been brought to Venice by a Byzantine princess and Coryate's use of this exotic implement brought him a notoriety he must have relished. In many ways Coryate was not so much a Grand Tourist as a traveller in the heroic mould of Marco Polo and Ibn Battuta; he died at Surat near Bombay from a surfeit of sack.

Coryate's fork is a small example of the part the Grand Tour played in revolutionising English art, thought and manners during the seventeenth century. The philosopher Thomas Hobbes, the poet John Milton and the architect Inigo Jones all made the tour and each was deeply affected by the experience. In 1610 Hobbes travelled as a tutor in the service of the Cavendish family. It was in this way that he first became aware of the new scientific ideas of the continental universities. During a later tour, undertaken in 1634, he was even able to meet Galileo.

Milton set out on his tour in 1638. In Italy the thirty-year-old poet and classicist was bombarded with aesthetic and intellectual stimuli. Arriving on 'the classic ground' was in itself a stirring experience but Milton also became immediately involved in the intellectual life of contemporary Italy. In Florence he became a member of an academy, calling itself the Svogliati or the Sophisticates. Like Hobbes he visited the aged Galileo. Everywhere he came into contact with the new styles of the High Renaissance and the proto-Baroque. In Rome, at the Casa Barberini, he heard for the first and last time in his life a full-scale opera, an art form then unknown in England. It lasted five hours and the sets and costumes were designed by Bernini. When he returned to England Milton took with him scores by Monteverdi and Gesualdo, among others. Direct reference to his Italian journey in Milton's poetry is limited to a mention of 'the leaves of Vallambrosa' in *Paradise Lost*, but it is impossible that the experience did not have a profound impact on his aesthetic sense; in Italy he was 'confronting an exotic world, opulent with colour, such as he had only seen in his dreams'. Milton was a puritan but one whose avowed moral principles were constantly at war with his sensuous response to the kind of ornate and refined beauty that he had encountered in Italy. In his old age the blind poet is said to have held olives in his hand to remind him of his journey.

In the widest sense the Grand Tour had a direct influence upon the transition from the daring and sometimes extravagant styles of earlier seventeenth-century English art, to the stricter classicism and correctness of Restoration and Augustan styles. It is in architecture that this influence is most spectacularly evident. On his second tour in 1613, Inigo Jones travelled in the entourage of the Earl of Arundel, and for the first time became aware of the work of the great Renaissance architect Andrea Palladio (1508–80). In Palladio's chaste and superbly proportioned classicism Jones found his ideal. He was able to collect the published works of Palladio (*I Quattro Libri dell' Architettura*) and also met his pupil and successor Scamozzi. In Venice he received strong encouragement from the ubiquitous Henry Wotton. Until Jones' Italian innovations Jacobean architecture had displayed a transitional and fanciful style, still in many ways late medieval; such buildings as Jones' Whitehall Banqueting House (begun 1619) and the Queen's House, Greenwich (begun 1616), must have seemed shockingly severe and modern with their strict application of classical orders and proportion.

Jones' second tour set English architecture on the path it was to follow throughout the eighteenth century. Arundel, his patron, also started a trend that was to continue for the next two centuries; he was one of the first of the English 'milords' abroad to combine his travels with art collecting on a grand scale. He even had a personal agent in Italy who, after his return, sent him weekly reports on any *objet d'art* that might be available for purchase. The Palladian style that Jones had pioneered proved admirably suited to the English eighteenth-century concern with proportion and good sense before all else. The Grand Tour was not sufficient in itself to end English conservatism and isolationism and once the Palladian style became established it proved impossible for the later, more florid, continental styles of the Baroque and the Rococo to take root in England. Continued visits of architects and their patrons to Italy served only to reinforce the style. In 1713 the architect William Kent was in Italy when he met two of his future patrons, Richard Boyle third Earl of Burlington and Thomas Coke, both immensely rich men and both following the example of Arundel in their avid collection of art treasures. In Padua Coke bought up a whole section of a monastic library and elsewhere collected colossal busts, torsos and bas-reliefs which were shipped to England from Leghorn (Livorno); he was still in his teens at the time. Burlington arrived home with a truly imperial booty, scattered among 878 items of luggage. It was by now customary for any self-respecting Grand Tourist to return to England with some tangible proof of his superior culture in the form of antiquities and art treasures. English ambassadors and consuls in Italy seem often to have spent as much time in art-dealing, sometimes of a dubious nature, as on their official duties. The wealthy of the new country display little compunction at depriving the old country of whole sections of its heritage. England was by now an imperial power with expanding colonial possessions and it is inevitable that its aristocrats and *nouveaux riches* should display imperialist attitudes when abroad.

The houses of the English eighteenth-century nobility soon began to look like carbon copies of Italian sixteenth-century originals, their interiors suitably adorned with Italian statues, busts and paintings.

The façade of Burlington House was an imitation of Palladio's Palazzo Porto; Mereworth Castle in Kent is a clumsy replica of the same architect's Villa Rotonda; Chiswick House is a better version of the same building. Such foreign importations, dictated by fashion, were not always suited to English conditions: in his 'Epistle to Burlington', Alexander Pope ridicules those builders who:

> . . . call the winds through long arcades to roar,
> Proud to catch cold at a Venetian door;
> Conscious they act a true Palladian part
> And if they starve, they starve by rules of Art.

In the second half of the eighteenth century there was a certain amount of reaction against Palladianism, but this again was directly influenced by the Grand Tour. The stylistic innovations of the Adams Brothers were inspired by Italian models observed by Robert Adam while on tour. Adam did not look to the Renaissance for his models but to the remains of Late-Classical architecture, especially the basilicas and baths of Rome. His researches even took him as far as the Dalmatian coast where he made extensive sketches of Diocletian's immense third-century palace at Split (Spalato).

At the same time the Palladian style still continued to spread further afield by means of the Grand Tour. Several Virginian plantation owners made the tour in the late eighteenth century and returned to America to build themselves mansions after the Palladian fashion. Thomas Jefferson was another American Grand Tourist who became an enthusiastic advocate of the style, and the University of Virginia was designed in accordance with his ideas. The White House itself was almost another replica in memory of the tour. In the twentieth century technology has made it possible for this process to achieve what one hopes is its final extreme; a Portuguese monastery can now be taken to pieces and re-erected for the private delectation of some transatlantic millionaire, and London Bridge can reappear like a fixed mirage in the middle of an American desert. Had the appropriate technology existed in the eighteenth century it is more than likely that the real Villa Rotonda of Palladio would have ended up in England alongside its replicas, purchased, no doubt, by some eighteen-year-old 'milord' with an inheritance.

'THE GREATEST BLOCKHEADS IN NATURE'

The eighteenth century is conventionally considered the Golden Age of the Grand Tour, especially the thirty years between 1763 and 1793. In many ways the tour seems a typical product of 'The Age of Reason' with its cosmopolitan outlook and conscious evocation of the classical past. In this atmosphere travel was easier, artistic styles and new knowledge spread more rapidly. As we have seen, the Grand Tour in its initial stages did much to bring a more civilised style of life to the aristocracy and bourgeoisie of England and France. By the eighteenth century France not only had Europe's largest population and strongest army but it had also usurped Italy's position of cultural dominance. Patte, a French court architect, declared, 'Paris is to Europe what Greece was at the time of its artistic glory: it provides the whole world with artists'. Frederick the Great of Prussia was a collector of the paintings of Watteau and the despots of Germany, Italy and Spain assiduously copied the glories of Versailles. England, meanwhile, had become the dominant commercial and colonial power. Economically and industrially Italy was stagnating while its population increased. For the Grand Tourist it continued to be the object of special veneration but even as early as the end of the seventeenth century the cultural and educational tourism that Bacon had defined begins to change its character.

In 1699 Addison embarked on a Grand Tour that was to last until 1704. His first contact with Europe was inauspicious; on disembarking at Calais he fell straight into the harbour. He understood no French, German or Italian, and to refer to Bacon, went very reluctantly 'to school'. Of the art treasures of Paris, he remarked, 'what particularly recommends 'em to me is that they don't speak French and have a very good quality, rarely to be met with in this Country, of not being too talkative'. This contrasts sharply with the more respectful attitudes of Jacobean tourists, who evidently felt that in visiting Paris they were visiting one of the principal homes of art. social refinement and learning. By 1770 *The Gentlemen's Guide* could speak glibly of 'the follies, vices and fopperies of that vain and superficial people' – the French have already become firmly typecast. The cultural superiority of Europe over England was by now much less marked and England's economic prosperity and colonial expansion very marked indeed. The growing power and confidence of England inclined the Englishman abroad to a much more complacent attitude. He no longer felt so obliged to become closely acquainted with a country's language, art, social customs and law. Easy disdain and a disregard for the present realities of the country visited became a prominent feature of tourist attitudes. In 1785, Dupaty, a French observer, made the following scathing and all too familiar remarks concerning English tourists:

> In a hundred there are not two that seek to instruct themselves. To cover leagues on land or on water; to take punch and tea at the inns; to speak ill of all the other nations and to boast without ceasing of their own; that is what the crowd of English call travelling.[3]

That Dupaty's remarks were not merely the product of French chauvinism is demonstrated by the even more withering observations of English writers. Lady Wortley Montagu, for example, complained that the young Englishmen abroad kept:

> ... an inviolable fidelity to the language their nurses taught them, their whole business abroad being to buy new clothes in which they shine in some obscure coffee-house, where they are sure of meeting only one another; and after the important conquest of some waiting gentlewoman of an opera Queen, who perhaps they remember as long as they live, return to England excellent judges of men and manners. ... I look on them as the greatest blockheads in nature, and to say truth the compound of booby and petit-maître makes up a very odd sort of animal.

With the new wealth of the English bourgeoisie the number of tourists had multiplied, and it would be unrealistic to expect them all to be on a level with Sidney and Wotton or Coke and Burlington. Nevertheless Lady Wortley Montagu's description is disturbingly close to the modern caricature of the English tourist with his herding instinct, philistinism, proverbial ignorance of any foreign language and, in contradiction to the ostensible purpose of travelling, his general tendency to avoid close contact with anything too alarmingly foreign; already in the eighteenth century he travels about inside his own environmental bubble, impervious to all but the rudest intrusions, his mind wholly taken up with the thought of the next stop for tea.

It might be argued that if the eighteenth-century Grand Tour was less grand than is sometimes thought, it was at least more leisurely and much less a matter of routine than twentieth-century tourism. Unfortunately even this must be qualified. In 1760 Dr Johnson complained of the tourist, 'that enters a town at night and surveys it in the morning and then hastens away to another place . . .'. In his travel book *The Rhine* (1794) Thomas Cogan is more sweeping:

> Should their road lead through Paradise, or should they have taken a long and tedious journey expressly to see the Garden of Eden, it is a question of whether our impetuous gentlemen would not tip the post boy half a crown extraordinary to mend his pace as they were driving through it.

Dr John Moore, a tourist in Rome, remarked on a young man who 'ordered a post chaise and four horses to be ready early in the morning and driving through churches, palaces, villas and ruins with all possible expedition . . . fairly saw, in two days, all that we had beheld during our crawling course of six weeks'. Such a Grand Tourist would have been more at home in the age of the organised coach tour. The principle of the souvenir snapshot was also established long before the appearance of the camera. The Grand Tourist in Rome would pose to have his portrait painted against a backdrop of a suitable high cultural tone, the Colosseum or the Forum and a scattering of atmospheric cypresses. As can be imagined the Roman souvenir portrait developed into a minor industry, providing a useful source of income not only for local artists but also for foreign artists who had come to Rome to study the glories of antiquity at first hand. By the second half of the eighteenth century there were tourists who could visit Rome and not even learn the whereabouts of the Colosseum. There were English cafés, English restaurants and English 'pensions', especially in the region of the Spanish Steps which, for obvious reasons, was also the chief area of operation for Rome's prostitutes. Boswell's diaries reveal a seemingly limitless supply of young Italian girls for the foreigner with money; of one he notes, 'Sister, a nun, Mother who sells daughters, talked of "vocation". Much enjoyment.' Boys were procured with similar ease for those with less orthodox tastes, and during the nineteenth century male prostitution catering largely for foreigners seems to have become something of an Italian speciality. These were not the only tourist industries; the eighteenth century also had its precursor of the package tour. A *vetturino* (or *voiturin*) was a kind of guide or one-man touroperator, who for a lump sum organised the transport of the passenger

and his luggage from A to B with prearranged stops along the way
and board, lodging and wayside meals included. The vetturino was
proverbially dishonest, but it was noticed that his clients were seldom
troubled by bandits and there were few travellers who did not make
use of one for some part of their tour. In the nineteenth century
Hazlitt warned, 'Let no one who can help it travel by vetturino'. The
tourist was already something of a victim, wealthy and an easy prey;
Lady Knight, who lived abroad between 1776 and 1795, complained
that, 'the English pay double for everything in every country'. If the
tourist is largely ignorant of a country's language and customs, and
strikingly more affluent than the majority of its inhabitants, then he
must expect to be exploited.

IDYLLS OF THE BOURGEOISIE

What men call gallantry, and gods adultery
Is much more common where the climate's sultry.
Byron, *Don Juan*

The Grand Tour was no longer an aristocratic preserve; it had been
invaded by the bourgeoisie. There were, of course, still considerable
numbers of tourists who travelled in Italy in a spirit of very real
veneration for its enormous cultural heritage; there were still creative
minds that benefited immensely from direct contact with this heritage,
for example, Robert Adam and the historian Gibbon. Yet even in
this rarefied field there is a noticeable change in attitude. This was
effected by two philosophic and artistic movements: the 'return to
nature' of Rousseau and his followers, and 'neo-classicism'.
    Rousseau's philosophic outlook went against the prevailing ration-
alist bias of eighteenth-century thought. He is the pioneer of the
romantic cult of sensibility rather than sense, and nature rather than
society. His 'educational' novel *Emile* caused an enormous stir when
it was first published in 1762. It stresses the corrupting influence of
society: 'Men are not made to be crowded together in ant-hills . . .
the more they congregate the more they corrupt each other.' Nature
is rational and society therefore irrational; the noble savage lives in
a state of innocence and equality that is lost once he becomes
civilised. In this we can discern a familiar process; as European

society becomes more highly urbanised and uniform in styles and customs, the lives of those outside the urban system are idealised and sentimentalised, while at the same time the real models of the noble savage were being ruthlessly exploited by the European colonial powers. In a highly artificial form the cult of the natural even reaches the aristocracy where it emerges as an attempt to enact pastoral convention – for example, Marie Antoinette's 'village', with its dairy, watermill and farm, all contained within the rigid formalism of the Palace of Versailles. In Rome the aristocracy liked to refer to their palaces as 'huts' and their gardens as 'pastures'. For all this Rousseau and his return to nature belong essentially to the new bourgeoisie. His ideas are the foundation of bourgeois escapist philosophy, and bourgeois revolutionary theory.

Rousseau's idea of nature was deeply influenced by his early travels. Until his public success he was a poor man and consequently he did much of his travelling on foot; once he became a public figure he did much to popularise the walking holiday. In his *Confessions* he praises the uplifting qualities of walking in wild mountain scenery. We take appreciation of the beauties of the alps for granted but the educated person of the eighteenth century most certainly did not; the conventional idea of good landscape was exemplified by the Loire Valley or the hills of Tuscany, moderation and proportion in all things! High mountains were mostly considered monstrous and frightful, inconvenient obstacles in the way of civilised man. When Addison admitted to experiencing 'a sort of agreeable shuddering at this most misshapen scenery', while crossing the alps, he was conscious that this was a highly unorthodox sensation. Gothic architecture was affected by the same disapproval, being the artistic equivalent of the 'misshapen' alps. The enthusiasm for the picturesque which begins to appear in the later half of the eighteenth century changed all this. The alps were still terrifying and awesome but the terror and awe were now pleasurable and thrilling. William Coxe was one of the first Englishmen to discover the attractions of Switzerland in the late eighteenth century, describing a glacier as, 'a stormy sea, frozen solid'; in 1816 Byron went one further and compared a glacier to 'a frozen hurricane'. After 1750 Chamonix began to become fashionable as a watering place and in the 1780s Mont Blanc itself was conquered. In 1790 William Wordsworth made a walking tour of Switzerland, still an unconventional way to spend a holiday at the time. The Romantic Movement combined with the technological innovations of the first half of the nineteenth century completed this reversal of attitudes. Man was both conquering nature and identifying with it. Byron said of alpine landscapes, 'Here to be lonely is not desolate . . .'.[4] In the 1820s the first tourist hotels appeared in Switzerland, and the Englishman was already established as the *hochtourist*, that is, the richest and most privileged of tourists.

The origins of the cult of mountain scenery are inseparable from Protestant morality, and it is thus only appropriate that its chief focus should be Switzerland, the land of Calvin and most bourgeois of all European states, and that its most ardent followers should be the nineteenth-century English. Glaciers, defiles, peaks and torrents are admirable because 'they seem to encourage a morality of effort and solitude', nature flatters puritan ethics. The contemplation of alpine scenery from the safety of the hotel is a labour-saving substitute for Rousseau's morally uplifting walk; mountain air regenerates and cleanses the city dweller, the sight of a mountain summit provokes moral ideas, and to climb them, with the assistance of local guides, is an aspect of civic virtue. Heroism and moral effort can thus be bought and enjoyed without appreciable risks or ill effects. This attitude is extended to embrace all landscape, which is only perceived by the official guide books when it becomes 'picturesque', that is, 'any time the ground is uneven'. This is quite the reverse of the seventeenth-century aristocratic tourist attitude, now it is precisely 'the gracelessness of a landscape, its lack of spaciousness or human appeal, its verticality, so contrary to the bliss of travel, which account for its interest'. The tenacity and exclusivity of this view throughout the nineteenth and into the twentieth century are pointedly revealed by Roland Barthes' analysis of the *Blue Guide* from which the above quotations are taken.[5]

Parallel to the bourgeois veneration of nature is the bourgeois veneration of antiquity. Marx has observed that, although in itself essentially unheroic, bourgeois society has a profound need for the heroic image or archetype; to find this it looks into the past. In touristic terms this means that 'the human life of a country disappears to the exclusive benefit of its monuments'. The people are reduced to 'a charming and fanciful décor'[6] whose only function is to enhance the open-air museum. This in turn reduces the significance of the monuments themselves, since, if the present reality of the country is suppressed, there is no sense of history; the monuments 'become undecipherable therefore senseless'. Everything becomes 'scenery', landscape, people and antiquities, empty and theatrical in the worst sense.

The English attitude had been backward-looking throughout the eighteenth century. In the time of Kent, Burlington and Coke, the world of Palladio and his contemporaries was already a part of Italy's 'glorious past'; but the work of subsequent Italian architects was largely overlooked. When new models were required Robert Adam looked even further back to 'the grandeur that was Rome'. He was not alone in this; in 1738 excavations began at Herculaneum and ten years later Pompeii was discovered. This attracted the attention of the influential German art historian Winckelmann (1717–68), who argued that nature should be studied in the works of the 'ancients', and that the figures of Greco-Roman myth presented ideal heroic models that had never been surpassed. This appreciation was based on a partial knowledge of Late-Classical art and when the genuinely Greek temples of Paestum in Southern Italy became known they were at first regarded with revulsion as crude and barbaric: they could not be adapted so easily to the requirements of the aristocratic or upper-middle-class salon.

The Grand Tourists of the sixteenth and seventeenth centuries had visited Italy for the sake of its contemporary art and architecture, its living artists, its scholars and universities, as well as its catalogue of ancient monuments. Although still highly active during the eighteenth century in many artistic and intellectual fields (notably music), Italy had lost much of its former prestige. Its conventionalised image was changing; it is seen exclusively as the land of antiquity (since Greece was still too inaccessible) and the voluptuous South. Meanwhile the poverty and oppression of the mass of living Italians was increasingly apparent. Even Addison, with his general impatience of foreigners, had been moved to observe, 'The poor inhabitant beholds in vain / The red'ning Orange and the swelling grain'. Gibbon's criticisms of Italy's social injustices go beyond such polite sentiments. Of the court of the Kingdom of Sardinia in Turin he remarked:

> The servility of the courtiers revolts me and I view with horror the magnificence of the palaces which had been cemented with the blood of the people. In a small and poor kingdom like this they must grind the people in order to be equal with the other crowned heads. . . . In each gilded ornament I seem to see a village of Savoyards ready to die of hunger, cold and misery.

Such awareness and moral outrage in a tourist is rare, although hardly surprising in the man who was to write *The Decline and Fall of the Roman Empire*. It was, in part, his first-hand observation of Italy's decadence that inspired him to undertake this great work. In general, the theatrical unreality of tourism tends to protect the tourist from such painful reflections; the picturesque and the historic cannot hurt.

The changing significance of Italy is well illustrated by Goethe's Italian journey (*Italienische Reise*). This journey began in 1786 but the desire to visit Italy, or ideally, Greece, had been a ruling passion for some years. For Goethe the classical world of Greece and Italy was 'a place of serene beauty, almost a pagan Garden of Eden, a civilisation where Rousseau's "noble savage" had been realised to perfection'.[7] Thus in Goethe's romantic classicism, antiquarian neo-classicism and the return to nature were combined. On first entering Italy he wrote, 'I enjoy this country as though I had been born and bred here and had just returned from a whaling expedition to Greenland'. In Rome he declared: 'I am here at peace.' He was so anxious to reach Rome that Venice, Bologna and Florence merited only 'whistle-stop' tours: Florence took him just three hours. Despite this Goethe was something of an 'alternative tourist'; he took few letters of introduction and, except in Naples, avoided high society. In Rome he lived among young painters and poets in cheap lodgings. He had come to Italy to 'live' and the conventions of the Grand Tour did not interest him. In 1787 Rome was an underpopulated and impoverished city, most of its inhabitants living in hovels, the Vatican itself surrounded by 'a maze of wretched and appalling slums'. Much of the area of classical Rome was given over to ruined gardens and pasturage. Violence was endemic. At the same time Roman street life was, to the Northerner, a revelation of candour and eroticism. The Italians might be poor, their government divided and oppressive, their laws chaotic and antiquated, but they certainly knew how to enjoy themselves! In this way the affluent Northerner nervously pushes unpleasant realities to the back of his mind, and with them his own inevitable sense of guilt. The Italians are spontaneous musicians, clowns and dancers. How many dance and song forms, transfigured in the music of the great eighteenth-century composers, were invented in their streets! Friedenthal, in his life of Goethe, even speaks of a 'love market'; abbés or young noblemen would arrange meetings between monied foreigners and the local bourgeois women. It was hardly necessary to resort to the prostitutes of the Spanish

Steps. Goethe himself took at least one mistress in Rome (the Faustina of the *Roman Elegies*) and, according to Friedenthal, it was only in Rome at the age of forty that he found 'complete erotic freedom'. Here he was free from the gossiping and moralising of his native Weimar. He did not feel trapped by his love affair since both parties recognised that it was impermanent; his Italian girl would have been grateful for the generosity of her rich visitor. In the first of the *Roman Elegies* the classical and the erotic happily combine as the poet taps out tentative Greek hexameters on his mistress's naked back. If the people detach themselves from the balletic-operatic backcloth they often do so as sexual objects.

For all its grinding poverty and inequality Italian life has come to represent liberation from the taboos of the tourist's home society. This already foreshadows some of the attitudes of the modern Western bourgeoisie toward Third World tourist destinations, particularly the attitudes of those younger more radically minded tourists who see 'The East' as the source of some kind of enlightenment or diffusely mystical revelation. For Goethe and the English poets, Byron, Shelley, Keats and Browning, Italy offered a direct release from the moral and physical restrictions of their countries of origin.

This was especially true of Byron and Shelley. In their minds the pagan mores of Italy and Greece were opposed to the sexually repressive system into which they had been born. The free Greek whose body and intellect were undivided is contrasted with the guilt-ridden Christian, at war with himself. On arriving in Italy in 1818 Shelley felt able to undertake a translation of Plato's *Symposium* in which the central theme of homosexual love is in no way disguised. In two poems written soon after this ('The Witch of Atlas' and 'Epi-psychidion'), he goes even further, moving towards the ideal of androgyny, that is, the breakdown of sexual differentiation. For Byron the sexual licence available to foreigners in Italy meant something rather less ethereal. Even Shelley, the translator of Plato, confirmed pagan and opponent of marriage, was shocked by Byron's association with the male prostitutes of Venice, commenting, in a letter to Thomas Love Peacock:

> He associates with wretches who seem almost to have lost the gait and phisiognomy of man and who do not scruple to avow practises which are not only not named, but I believe seldom even conceived in England.

In the same letter he makes some attempt to extenuate Byron's conduct on the grounds that Italian women are 'the most ignorant, the most disgusting, the most bigotted, the most filthy' in the world. Even 'Countesses smell so of garlic that an ordinary Englishman cannot approach them'. How far have the Italians fallen in the eyes of the English intellectual abroad! Byron himself described Venice as 'Thou sea Sodom', but while he was there continued to live '*dans une débauche affreuse*'.

In a more sympathetic mood he had once lamented the decline of Venice. The Venice that had been visited by the first English Grand Tourists had still been a thriving centre of art and commerce. Byron found 'Thirteen hundred years / Of wealth and glory turned to dust and tears'. He lamented the degeneracy of its inhabitants, who 'creep / Crablike through their sapping streets' yet was himself an active participant in their corruption. Venice was already sinking to the status of a single, enormous 'tourist sight', apt setting for Thomas Mann's tale of corruption and death, and Visconti's self-indulgently nostalgic adaptation of the same.

In 1812 Byron had published Cantos I and II of *Childe Harolde*. This ineffably boring and inept poem was responsible for the popularisation of a new image of the Englishman abroad. The leisurely young lord travelling for amusement and edification becomes a melancholic wanderer, a 'rebel without a cause', 'misanthroping among ruins and desolate places'.[8] Naturally the wanderer has sufficient independent means to enable him to be 'driven o'er shoals of guilt or oceans of excess' in proper romantic style. *Childe Harolde* was an enormous popular success and the mannerisms of its eponymous hero were widely imitated. The romantic wanderer travels because he is society's outcast, whether by choice or force of circumstance. Italy and Greece are his preferred destinations although, of course, a true wanderer will not admit to having a destination. In these countries he could find ample evidence of present Tyranny and past Vanity with which to confirm his pessimism. When his restless spirit tired of the contemplation of ruins and oppressed peasantry he could lose himself in some alpine desolation, there to 'worship nature with a thought profound'. As Byron himself observed, these attitudes have more to do with puberty than philosophy. *Childe Harolde* is the prototype of the anti-tourist; the wanderer is still a tourist, but a tourist who has 'dropped out', both from his home society and from conventional tourism.

As the journey to the South takes on the character of an escape from repressive and unsympathetic social structures the tourist tends to merge with the voluntary exile. Throughout the nineteenth century colonies of North European exiles gathered in Florence, Sienna, Rome, Naples and, most notoriously, Capri. In 1846 the poets Elizabeth Barrett and Robert Browning eloped to Italy in defiance of Elizabeth's neurotic, authoritarian father and remained there until her death in 1861. In the work of nineteenth- and twentieth-century authors Italy often seems a country more emblematic than real – a place where the language, the light, the landscape, the people are uniquely gracious/charming/beautiful. In the twentieth century the novelists E. M. Forster, D. H. Lawrence and Ronald Firbank were all deeply attracted to Italy, Firbank dying in Rome in 1926; all to a greater or lesser extent were homosexual. In Forster's Italian novels (*A Room With a View* and *Where Angels Fear To Tread*) conventional, upper-middle-class English people experience revelations, become hysterical, suffer breakdowns under the disorientating impact of Mediterranean light and Mediterranean manners. In *Where Angels Fear to Tread* (1905) Miss Abbot, a spinster of Sawston whose time is usually taken up with buying 'petticoats for the corpulent poor', declares of her first visit to Italy:

> All that winter I seemed to be waking up to beauty and splendour and I don't know what; and when the spring came, I wanted to fight against the things I hated, – mediocrity and dullness and spitefulness and society. I actually hated society for a day or two at Monteriano. I didn't see that all these things are invincible and that if we go against them they will break us to pieces. . . .

The travels of the seventeenth- and eighteenth-century Grand Tourists reinforced their sense of belonging to 'an international élite', determined on safeguarding its interests; the bourgeois and post-romantic tourism of the nineteenth and twentieth centuries contains a strong element of rejection of social class. A character in *Where Angels Fear To Tread* stresses the importance of 'loving and understanding the Italians, for the people are more marvellous than the land'. He refers to the ordinary, working people of Italy, but when a member of his own social class actually marries just such an Italian he is horrified. He appreciates that the face of the average Italian male has beauty and charm but one does not want to see it opposite one at dinner: it is 'not the face of a gentleman'. Loving and understanding the Italians remains an intellectual pose, they can only be loved as picturesque objects, kept at a suitable distance. Yet if the right degree of unreality or 'mystification' is preserved and the population remain 'actors in a vast classical ballet, a nice, neat commedia dell'arte, whose improbable typology serves to mask the real spectacle of conditions, classes and professions',[9] then tourism would seem to have a subversive potential. The beauty and sensuality of Mediterranean landscape and peoples can provide the bourgeois Northerner with a position from which it becomes possible to see the inadequacies of his own society more sharply; so for the first time in her life a Miss Abbot can hate society 'for a day or two at Monteriano'.

D. H. Lawrence was a virulent critic of English society and his tourism was, explicitly, an escape from the alienation of the industrialised world. In Italy and Sicily the earth was 'sappy', it was possible to return to 'basic human rhythms'. In the novels *The Lost Girl* and *Aaron's Rod* the central characters find a new life in Italy. His 'new life' is a kind of atavistic regression represented as a liberation from the inhuman mechanisms of civilisation and a return to instinctual, inchoate feeling centring on Lawrence's phallic cult. It is arguable that this liberation is merely the exchange of one form of subjection for another, the principal difference being that one is, supposedly, more natural than the other. This is post-Freudian pastoral convention and quite as artificial as the original. England represents machines, alienation and the super-ego; Italy represents the earth and the id. There is a strong element of condescension in this; Lawrence's first travel book, *Twilight in Italy*, contains the following statement vis-à-vis England and Italy: 'It is better to go forward into error than to stay fixed inextricably in the past.'

Italy, along with the whole Mediterranean world, is 'fixed inextricably in the past'. No longer the centre of the civilised world its backward rural life and decaying cities enchant and fascinate. It becomes a suitable area of relaxation and pleasure for the inhabitants of the industrialised world. What was originally a culturally motivated tourism has now become, in some ways, anti-cultural – a flight from civilisation and progress in search of 'a world of pleasure'. The Mediterranean area seems to approximate to the images of Eden and Arcadia. There is, of course, trouble in paradise but any disturbing effects are nullified by a kind of alchemical conversion, by which ignorance becomes 'charming simplicity', superstition becomes 'colourful ritual', back-breaking labour and primitive farming techniques become 'closeness to the soil'. Even poverty is seen as a blessed absence of 'filthy lucre', not as the presence of suffering. The tourist's relative affluence in the face of this poverty also enables him to play the role of aristocrat – and like the aristocrat he sees his condescension to the poor as something admirable, a 'beautiful emotion'. He is, after all, still a member of 'an international élite' determined on safeguarding its own interests – that is, the bourgeoisie of the North Atlantic Community. When visiting a backward country he must maintain the standards of that élite; any real connection with the natives would be a betrayal of his class.

It is commonplace that the touristic Eden only seems so to the tourist; the inhabitants covet the machines that will destroy the resemblance. The example of the affluent visitor will only increase the longing for the implements of progress. The liberation that tourism seems to promise the inhabitants of the industrialised world is largely illusory. The world of pleasure is constantly in retreat and its seekers must spread out further to more distant and exotic destinations. The Pleasure Periphery continually expands, assisted, in the twentieth century, by a massive industry. In the 1860s Thomas Cook, the pioneer and prophet of this industry, proclaimed:

God's earth in all its fullness and beauty is for the people.

3 Thomas Cook: Tourism and the advancement of human progress

The birth of organised mass tourism is almost biblical in character, endowed with all the high moral tone of nineteenth-century evangelism. In 1841 a book salesman, Baptist preacher and tract distributor of Derbyshire was on his way to a temperance meeting in Leicester when he was inspired with 'the idea of engaging a special train to carry the friends of temperance from Leicester to Loughborough and back to attend a quarterly delegate meeting'. The man was Thomas Cook and his idea was put into operation with characteristic speed and efficiency. A few weeks later 570 travellers made the journey by the Midland Counties Railway at a specially reduced fare. This venture was soon followed by excursions to such beauty spots as Matlock and Mount Sorrel, and in 1843, 3,000 school children were taken on a trip from Leicester to Derby. Soon 'excursions' took up much of his time and Cook was declaring: 'We must have RAILWAYS FOR THE MILLIONS.' Despite these activities he still found time in 1846 to publish a book of temperance hymns, which included the imperishable lines:

> Six hundred thousand drunkards march
>   To wretchedness and hell;
> While loud laments and tears and groans
>   In dismal chorus swell.

It is arguable that Cook's real beginning as a 'mass excursionist' was the Liverpool–Caernarvon trip of 1845. The tourists travelled by rail to Liverpool, from where they took a steamer to Caernarvon – with an ascent of Snowdon as a grand climax. The advertisements for the trip caused a sensation and the response was so overwhelming that a second trip had to be arranged. Cook thought of everything; he made a preliminary survey of accommodation and facilities and produced a *Handbook of The Trip to Liverpool*. Borne up by his success Cook experienced his second 'revelation', this time in more dramatically appropriate surroundings: 'From the heights of Snowdon my thoughts took flight to Ben Lomond and I determined to try to get to Scotland.' The excursionist invasion of Scotland soon followed in 1846 and 1847. From 1848 to 1863 Cook conducted circular tours of Scotland, with 5,000 tourists a season. During the same period the Lake District, the Isle of Man and Ireland were all 'opened up'. In 1848 Cook also initiated the first tour of a 'stately home' when the Duke of Rutland opened Belvoir Castle to his excursionists. Soon after the Duke of Devonshire welcomed 1,200 excursionists to Chatsworth. With the citadels of the landed aristocracy falling before him it is no wonder that a man of Cook's 'humble origins' saw ever wider and more enticing prospects opening before him:

> I had become so thoroughly imbued with the Tourist spirit that I began to contemplate Foreign Trips, including the Continent of Europe, the United States and the Eastern Lands of the Bible.

In the first half of the nineteenth century the last major obstacles in the way of organised mass tourism in Europe were being removed. A year after Waterloo the first Channel crossing by steamer was made (the site of the battle itself becoming a major tourist attraction). By 1821 a regular service was operating between Dover and Calais. In 1828 the first railway tracks were laid in France and Austria, and in 1844 the railway reached the inhospitable terrain of Switzerland. This revolution in transport technology produced an immediate expansion in European tourism. The ground was already well prepared – most obviously by the continuing tradition of the Grand Tour – but also by the increased popularity of spas and seaside resorts in the latter half of the eighteenth century. By the mid-nineteenth century holidays away from home had become customary for a larger social group than ever before. Cook's initiative and organising genius provided the final impetus.

Cook was the perfect entrepreneur, a brilliant opportunist, quick to sense the needs of his clientele, and convinced of the absolute rightness of what he was doing. There was no clash between his philanthropic morality and his business sense, in fact the two became increasingly inseparable. The railway he regarded as a great and beneficial social force. His excursions were conducted on the Benthamite principle of 'the greatest benefit for the greatest number at the lowest cost'. He spent much time and effort persuading the directors of railway and steamship companies that this was not only altruistic but good business. He was fully aware that he was a great innovator – organised travel on the scale of the Liverpool–Caernarvon trip had never been seen before. He saw 'excursionism' as an agent of democratisation, and in 1861 he demonstrated the sincerity of his democratic principles by organising an excursion of 1,500 to 1,600 people to support a working men's demonstration in Paris. Cook made a loss of £120 and described the venture as a 'labour of love minus profit'. Nevertheless, a similar excursion was organised in the following year.

Despite this promising beginning a politically aware tourism has shown no signs of materialising; one cannot imagine modern tour operators supporting the struggles of French students and workers in any recurrence of the 1968 May riots. Cook remains organised tourism's noblest apologist; without qualification he saw his work as 'appertaining to the great class of agencies for the advancement of Human Progress'.[1] This vision has not been fulfilled; as we shall see in later chapters tourism has proved remarkably ineffective as a promoter of equality and as an ally of the oppressed. At the time of Cook's first innovations what was most evident was the fact that people of only modest means now had more opportunities for travel than ever before, and the number and variety of destinations open to them was constantly growing. In the winter of 1850–51 Cook was already negotiating for a tour of America, but his attention was diverted when he was offered the opportunity of conducting excursion trains to the Great Exhibition of 1851. Altogether, Cook conducted 165,000 people to and from the Crystal Palace. After this success the Paris Exhibition of 1855 must have seemed the ideal opportunity for the first excursionist invasion of the continent. But here Cook met with opposition. The companies controlling cross-Channel traffic were unenthusiastic and all he could get was 'a trip to France' from Leicester to Calais. Cook was not so easily discouraged and in the following year he succeeded in organising his first 'grand circular tour of the continent'. The itinerary covered Harwich, Antwerp, Brussels, Cologne, the Rhine, Strasbourg, Paris, Le Havre and Southampton. The tour was so successful that it had to be repeated six weeks later. The numbers involved in these first continental tours were only around fifty however and until the early 1860s Britain remained Cook's main field of activity. It was not until the late 1850s that he began to make any great profit from tourism and he was still equally active as a social reformer, campaigning vigorously for the repeal of the Corn Laws.

Thomas Cook's conquest of Europe began in earnest in 1862 when he made arrangements with the Brighton and South Coast Railway for passenger traffic to the continent via Newhaven and Dieppe. Cook's Paris excursions are the first true 'package tours'; all the details of transport and accommodation were prearranged, and the tourists were generally of modest means. Cook had replaced the *vetturino* system of the Grand Tour, and carried out his duties with much greater efficiency and honesty. It was not long before his example was imitated; in 1863 the Stangen travel agency was established in Breslau. Stangen[2] soon moved his centre of operation to Berlin and became a successful rival of Cook.

In 1863 Cook visited Switzerland where his ideas were greeted with enthusiasm by hoteliers and railway proprietors, and the first 'personally conducted tour' of the country followed. In 1864 Cook wrote:

> France and Switzerland now present to me new and almost unlimited fields of tourist labour. At the moment I am surrounded in Paris with some five or six hundred enterprising tourists and am expecting an addition of four or five hundred more tonight. Already a party of a hundred has started for Switzerland. . . .

His next, inevitable, stop was Italy, that most illustrious and venerable of tourist destinations. Cook first made a personal survey of Turin, Milan, Florence and Genoa, to familiarise himself with their touristic attractions and facilities. In 1864 the first guided tour of Italy left England with applications far in excess of the available tickets. Even the impact of the South did not lead Cook to compromise his temperance principles and, although he could not prevent his tourists from sampling the local wines, he did advise them not to 'invest their money in diarrhoea'. The 1860s also saw the introduction of Cook's railway and hotel coupons. With his usual thoroughness Cook personally tested the system by travelling through Italy to Vienna, down the Danube into Hungary and from there via the Tyrol into Switzerland. (By the 1890s, 1,200 hotels throughout the world accepted his coupons.) Starting in 1868 Cook arranged regular circular tours of Switzerland and Northern Italy. Despite the existence of rivals such as Stangen the tourist's Europe was overwhelmingly dominated by Thomas Cook.

He was not without his critics. Charles James Lever, the Irish novelist and critic, repeatedly attacked Cook in the pages of *Blackwood's Magazine*. The new breed of tourist inspired him with a hearty contempt; he described the Italian cities as 'deluged with droves of these creatures – for they never separate and you see them forty in number pouring along a street with their director, – now in front, now at the rear, circling them like a sheepdog. . . .' According to Lever the men in these parties were 'mostly elderly, dreary and sad looking; the women, somewhat younger, travel-tossed, but intensely lively, wide-awake and facetious'. Ruskin lamented the passing of the more leisurely travelling habits of the Grand Tour, but the more usual attitude is represented by a 'poem' written by one John Close which includes the line: 'We say all hail to Cook, this philanthropic man. . . .' Mark Twain declared with breathless enthusiasm:

> Cook has made travel easy and a pleasure. He will sell you a ticket to any place on the globe, or all the places and give you all the time you need and much more besides. It provides hotels for you everywhere . . . and you cannot be overcharged for the coupons show just how much you must pay. . . .

Cook had made his first exploratory visit to America in 1866. He found 'American Express' already in existence but with no fully developed excursion system. The first excursion to America was made later in the same year. A year earlier 'Thomas Cook & Son' had established their first official London office at 98 Fleet Street. John Mason Cook·now joined his father as a permanent partner and took charge of the London office. From now on the history of Thomas Cook & Son was one of continuous expansion and growing prestige. An excursion of 20,000 people to the Paris Exhibition in 1867 received the personal blessing of Napoleon III. In the new age of organised tourism the Ruskinian nostalgia for the aristocratic discomforts of eighteenth-century travel and Lever's élitist scorn were equally cries in the wilderness. Few people apart from Lever seem to have speculated on the effect that the new breed of lower-income, protoxenophobic, linguistically ignorant tourist would have on the native population of the countries they visited:

> they deride our church ceremonies, they ridicule our cookery, they criticise our dress, they barbarise our language. How long are we to be patient under these endurances?

Occasionally the onward march of 'Thomas Cook & Son' was impeded by vociferous local opinion. When Cooks bought up the Vesuvius funicular they refused to pay the mountain guides the £900 they had extorted from the previous owners. In retaliation the guides burned down the station, threw the carriages into a crater and cut the line. Such Latin passion was no match for the methodical Cook who simply closed the whole enterprise down and waited until the lack of tourists brought the rebellious natives 'to their knees'. This was accomplished in only six months.

Thomas Cook & Son soon began to wield near-governmental power and influence. A contemporary remarked, 'The world belongs to Thomas Cook'. In 1872 Cook made his first round-the-world tour, commenting: 'This going round the world is a very easy and almost imperceptable business. . . .' Despite this it was Stangen's German agency that arranged the first touristic round-the-world trip in 1878. By this date Thomas Cook & Son were fully engaged in the Near East. As early as 1868 Cook had undertaken an exploratory tour of Constantinople, Beirut, Jaffa, Alexandria and Cairo. In December 1868 he advertised a tour of Palestine and the Nile for the following spring. The Palestine tour involved much negotiation with local sheikhs, looking forward, perhaps, to Cook's recent tribal tour of New Guinea (see p. 170). The tourists travelled in great state and stayed in lavishly equipped tents. Such was the monopoly of Thomas Cook & Son in this area that in 1898 they were responsible for all the arrangements for Kaiser Wilhelm II's pilgrimage to the Holy Land.

The extent of Cook's power and influence becomes most nakedly apparent in Egypt. In 1870 John Mason Cook was officially appointed by the Khedive to act as government agent for passenger traffic on the Nile. In 1875 he persuaded the Khedive to agree to a passenger steamer service from the first cataract to the second and soon after was appointed sole agent for the postal service on all government steamers. In 1880 the Egyptian government gave Cooks exclusive control of all passenger steamers. This gave Cooks a position of such decisive importance in the life of the country that it was hardly an exaggeration to say (as G. W. Steevens did) that: 'The nominal suzerain of Egypt is the Sultan, its real suzerain is Lord Cromer. Its nominal governor is the Khedive, its real governor . . . is Thomas Cook.' It was a small step from this to direct involvement in politics, and when pleasure traffic on the Nile ceased during the revolt of Arabi Pasha in the 1880s, Cooks turned to transporting soldiers. The British War Office relied on Cooks for the rapid movement of its 'top-brass'. After these disturbances (and the Gordon fiasco) Cooks had to build up their fleet again as the original steamers had been lost. By 1890 they had fifteen steamers which operated as floating hotels. In 1887 Cooks had opened a hotel at Luxor. This was not only the first luxury hotel in Luxor, but the first Cooks hotel anywhere. It was immediately successful and work soon began on a second hotel.

From the first, Cooks in Egypt was a very different enterprise from Cooks in Europe. It was altogether grander and more luxurious; it was, in an exact sense, imperial. Cooks were not merely representative of British imperialism in Egypt, they were essential to its operation. This was no longer the democratising, philanthropic venture of the 'fifties and 'sixties, this was tourism for aristocrats and colonials, and can be compared with Roman tourism in Egypt. As we have seen (Chapter 1) most Roman tourists in Egypt were government officials or soldiers on leave. For the British, Egypt was both a dependent state and a convenient stopping-off place on the most direct route to India. The character of this Victorian and Edwardian tourism in Egypt is typified by its hotels with their resoundingly regal names: the Windsor Palace in Alexandria, the Semiramis in Cairo, and the Winter Palace in Luxor. Such hotels were, literally, palatial. The Semiramis in Cairo, though somewhat gone to seed, still retains a hall of mirrors 'à la Versailles', a hideously ornate dining-room and a superfluity of potted palms in scrupulously polished brass bowls. The Winter Palace at Luxor easily outdoes this: it is a huge bright pink sandstone monstrosity with its public rooms largely intact with their parquet floors, mahogany chairs and general air of sumptuous gloom. Private rooms and suites are named after British aristocrats, archaeologists and politicians. The hotel completely dominates the town and commands a superb view across the Nile to the cliffs of the Royal Necropolis of Thebes. A monument to nineteenth-century Europe's imperial pretensions thus appropriately confronts the funerary monuments of one of the earliest empires. It is even a little poignant that the old Winter Palace has now been largely superseded by the New Winter Palace – a compact, air-conditioned upstart parasitically attached to its northern wing.

In the nineteenth century Egypt was a distal and autonomous province of the decrepit Ottoman Empire. Having witnessed the grandeur and decay of Pharaonic, Ptolemaic, Roman, Fatimid and Mameluke Empires, its political power and cultural vitality had been in abeyance for some centuries. It constituted an ideal open-air museum where it never rained. It could be toured in the most leisurely fashion in luxuriously equipped house-boats. Egypt also provided the artists of the European 'decadence' with some of their favourite motifs – notably the Sphinx which appears so prominently in the work of Oscar Wilde and Gustave Moreau. Impressed by the 'inhuman scale and ruthless power' of Pharaonic architecture, self-styled decadents and aesthetes were prone to meditate on the sinister fascination of ancient Egypt. The marvellous 'Arabian Nights' sky-line of Cairo complemented another *fin de siècle* obsession. The East of Byzantium and Islam held a particular fascination for some nineteenth-century French writers – Gautier, Flaubert and Nerval among others. A visit to the Near East was considered excellent therapy for the romantic disappointed in love. In the 1840s Gérard de Nerval had set up house in Cairo with a Javanese girl he had bought in the slave market. Her habit of filling her bed with onions (for the sake of their soothing scent and their religious connotations) soon proved trying, however, and Nerval offered to send her to Gautier.[3] Thomas Cook & Son made it possible for decadents and aesthetes to visit Egypt without sacrificing any of their sybaritism, and Oscar Wilde's lover, Lord Alfred (Bosie) Douglas, was among those to take advantage of this. This tradition was maintained by Ronald Firbank, Wilde's great successor as the apostle of wit and dandyism, who made a Nile tour in the 1920s, during the course of which he is said to have suppressed a mutiny single-handed.

By the 1880s Thomas Cook & Son was an institution of the British Empire. When John Mason Cook left for India in 1880 he went with Gladstone's personal blessing, and seems to have seen his mission in diplomatic terms: '. . . while it would be well to arrange for the visits of Englishmen to India; it would be even more serviceable if the wealthy natives of India could be induced to visit Europe'. Tourism as an agent of 'Human Progress' has here become an agency for the consolidation of Empire – a means by which the ruling class of the conquered country can be induced to identify more closely with the ruling class of the conquering power. John Mason Cook established offices in Bombay and Calcutta and formed the 'Eastern Princes' Department'. In 1887 this department arranged the visits of Indian Princes to Queen Victoria's Jubilee celebrations. These princely travelling parties were often extraordinarily ostentatious, and were likely to include such items as 200 servants, 10 elephants and 33 tame tigers. The Eastern Princes' Department was still in existence in the 1950s when John Pudney wrote his life of Thomas Cook.[4]

It would be unfair to think of Cook's involvement in India as entirely a matter of the successful management of princely extravagance. The company was also charged with the task of reorganising the pilgrim traffic from India to Mecca, which had, until then, been scandalously misconducted. Cooks were given a virtual government monopoly, and like Christian pilgrims to the Holy Land, Indian Moslems were soon enjoying the benefits of their superior honesty and organising ability.

By taking advantage of nineteenth-century advances in transport technology Thomas Cook & Son had effected a revolution in tourism by the end of the century. No longer the preserve of peripatetic aristocrats and eccentrics, tourism was now an industry. Armed with Cook's hotel and rail coupons, the tourist could demand uniform prices and standards of service and accommodation. This new standardisation was double-edged in effect; on the one hand it meant greater comfort and convenience and less need for decision-making on the part of the individual tourist; on the other hand it meant a decrease in the elements of real novelty and adventure in tourism. The tourist was less likely to experience discomfort or embarrassment but also less likely to make any real contact with the country visited. Cook's conducted tour system reduced the tourist destination to a limited number of approved sights.

Cook had also expanded tourism's geographical scope. If the cities of Italy were felt to be overrun with 'dreary, sad looking' men and 'facetious' young women, the aristocrat and adventurer could now look further afield with equanimity to Egypt, the Holy Land or India where Cook's tourism took an essentially different form. In Europe Cook's organised tourism extended the privileges of the upper classes to the bourgeois and the petit bourgeois of the industrialised nations; in relation to the peasantry of Italy the ordinary English tourist assumes a quasi-aristocratic status. In the dependencies and colonies of Empire the tourism of palatial hotels and houseboats expresses and reinforces rigidly hierarchic distinctions between white ruling classes and coloured subject peoples; it is entirely dedicated to the convenience and amusement of aristocrats and colonials. Ironically, one of the ostensible motivations of this tourism remains the admiration of the subject people's 'Glorious Past'.

4 The World, the Flesh and the Devil

MORAL PLEASURE

He felt the breath of centuries of wickedness and disillusion; how
many civilisations had staled on that bright promontory! Sterile
Phoenicians, commercial-minded Greeks, destructive Arabs,
Catalans, Genoese, hysterical Russians, decayed English, drunken
Americans, had mingled with the autochthonous gangsters – everything that was vulgar, acquisitive, piratical and decadent in capitalism had united there, crooks, gigolos, gold diggers, and captains of
industry through twenty-five centuries had sprayed their cupidity
and bad taste over it. . . .'

Cyril Connolly, *The Rock Pool*

The Grand Tourist was not interested in visiting tourist resorts. A town
that existed chiefly to house and divert visitors would not have the
requisite history and culture to attract him. Resorts as such developed first in the home countries of the north-western Europeans, on
the inner peripheries of the metropoles. They began as health resorts
or spas.

The spa which had existed in Western Europe since Roman times
(and earlier than that in Gaul) centred on a spring whose waters were
considered to have health-giving properties. Bath itself was the
Roman Aquae Sulis revived; such French spas as Vichy and Aix-les-
Bains also dated back to Roman times. By the second half of the
eighteenth century the purely curative aspects of these resorts were
largely eclipsed by their social and fashionable aspects. In England
Richard (Beau) Nash reformed Bath, banishing duelling and lunatics
from the streets. It soon became the cynosure of social elegance – a
place for the civilised making and unmaking of marriages. In
Germany the 'baden' (Baden-Baden, Wiesbaden, Karlsbad, Marienbad) were as often as not gambling resorts in disguise. Seaside
resorts like Brighton, Scarborough, Deauville and Trouville were at
first seen as resorts for health rather than pleasure. Bathing at the
English seaside resorts in the eighteenth century cannot have been a
very pleasurable activity; it was considered unhealthy to bathe in
summer when, it was believed, noxious 'saline effluvia' hung over the
sea – sinister, invisible and deleterious to the health of the bather.
Bathing in the frigid seas of October and November was considered
beneficial for an extraordinary variety of ills, including mental ill-

nesses; bathing at Weymouth was one of the many drastic 'cures' for madness to which George III was subjected. There were those who remained unconvinced of the benefits of spas, as the following passage from Smollett's *Humphrey Clinker* demonstrates:

> Good heavens, the very thought makes my blood run cold. We know not what sores may be running into the water while we are bathing, and what sort of matter we may thus imbibe; the king's evil, the scurvy, the cancer and the pox.

In general the pursuit of health became a convenient cover for the pursuit of pleasure. Taking the waters, brisk seaside walks and bathing in an autumn sea endowed pleasure-seeking with the essential appearance of moral qualities (physical exertion being inseparable from 'moral effort' to the bourgeois mentality). Despite this Regency Brighton was quite blatantly a pleasure resort before all else. Within easy reach of the fashionable social world of London, it became famous as the favourite resort of libertines. Its general air of licence and extravagance is epitomised by the high-camp architectural fantasy of the Brighton Pavilion, with its 'Chinese' interior décor and 'Moghul' cupolas. Such undisguised pursuit of the pleasurable and exotic was disapproved of in Victorian England. Nevertheless spas and seaside resorts were an essential adjunct to the prevailing moral hypocrisy of nineteenth-century Europe. They isolated the infection; the upper classes could maintain the moral proprieties in their metropolitan centres, while in their health resorts they could throw their money away and take lovers. 'Quarantine resorts' might be a better description.

The nineteenth century also saw the development of a large-scale pleasure zone at some considerable distance from the metropolitan centres, namely the French Riviera, centring on Nice, Cannes and Monte Carlo (or – as the French called them – the World, the Flesh, and the Devil). By the end of the century the Riviera was unmistakably a manifestation of the Pleasure Periphery at its most extravagant and decadent. Its development only became possible when escape to the South had become a major feature of European tourism, but this development still followed the pattern of the more northerly 'health resorts'. Until the 1920s it remained a winter resort area – the heat of summer was considered not only intolerable in itself but a danger to health. If a resort was too obviously a centre of mere dissipation and pleasure-seeking public reaction could be violent, as the first

promoters of Monte Carlo were to discover. As late as the 1920s
Cannes was anxious to compare itself to the English health resort, in
order to attract the respectable English clientele, an official guide
proudly declaring that: 'Cannes is sometimes called the Mediterranean Cowes.'

LORD BROUGHAM AND THE DAUGHTER OF THE SIRENS

In the eighteenth century Nice was a port of some importance. In
1766 Smollett's *Travels in France and Italy* was published, and as a
result the town soon became a fashionable health resort for the
English aristocracy. Smollett, who was a consumptive, praised Nice's
health-giving air: 'This air being dry, pure, heavy and elastic must be
agreeable to the constitution of those who labour under disorders
arising from weak nerves, relaxed obstruction, perspiration fibres, a
viscidity of lymph and languid circulations.' The Duke of York, the
Duke of Gloucester, the Duke of Bedford, the Duchess of Cumber-
land and the renowned dandy Lord Bessborough duly made Nice
their winter residence, there to enliven their 'languid circulations'.
By the 1780s Nice even had its own English quarter known as
Newborough. A contemporary observer remarked that 'the place is
flourishing, owing very much to the resort of foreigners, principally
English, who pass the winter here for the benefit and pleasure of the
climate'. A certain James Edward Smith declared himself 'disgusted
with the gross flattery paid . . . to strangers and to the English in
particular'. As in Switzerland the Englishman was the 'hoch-tourist'.
The process of Nice's conversion into 'an English watering place' was
temporarily interrupted by the French Revolution and the Napoleonic Wars. The English aristocracy fled and their mansions were
briefly given over to the people.

The comparative prosperity and sophistication of eighteenth-
century Nice were exceptional. In 1785 Monaco consisted of 'two or
three streets upon precipitous rocks; 800 wretches dying of hunger;
a tumbledown castle and a battalion of French troops'. Throughout
the period of the Grand Tour the Riviera had been avoided by
travellers. In the seventeenth century the coast was still infested with
brigands and 'barbary pirates'. In the eighteenth century roads were

bad and those tourists who travelled to Italy via the southern route usually sailed from Marseilles, Nice or Antibes to Genoa. Most tourists avoided even this slight contact with the future Côte d'Azur, preferring to face the 'misshapen scenery' of the Mont Cénis pass. In the nineteenth century when its vogue had begun it could still inspire Swinburne to magnificent invective:

> ... a calcined, scalped, tasped, scraped, flayed, broiled, powdered, leprous, blotched, mangy, grimy, parboiled country WITHOUT trees, water, grass, fields, – WITH blank beastly senseless olive and orange trees like a mad cabbage gone indigestible; it is infinitely liker hell than earth and one looks for tails among the people. And such females with hunched bodies and crooked necks carrying tons on their heads and looking like Death taken seasick.

It was, however, another Englishman who, in 1834, first discovered the charms of an obscure Rivieran fishing village called Cannes. It is characteristic that Lord Brougham should have made the discovery while trying to reach Italy. He was forced to turn back by an outbreak of cholera in Provence. In Cannes he tasted bouillabaisse and the wines of Var, and promptly fell in love with the place. He returned every winter for the next thirty-four years. The official 1922–23 guide book of the Cannes Syndicat d'Initiative is most imaginative when explaining the reasons for Lord Brougham's particular love of Cannes:

> He was charmed by the rosy sunsets (which suggest to poets the blood of barbarous hosts and Roman legions slaughtered in the bay reflected in the heavens and marking their apotheosis).

This invaluable document, which would seem to be the work of a frustrated symbolist poet with an inadequate grasp of English, is equally inspired in its treatment of history: the origins of Cannes, that 'daughter of the Sirens' are 'lost in the Night of Time', but it was a fashionable resort in Roman times; 'During three centuries Cannes had no occasion to envy Bahia or Sorrento, for it rivalled them in palaces beautiful with marble colonnades and gates of brass encrusted with precious stones'. Although this account owes more to imagination than archaeology and succeeds in confusing Italy with Brazil (Bahia/Baiae) it does, inadvertently, remind us of an historical truth: the Baian littoral of Imperial Rome was the only previous resort development comparable in scale to the French Riviera of the nineteenth and twentieth centuries.

Whatever the conjectural glories of Cannes in Roman times Brougham did his best to promote improvements in nineteenth-century Cannes. He agitated for funds to build piers and harbour facilities. In England he advertised its charms so enthusiastically that other members of the English upper classes began to follow his example. By the time Brougham died in 1868, Cannes was a full-scale winter resort with all the necessary cumbrous and palatial facilities. It should be noted that these hotels and villas were situated at Cimiez, in Nice, which was some distance away from the sea. Aristocracy and royalty visited Cannes for the sake of its air; Cimiez was, in the words of the guide-book, 'delicately screened from most of the winds'. There was still something less than absolutely respectable about beach activities – something distinctly plebeian.

'INNOCENT BATHERS ARE ENTICED . . .'

The history of Monte Carlo's rise to fame and fortune is of particular interest. It constitutes the first example of an underdeveloped state converting itself into a 'pleasure reserve' of the European aristocracy, as a solution to a desperate economic situation. As an independent state Monaco could promote the less morally respectable forms of diversion that were impermissible in the neighbouring French resorts. In the 1850s Monaco had been reduced to bankruptcy by the revolt of Menton and Roquebrune against the taxes on olive-oil and fruit that were its chief source of income. Prince Charles III and his mother Princess Caroline consequently decided to develop their state as a winter resort on the lines of Cannes and Nice – with the added attraction of a casino. The princess sent her private secretary M. Eyneaud to Baden-Baden to investigate the profitability of the casino there. Eyneaud was favourably impressed, but pointed out the necessity of disguising a gambling resort as a spa.

The whole project was nearly a disaster, an object lesson in injudicious investment and incompetent tourism planning. The first concession of thirty years was granted to Napoleon Langlois and Albert Aubert. This gave them the right to provide a variety of amenities, 'notably balls, concerts, fêtes, games such as whist, écarte, piquet,

GRAND AND MASS TOURISTS
Eighteenth-century visitors to the Colosseum, Rome (above)
Twentieth-century tourists watch the Changing of the Guard, Buckingham Palace (below)

EXTENDING PERIPHERIES
Thomas Cook's first outing, 1841 (above)
Jumbo jet (below)

faro, boston and reversi, as well as roulette with either one or two zeros and trente et quarante . . .'. The Villa Bellevue was duly opened as a casino in 1856 with garbage cans inauspiciously cluttering its entrance. Monaco was without adequate communications with the neighbouring French resorts and had few hotels. The Villa Bellevue was dilapidated and the casino was soon losing as much as £2,800 a day. Between 15th and 20th March 1857 it received only one visitor who left with the princely sum of two francs in winnings. In the same year Langlois and Aubert sold out to one Frossard de Lilbonne, who, in turn, sold out to a M. Daval, another impecunious incompetent. The casino somehow survived and in 1859 began to make a profit of £50 a day. It was in 1860 that Eyneaud first approached François Blanc who had successfully operated a casino in Bad Homburg for some years.

Blanc immediately embarked upon building the new casino, and rebuilding the royal palace and the Hôtel de Paris. He imported French architects, Italian labourers, Scottish landscape gardeners, and paid the army. He agreed to increase the sum due annually to Prince Charles, and also undertook to improve the road between Nice and Menton. For the first time efficient transport was organised between Nice and Monaco by road and sea. Blanc began to put pressure on the railway company to extend the line to Monaco. The price of land immediately shot up. The 'Société des Bains de Mer at Cerde des Etrangers' was founded with capital of 15 million francs, and 30,000 shares at 500 francs each. Among the first shareholders was the future Pope Leo XIII, then a cardinal.

Until his death in 1881 Blanc was the virtual ruler of Monaco. His prestige was enormous, and the English aristocracy began to visit his casino, among them Lord Strafford, the Duke of Hamilton and Lord Brougham. Lord Brougham spoke of discussing 'politics with statesmen, art with the leading artists and finance with M. Blanc'. Blanc was regarded, with justice, as one of the world's great financiers.

Brougham gave Monte Carlo the tourist establishment's seal of approval, but the local inhabitants were less than enthusiastic. A French pamphleteer wrote:

Near rustic cottages Satan has installed, with all his vulgar seductions, one of his most funereal industries. . . . In this corner of Paradise, amid giant olives, orange groves and fig trees, blessed with air so pure . . . here the genius of ill has established a gaming house. Youths who throw away family fortunes, tradesmen with numbers of children daily meet with ruin and dishonour. Innocent bathers are enticed into the labyrinth of evil, this cathedral of vice, the casino of Monaco. . . .

John Addington Symonds went even further, describing the casino as a 'large house of sin blazing with gas lamps by night, flaming and shining by the shore like pandemonium or the habitation of some romantic witch. . . .' How easily Monaco's pleasure reserve becomes transformed into a gothic nightmare of the repressed bourgeois imagination! Symonds's diatribe also demonstrates the irresistible appeal of such places: sin, voluptuous dissipation and reckless waste were monstrous but fascinating and desirable ('the habitation of some romantic witch'). Monte Carlo's casino thus becomes a 'flower of evil'. This kind of criticism can only have helped to ensure its success.

Opposition was especially virulent in Nice where 700 people sent a petition to Paris demanding the supression of gambling in Monaco. Two blackmailers covered the hoardings at Nice railway station with luridly allegorical depictions of ruined widows, suicides and orphaned children. It seems likely that this moral fulmination had a strictly economic base. The people of Nice and Cannes did not relish the prospect of such a glamorously sinful rival. Petitions and blackmail were to no avail, and in 1868 the railway reached Monte Carlo. His success assured, Blanc distributed charity in Nice, in hopes of pacifying his critics, but the money he gave towards the Cannes 'Battle of Flowers' was used to make grotesque effigies of himself and Prince Charles.

It is unlikely that either Blanc or Prince Charles were much disturbed by these attacks; both were profiting immensely from their investments. Blanc's Hamburg casino was still highly lucrative and Monte Carlo made him so wealthy that he was able to contribute £80,000 of his personal fortune towards the indemnity imposed on France at the conclusion of the Franco-Prussian War. By 1871 Monte Carlo could boast 80 furnished apartments, 4 doctors, 19 hotels, 24 villas and 18 cab drivers. Within the next ten years this increased to 433 furnished apartments, 31 doctors, 35 hotels, 116 villas, etc.

Monaco owed all this to its casino. Sabine Baring Gould in his *Book of the Riviera* of 1905 quotes a certain Miss Dempster: 'It is the green table that keeps the gardens green and the violins in tune; that has brought 30,000 residents and so many hundred prostitutes to the town. . . .' Even the new cathedral had been financed by the proceeds of the casino. None of Monaco's new buildings pleased the vituperative S. B. Gould who compared the 'distant effect' of the cathedral to 'an infant peacock spreading its tail before it has any feathers to display'. The casino and theatre had been designed by Charles Garnier, the architect of the Paris Opera, but in Gould's eyes they were irredeemably vulgar, displaying, 'no token of genius or sense of beauty'. He allowed that gambling would inevitably appeal to 'the lowest types of humanity' (whom he considered to be 'the North American Indians, the half-caste Peruvians and Mexicans', as well as 'the unintellectual and those without mental culture throughout Europe'). In consequence it was sensible that places should be provided for their degraded pursuits, but he laments, 'that one of the fairest spots in Europe . . . should be given over to harlots and thieves and Jew moneylenders, to rogues and fools of every description'. Gould's moral strictures are somewhat blunted for us by their tendency to become confused with their author's numerous racial prejudices, but in this case the criticism is valid. One of the most distressing aspects of mass tourism is its tendency to choose precisely those areas of the world most distinguished by natural beauty and historical interest, as centres for its most unintelligent and neurotic pursuits.

Gould is also outspoken on the subject of gambling suicides. He speaks of a conspiracy on the part of the authorities (including the church) to suppress any hint of scandal:

> directly a man has shot or hung himself he is whisked away by the police and the body concealed till it is ascertained that no-one is particularly interested in his fate. Then at the end of the season, the bodies of the suicides are packed in cases that are weighted and the boatmen sink them far out to sea between Monte Carlo and Corsica.

Even this, we are told, is an improvement on earlier techniques of disposal. The bodies had been crammed into 'holes and cracks in the limestone on which the casino stands'. After a time this was found to be too insanitary, and, according to a certain Captain Weike, sixty corpses were removed from one such rift in 1898. Captain Weike was also the author of a pamphlet, banned in the French resorts, that alleged extensive cheating on the part of the casino management.

Though it may have been founded on the corpses of suicides Monte Carlo's 'labyrinth of evil' could not be dislodged from its rock. Even the earthquake of 1887 proved ineffective in this respect. The Rivieran resorts had been celebrating Shrove Tuesday with masked balls, when the earthquake struck at five in the morning; guests ran screaming into the streets still dressed in the costumes of Pierrot or Columbine, Julius Caesar or Nero. Those who thought this might be divine judgement of Rivieran dissipation must have been disappointed that the earthquake's ravages showed no sign of 'moral choice', for although sedate Menton was badly hit, Monte Carlo was virtually unscathed, its 'cupidity and bad taste' inviolate.

LAST RITES

The development of other resorts was rather less hectic – and it was usually the English who first 'discovered' them. Dr Henry Bennett settled in Menton in 1859 and advertised its charms in his writings. It was considered especially beneficial to consumptives, and if Monte Carlo was the best place to be ruined Menton was considered the best place to die. According to S. B. Gould, doctors would recommend it to their incurable patients so that they might die there without causing them any embarrassment. Menton's cemeteries bear horrifying witness to this.

In the 1860s the Italian Riviera also began to be popular with the English. The novelist George Macdonald settled in Bordighera and an English colony soon grew up around him. In 1861 San Remo opened its first hotel catering for English visitors, and by the end of the century it had become a cosmopolitan resort, rivalling the major French resorts. Its 'sedative' climate was considered especially good for insomnia.

In the 1890s Queen Victoria first visited Cannes, along with her favourite ghillie John Brown, her donkey Jacko, her French chef, Hindu bodyguard, her doctor and '*quelques autres pièces de domesti-cité*'. The English aristocracy were followed by the Russian Grand Dukes, who vastly exceeded them in sheer extravagance. They were enthusiastic but spectacularly unsuccessful gamblers – and hence a great boon to the Rivieran economy. When the Czar visited Nice he was preceded by 100 courtiers, diplomats and servants. On the coast at the same time were Queen Victoria, Franz Josef, 'most of the

Balkan kings, half the English peerage and the Almanach de Gotha'.[1] It is hardly surprising that the Riviera at the turn of the century was five or six times *more* expensive than the Riviera of the 1950s and 'sixties.

As Europe moved steadily closer to catastrophe, its ruling class could retreat, each winter, to the haven of their own geographically distinct pleasure-reserve. This is most evident in the case of the Russian aristocracy; on the Riviera they could enjoy, without restraint, the fruits of their privileged position within an archaic and corrupt social system, without having to witness any of that system's ill effects. The more they were enabled to escape from the social and political realities of their home country, the less inclined they were to accept the necessity of change, and the more inevitable their violent overthrow became. On the Riviera their only social responsibility was to spend freely. The indigenous inhabitants of a fully developed Pleasure Periphery must, to a large extent, suspend the operation of their critical faculties. The host cannot criticise the peccadilloes of his guests when they are the source of his income. At best, the host will adopt a neutrality that tacitly condones and, at worst, he will actively incite the guest to greater excesses.

Thus the European aristocracy found their every whim and eccentricity accommodated. They gambled, made love (with each other or with their servants) and, occasionally, killed themselves from excess of *ennui*. An extensive repertoire of bizarre private rituals was invented to keep this *ennui* at bay. Prince Tcherkovsky, who had a villa at Cimiez, maintained a staff of eighty-seven; of these forty-eight were gardeners whose chief task it was to change every flower in their master's garden each night, so that he might be spared the boredom of viewing the same prospect on two consecutive mornings. Another prince had strawberries delivered to his suite every morning, in defiance of the season. He did not eat the fruit, this was a vulgar function performed by a liveried Cossack servant. The prince would merely crush them with a spoon and explain that, although he could not bear the taste of strawberries, he adored their perfume. The most sophisticated forms of pleasure are those which go against nature. Flowers are by nature sedentary, therefore Prince Tcherkovsky's had to be moved; it is in the nature of fruit to be eaten, therefore it is savoured for its scent alone.

This heroic struggle against boredom did not bring unqualified benefit to the Riviera. Augustus Hare, that most fascinating of

Victorian bores, visited the coast in 1896, and his impressions are far from being entirely favourable. Nice, he dismissed as a 'great, ugly, modern town with a glaring esplanade'. At Nice the view from the Cimiez Grand Hotel had been ruined by the building of 'the frightful Hotel Regina'. The surrounding hills he found covered with the repellent abodes of rich Englishmen.

> ... whose main object seems to be the effacement of all the natural beauties of the place, to sow grass which can never live, to import from the North shrubs which cannot grow, and to cut down and root up all the original woods and flowers. ...

This is a further variation of the 'against nature' theme, but one that aims at reassurance; by introducing the English lawn and its temperate attributes into the exotic flora of the South, one can enjoy all the benefits of Mediterranean air without having to accept a too-evidently foreign environment.

Hare found Saint-Raphaël 'without beauty or interest' but Ste Maxime he approved as 'excellent for people who do not like golf or gaiety'. Hare's comments strikingly recall those of Seneca, Horace and Symmachus concerning the Baian littoral. Like Hare they criticised the excesses of the villa owner, and in general the vulgar extravagances of behaviour a pleasure zone encourages.

Although the *fin de siècle* aristocratic mode of Rivieran tourism remained essentially unchanged in the first decade of the twentieth century there were some innovations. At Nice the Cimiez hotels were gradually deserted in favour of opulent new hotels on the seafront – most notably the Carlton. Cimiez hotels like the Alhambra and the Winter Palace rapidly declined and those that remain standing today have mostly been converted into apartments, schools and clinics. In 1905 Henry Ruhl opened the Ruhl Hôtel on the Promenade des Anglais at Nice. This was followed in 1912 by the Hôtel Negresco. The Carlton and the Negresco have retained their air of *belle époque* splendour, the Negresco still suggesting 'the set of some curious eighteenth-century French comedy being directed by Fellini'. In 1957 its original décor was saved from modernisation by the intervention of nostalgic Americans to whom it represented '*le vrai style européen*'.

It was during the heyday of the Carlton and Negresco that rich Americans, the Vanderbilts and Rockefellers, began to appear in considerable numbers on the Riviera. James Gordon Bennet, the founder of the *New York Herald Tribune*, settled at the Hôtel du Cap at Antibes, and saved it from bankruptcy in the process. He became famous for his 'huge breakfast parties' and his choice of the Hôtel du Cap was prophetic of the tastes of post-war American expatriates. The appearance of Americans on the Riviera was something of a new departure; during the nineteenth century they had, in general, remained faithful to the idea of the Grand Tour. They were late-comers on the European tourist scene and were still largely concerned to absorb a little of the culture of the old world. Because of the distance involved a European tour was also likely to be a 'once in a lifetime' thing for all but the richest Americans. It was only after the Great War that Americans were to emerge as pioneers of a new tourism dedicated to the sophisticated pursuit of simple pleasures.

During the 1913–14 Riviera season 50,000 holiday-makers spent a total of 50 million in gold francs. The grand, masked ball continued, the guests apparently oblivious of the menacing events occurring outside the charmed circle of the chandeliers' light. At the end of the season they fled north again, like vampires running before strong sunlight. In the quiet of the Riviera out of season bells rang announcing the commencement of hostilities, announcing, also, the end of a style of tourism.

5 Simplicity without Innocence

Even though it happened in France, it was all somehow an American experience.

Gerald Murphy

As soon as the armistice had been signed wealthy American tourists began to arrive in Europe; they came in a new spirit of confidence and (even) superiority. The great aristocracy of Europe had failed in the decadence, the Great War and the Russian Revolution of 1917. The nouveaux riches of the new world need no longer feel inferior or gauche before an old world of superior culture and refinement. Many Americans felt that England would soon sink to the level of a politically insignificant 'pastoral country'. They 'would then visit it in much the same spirit as the Romans of the early Empire went to the ancestral ruins of Troy'[1]. In Britain of the 'twenties there was considerable resentment of Americans who were felt to be buying up the country's heritage 'with more acquisitiveness than real taste'. These transatlantic 'culture vultures' soon surpassed the English eighteenth-century Grand Tourists. The English lords might have built replicas of Palladian villas on returning from their tours but they had never succeeded in bringing the originals home with them; during the 'twenties 'Great Lodge' in Essex and Agecroft Hall in Lancashire were dismantled, shipped and re-erected in the States.

If the British felt that the Americans had unfairly profited from the woes of Europe, American intellectuals, in turn, felt slight sympathy for the British. In F. S. Fitzgerald's *Tender is the Night*, the hero, Dick Diver, finds 'something antipathetic' about the English:

England was like a rich man after a disastrous orgy who makes up to the household by chatting with them individually, when it is obvious to them that he is only trying to get back his self respect in order to usurp his former power.

This anti-British feeling was linked with an anti-aristocratic feeling; when Sarah Murphy's sister Mary Hoyt Wiborg took to associating with the titled English the Murphys broke with her entirely. There is a general impression in *Tender is the Night* that the English aristocracy is repellent, cold and, in the final analysis, homosexual. Britain is not so much quaint and 'olde worlde' as effete and sterile.

In a sense this was literally true since an entire generation of English males had been decimated by the War.

France was the American intellectual's preferred country. She accepted the status of 'old world' with consummate style and grace. Before the War, Paris had been the centre of the Decadence – the principal scene of that importation of the exotic that accompanies the development of a Pleasure Periphery. There had been exhibitions of Oriental and African art and visits by Balinese gamelan orchestras. The combination of these exotic and primitive motifs with the *fin de siècle* art of Europe produced the modern style. Thus it was inevitable that, in the 1920s, Paris should remain the centre of the artistic world, although, significantly, many of its most important artists were foreigners (Picasso, Miró, Stravinsky, Ezra Pound, and so on).

For Gertrude Stein 'England had the disadvantage of believing in progress, and progress had really nothing to do with civilisation'. For an 'old world' to adhere to the idea of progress was merely graceless refusal to admit defeat. In contrast France 'could believe in civilisation in and for itself'; she responded to these ambiguous compliments with an enthusiasm for Americana, particularly the music of the American negro. In 1923 Darius Milhaud's ballet *La Création du Monde* received its première. The score combined elements of blues and ragtime with 'neo-classical' stylisations, and in the same programme was a satirical ballet called *Within the Quota* – music by Cole Porter, set design and costumes by Gerald Murphy. The backdrop for this self-conscious exercise in Americana was a parody of the front page of a Hearst newspaper bearing the headline: UNKNOWN BANKER BUYS ATLANTIC.

The American tourists were, themselves, in flight from the philistinism and puritanism of their home country (epitomised by Prohibition). Europe's *ancien régime* had collapsed, and the resulting increase in social mobility combined with the more informal social habits of the Americans to produce a new style of tourism.

In the early 1920s the Riviera was still underdeveloped as a summer resort. Nor could it recover its status as a winter resort; the demise of the Russian Grand Dukes had greatly weakened its economic base. In Nice soup kitchens run by impoverished princesses catered for the tastes of other impoverished émigrés. In Cannes, as a gesture of charity (and perhaps gratitude for earlier munificence) White Russians were put in charge of garbage disposal. Still others became taxi drivers, driving, no doubt, with all the erratic temperament of those who have come down in the world. The 'international set' of which they had been the leaders, still spent its summers at 'Trouville, Deauville and all the other villes'.

The official guide of the Cannes Syndicat d'Initiative of 1922–23 was still chiefly concerned to promote the town as an aristocratic winter resort: 'First and foremost, no resort in Europe has a fairer winter climate. Fogs are unknown. . . . A brilliant series of Gala Dinners and Masked Balls is held throughout the season. . . .' At the same time the guide is already (illiterately) anxious to dispel fears of the Riviera's intolerable summer heat: 'The climate of the French Riviera, contrary to the reports published it [*sic*] most temperate during the summer months.' In contrast Helena L. Waters' *The French and Italian Rivieras* (published 1924) is a perfect hypochondriac's guide: 'The many curves and indentations of the coast . . . are a source of danger, for they give alternate sun and shade with a great difference in temperature and are the cause of many bad throats with people who are susceptible to them.' She also warns against the dangers of watching winter sunsets, which pastime, she avers, often leads to pneumonia. By 1924, however, there were already signs that the Riviera's status and character were undergoing a major change.

The expatriate Americans Gerald and Sara Murphy spent the summer of 1922 on the Normandy coast at Houlgate; they found it chilly and wet. In the same year their friend Cole Porter had rented a château at Cap d'Antibes. The Murphys gratefully accepted his invitation to visit, Gerald later commenting:

> Cole always had great originality about finding places, and at that time no-one ever went near the Riviera in summer. The English and the Germans – there were no longer any Russians – who came down for the short spring season, closed their villas as soon as it began to get warm. None of them ever went in the water you see. . . .

Porter himself never returned to the Riviera but in 1923 the Murphys were already established. They persuaded André Sella, the proprietor of the Hôtel du Cap, to stay open during the summer, and themselves began to clear La Garoupe beach of its layer of seaweed.

A PASTORAL QUALITY
I adore simple pleasures; they are the last refuge of the complex.
Oscar Wilde

Edouard Baudouin, Gerald Murphy, Elsa Maxwell, Frank Jay Gould and Benjamin Ficklin Finney Junior all claim or are claimed by others to have saved the Riviera from bankruptcy by transforming it into a summer resort. Baudouin and Gould did much to turn Juan-les-Pins into a fashionable summer resort. Of all these pioneers, it is noticeable that only one is French; in the 1920s Americans dominated innovations in European social fashions, and no Americans in Europe were more closely and imaginatively in touch with its new artistic movements than Gerald and Sara Murphy. They have a further advantage over their rival claimants in that their Riviera lifestyle provided much of the material for F. Scott Fitzgerald's great novel *Tender is the Night*. This brings us up against the confusing question of the relation of *art* to *reality*. The Murphys were the original models for the Divers – the American couple who are the central characters of the novel, but as the novel progressed the characters of Gerald and Sara Murphy were invaded by those of Scott and Zelda Fitzgerald. For all this, many of the observations of the Divers' lifestyle remain applicable to that of the Murphys and their intimate circle (of which the Fitzgeralds were a part).

In 1923 the Murphys began the conversion of what was to become the Villa America, one of the models for the Villa Diana of *Tender is the Night*. Their example was soon followed by Pablo Picasso and his wife who rented a villa at Antibes. According to Gerald Murphy, Picasso developed a 'habit of creeping up behind people on the beach, waiting for them to stoop over to pick up a shell or something and then photographing them from the rear'. In 1923 the Murphys were also visited by Gertrude Stein and her lover Alice B. Toklas. They were followed by Fernand Léger and his wife, Rudolph Valentino, the Count and Countess Etienne de Beaumont, the Hemingways and the Fitzgeralds. The Hôtel du Cap was soon full to capacity throughout the summer. Benjamin Ficklin Finney gave costume parties on the beach at midday; Gerald Murphy served dry sherry from the bathing huts.

All this activity – and studied inactivity – centred on the beach. Not only was the Mediterranean sun no longer shunned but the most important social activities were conducted under its full glare. A new style of leisure was being created, a style which, for all its sophistication, goes back to the childish idea of pure play.

The waning of the Rivieran 'heliophobia' is, at one level, a direct result of American influence. American tourists often originated from regions with subtropical or 'Mediterranean' climates, and consequently they found the traditional summer resorts of the European upper classes too cold. America was already developing its own peripheral resorts in Florida, Cuba and Mexico, and the more informal habits of these places were imported into Europe. Edouard Baudouin was inspired to open the casino at Juan-les-Pins during the summer by a film of Miami showing American women in beach pyjamas. (Despite this, Ina Clare, the first woman to enter the Juan-les-Pins casino wearing beach pyjamas, only succeeded in doing so by creating a 'scene', sufficiently histrionic to worry its proprietors more than her pyjamas.) Gerald Murphy was a dedicated dandy and a great innovator in the field of 'functional' beach attire. This is referred to in *Tender is the Night* when Nicole Diver remembers how she and Dick Diver had bought 'sailor trunks and sweaters . . . in a Nice back street, garments that afterwards ran through a vogue in silk among the Paris couturiers'. Even in England men's fashions became somewhat less staid as a result of the Rivieran influence, 'sports shirts, coloured flannel and linen trousers' began to appear. The French sailor's striped jersey and white work cap worn with white duck pants soon became a kind of uniform at Cap d'Antibes. In Europe as a whole the elaborately modest, heliophobic beach wear of pre-war days gradually began to disappear.

These mannerisms were not evidences of any real simplicity characteristic of the Murphys and their circle. The style of life they invented on the summer Riviera was, consciously, a work of art. Gerald Murphy believed that 'only the invented part of life was satisfying, only the unrealistic part'. He was a dandy and like the doyen of all dandies and aesthetes, Oscar Wilde, he believed that life should imitate art. On the Riviera he was concerned with the pursuit of the elegantly simple as an aesthetic ideal. The Murphys' style may have seemed casual, youthful and fresh, it was in fact as artificial as Picasso's Antibes paintings, with their nymphs, fauns, goats and pan-pipes executed in shades of yellow and blue. Fitzgerald captures this quality perfectly when he speaks of the Divers' 'expensive simplicity', 'the nursery-like peace and goodwill, the emphasis on the simpler virtues', which 'was part of a desperate bargain with the gods'.

The pursuit of the simple was expressed in a variety of ways in Europe in the 'twenties. England, for example, had its fundamentalist 'back-to-the-landers' who 'had small holdings in picturesque villages; kept chickens and goats; spun, wove and dyed cloth; ran communal hand presses; did lino cuts; bottled fruit and home made wines; wore peasant dress . . .' and so on. The Murphys were both too affluent and too urbane to indulge in such excesses of simplicity, but while on their beach they did wear the clothes of a lower class, 'sailor' if not 'peasant' dress. The Murphy/Fitzgerald Riviera takes on the quality of a Watteau *fête-galante* in 'twenties costume, a social equivalent to the neo-classicism of so much art of the period. In her later life Sara Murphy remarked of her years in Paris and on the Riviera: 'It was like a great fair, and everybody was so young.'

Their Americanisms had combined with fundamental cultural traits in Europe. There was a general reaction on the part of the intelligentsia against the pre-war modes of aristocratic leisure, to which the bourgeoisie had aspired. The Murphys loathed what they referred to as '*sheer* society' and scrupulously avoided the rich 'society people' who, by the end of the 'twenties, had begun to visit the summer Riviera. The aristocrats who were admitted to their circle were those who had rejected, to some extent, the moral values and ritualised social habits of the *ancien régime* in favour of more unorthodox, Bohemian models. As the Murphys and other American expatriates were in flight from bourgeois philistinism, an urge to idealise some social class other than the bourgeoisie or the aristocracy becomes evident. The members of the industrial proletariat could not be converted readily into the figures of pastoral myth (or Barthes' 'nice, neat, commedia dell'arte'). There remained the preindustrial lower classes – the peasant, the fisherman – specifically the poorer inhabitants of Europe's Mediterranean regions ('. . . for the people are as beautiful as the land').[2] The process of idealisation and conventionalisation was already highly developed at the turn of the century (see Chapter 2) but the Great War and the Russian Revolution gave it a new and powerful stimulus. In the eyes of a left-wing intelligentsia the *idea* of the peasant had acquired new lustre; increasingly, it seemed that the hope of the world lay not with the urban proletariat, as Marx had predicted, but with the oppressed, agrarian peoples. On a much simpler level the peasantry pleased aesthetically (with their traditional dress) and morally (with their adherence to essential virtues). But the local inhabitants of the underdeveloped Rivieran and Provençal villages that the Murphys preferred only figure in their pastoral as 'extras' and functionaries.

Even more fashionable than the Mediterranean poor were the American negroes. The novels of the 'twenties by Ronald Firbank (e.g. *Prancing Nigger*) and Carl Van Vechten (e.g. *Nigger Heaven*) treated the negro with sympathy and appreciation. *The Long Weekend* speaks of the excitement felt by fashionable society in England at sharing a dance hall with 'these simply sensual people'. The Murphys themselves were pioneers in the collection of Black American music; their yacht *Weatherbird* had a record of that name by Louis Armstrong sealed in its keel. The Negro had been discovered to have a vital culture of his own, he was also distinct from the philistine bourgeois and the decadent aristocrat by one unalterable factor – namely his blackness.

ÉLITE SYNCOPATIONS: An Aspect of Pastoral Examined

Here I am before the sea; it is true that it bears no message. But on the beach, what material for semiology! Flags, slogans, signals, signboards, clothes, suntan even, which are so many messages to me.
Barthes

Sun tan is not merely a question of surface tone; it connects directly the questions of class and race. The deliberate cultivation of a darkened skin tone by a leisured class is not to be found before the 1920s. Robert Graves and Alan Hodges suggest that sunbathing, like nudism and hiking, was a creation of the Weimar Republic. During the war the Germans had found sunbathing a useful treatment for 'deficiency diseases' in children. Sunbathing became a part of a hearty, outdoor, and largely proletarian style of recreation. This does not explain its adoption *as a fashion* by those leisured and privileged classes that had avoided it previously. The fashion for sun tan is one sign of the profound change in the attitude of tourism's pioneering élite.

In regard to sun tan the new attitude was a complete inversion of the old. This was still very apparent in the 1930s when Patience Strong composed a poem on the subject. This begins with 'lovely girls in scant attire / stretched out full length . . . beneath the Sun's fierce fire'. They are compared with 'mermaids' and 'golden statuary':

the mermaid is a sexual symbol of great antiquity while the 'statuary' is obviously pagan and classical. In the midst of this torrid scene our poetess suddenly sees a girl who carries a parasol, wears 'a white and flowing dress, long white gloves, a shady hat'. Thus protected 'her cheeks were pink as roses and her throat as white as milk'. It turns out that the girl is 'The Ghost of Yesterday', she fades to agonised cries of 'Come back! Come back!' She is the ghost of the pre-war style of holiday leisure – with her virginal whiteness and her air of refinement – removed from the vulgar sensuality of the new Rivieran style.

Until the 1920s the European leisured classes had cultivated their 'milk and roses'. In Roman times ladies of refinement had swathed themselves in the fine silks of Kos to filter the coarsening rays; gardens and parks were provided with elaborately shaded walks, pergolas and colonnades. In general, the ruling classes of white imperialist states avoided darkened skin tone when this was possible. Any deliberate cultivation of a tan would have savoured too much of identification with lower (largely rural) classes and coloured subject peoples. Thus the ladies of the British Empire in India did not relax the cumbersome proprieties of Victorian dress to suit the climate. Similarly, for the females of the landed aristocracy in Europe, a pale complexion was the symbol of their superior delicacy, their idleness and seclusion. When these aristocracies and their empires became decadent and began to collapse, this hierarchic attitude to skin tone also began to collapse.

If the élite of the 'twenties summer Riviera did not invent sun-bathing as a leisure habit, it raised it to the level of high fashion. It was not merely a question of summer beach activities inevitably leading to some kind of a tan – like 'sailor sweaters' and evening visits to Provençal villages – the sun tan became an essential picturesque element in the pursuit of 'expensive simplicity'. It was now sought after for precisely the reasons it had been avoided. It was associated with the simple virtues and closeness-to-the-soil of the peasant, and it was associated with what a liberal intelligentsia conceived to be the superior spontaneity and natural sexuality of blacks.

The summer Riviera was closely linked with fashionable and artistic Paris and by the 1920s the myth of the insatiable sexuality of black people was already long established there. It had figured largely in the French Decadence. In the 1920s these mixed feelings give way to a franker appreciation on the part of the intelligentsia at least. The discovery of black music and culture endowed the Negro with a certain respectability. It even became possible to compare black and white races to the detriment in certain respects of the latter. To be pallid was to be effete; to be intellectual was to be alienated from the body. In a book like *Lady Chatterley* the author seems to move towards condemnation of the males of the aristocracy and the upper middle class, purely on the grounds of sexual inadequacy. To praise the negro for his spontaneity, sexual vigour and natural feeling for syncopation was, of course, a liberal rephrasing of racism now tinged with masochism.

For the post-Freudian generation of the aware, instincts were 'IN'. The clash of the urbane and fashionable with certain aspects of the primitive and natural produced an erotic excitement.

Coco Chanel seems to have been the first to make sun tan an indispensable accessory to a fashionable 'new look' – a look that emphasised the expensively casual ('It doesn't matter how much it costs as long as it looks cheap.'). As the fashion spread any consciousness of its original motivations and 'artistic overtones' rapidly disappeared. The hot summer of 1928 finally popularised sunbathing in England, and scantier bathing costumes, beach pyjamas, 'Mexican' sun hats and sun tan oil soon became a familiar feature of English, as well as French, beaches.

Although black culture was appreciated in the 'twenties by white Americans and Europeans, black artists themselves were still regarded very much as talented children and if, as Barthes suggests, 'even sun tan' has a message – the message is essentially that the sunbather is a child of nature. The bourgeois on their Mediterranean beaches can entertain the illusion of learning to love their bodies again as they did in childhood (see p. 88). The body not only becomes more visible, as the sun tan progresses, but in the process of being exposed to it is made more desirable. At the end of the holiday the sun tan is carried back to the city as a fading trophy that can be restored next summer. The sun tan becomes a mark of class distinction just as the aristocratic 'milk and roses' had been. The metropolitan bourgeoisie did not need to emphasise its separateness from the rural working class; the countryman was sufficiently remote to be idealised. Not so with the urban proletariat: a deep sun tan was the visible proof that the bourgeois had the money and leisure to escape from the north-west European metropolises to the South and the

Sun of the Mediterranean. For a sun tan always provokes the question 'Where have you been this year?' In the 1920s and 'thirties the French Riviera would have been sufficiently prestigious; today one would do better to name some remote Saharan oasis or perhaps the Seychelles or Bali. What had been motivated by aesthetic preference, in its most sensuous aspect, becomes another item in the bourgeois display of wealth. Even when the Mediterranean holiday becomes more widely accessible to the working class in the 1950s and 'sixties the question of status and prestige is still an important factor; bourgeois values have simply been transferred.

For many Mediterranean holiday-makers, acquiring a sun tan has become the principal reason for taking a holiday. Sun tan is in every sense a cult with its own obsessive ritual, its sacrifices, its specialised costume and implements. Many tourists who come from temperate regions experience great difficulty in acquiring a tan; they have to suffer to become beautiful. It is physically painful for them to change their skin, to become this different desirable creature at play on the beach, worshipping the sun. To attempt this transformation and to fail is social disaster. Not only does sunburn make its victim unattractive (the raw rather than the cooked), it makes it painful for them to be touched by others. A minor industry has grown up around this fear. We are offered a whole range of products (many of them perfectly useless) that claim to enhance the tanning process – remove the pink and painful intermediate stage and make the final result a deeper, more coppery gold.

This industry's advertising naturally does all it can to strengthen and perpetuate the myth and in this it is enthusiastically supported by the brochures of travel agents and National Tourist Bureaux – which are liberally adorned with bronzed girls and (on occasion) their mates. Sometimes this 'golden statuary' is linked to an item of local colour or historicity. Let us examine two such examples with, respectively, Tunisian and Greek settings. In the first a blonde, bronzed, bikinied girl clasping snorkel and fresh fish rides a camel – her expression a rather desperate attempt at Eastern Magic crossed with Amazonian hauteur. In the second a generically similar model reclines dreamily against a Greek column – our modern pin-up thus becoming some revenant goddess in the ruins of her temple; her expression, alas, is merely soporific. Perhaps this second juxtaposition is implying that you too can attain classical beauty and pagan sensuality for only £50+ inclusive? Quite frequently the blonde-haired, gold-skinned model (who is more likely to be Swedish than Tunisian or Greek) entirely obliterates her surroundings, all that is required is sunlight and a Freudian hint of seaspray.

It is clear that our automatic assumption that a tan makes a person more attractive is the product of recent social conditioning peculiar to the North Atlantic Community (Arabs are seeking to whiten their complexion). The artificiality of this adoption of an ideal of 'natural beauty' is strikingly revealed in the further range of products that make it possible for us to become 'children of the sun' (heliophiles) without the assistance of the sun. What could be more piquant than a tan acquired suddenly, at night, in winter, in the city? And is this artifice still supposed to signal that we are children of nature, desirable, available? The erotic element in the sun tan achieves near-epicene complexity when we become aware that tan and pallor are juxtaposed on the same body. I refer, of course, to the piebald nude models of pin-up magazines who have evidently sunbathed in their bikinis. This produces an effect curiously ludicrous and decidedly prurient. The pallor of the erogenous zones lends them a spurious, virginal mystique, and preserves the idea that despite their nakedness they are still secret and forbidden. The milk and roses complexion of the lady of refinement emphasised her ethereal elevation above the mass; the pallor of the pin-up girl's breasts suggests exclusivity of a different order; they are offered exclusively to readers of the magazine in which she appears. Perhaps the partial whiteness of the nude is also a reassurance of racial identity, for a sun tan that has gone beyond gold/brown to near black is generally considered less attractive. Since it is a phenomenon of white, bourgeois, capitalist states the sun tan craze does not imply any real breaking down of the barriers of colour and race. It merely flirts with the idea of the erotic aspect of colour, and perhaps symbolises a partial absorption into 'the System' of blackness, thus rendering it less threatening (priapism domesticated). The logical continuation of this process was the appearance in the 1960s of blacks decked in all the most superfluous luxuries of the affluent society in the pages of *Vogue*.

The sun tan craze is a microcosm of the whole tendency of mass tourism. Arriving with the final dominance of bourgeois philosophies and ideals, based on an illusory idea of another class or race – it is first adopted by an élite, then taken up by the mass of the bourgeoisie, mythologised and industrialised.

THE INCORRUPTIBLE CORRUPTED

... he considered the world of pleasure – the incorruptible Mediterranean with sweet old dirt caked in the olive trees, the peasant girl near Savona with a face as green and rose as the colour of an illuminated missal. He would take her in his hands and snatch her across the border ... but there he deserted her – he must press on towards the Isles of Greece, the cloudy waters of unfamiliar ports, the lost girl on shore, the moon of popular songs.

F. S. Fitzgerald, *Tender is the Night*

The above passage sums up an entire popular mythology which has had a direct influence on tourism. This mythology promulgates a world governed according to the philosophies of popular songs, given over to the worship of youth and the cult of moist-eyed, romantic innocence. It attained its fullest expression in the films of the 'twenties and 'thirties 'with their myriad faces of girl-children, blandly represented as carrying on the work and wisdom of the world'. It is also expressed in the thousands of framed prints that, until recently, adorned so many petit-bourgeois living-rooms: the young lovers are poised against some Riveran balustrade; above them the moon and stars, beyond them a palm-fringed esplanade and calm sea. This imagery is cinematically derived and it is appropriate that the Victorine Film Studios should have been set up at Nice in 1923 by Rex Ingram. A film colony was soon added to the Riveran élite; among others, it included Mary Pickford, Douglas Fairbanks and Harpo Marx.

The process of 'discovery' by the intelligentsia continued. The Bloomsbury Group discovered Villefranche and Katherine Mansfield and Aldous Huxley settled at the Hôtel Welcome. Phillip Barry and H. G. Wells, meanwhile, arrived in Cannes. The Riviera continued its tradition of accommodating the world's eccentrics. In Nice Frank Harris hired twelve-year-old girls to dance naked in his garden. Henry Clews, an American millionaire and sculptor, bought the Château de la Napoule; Charles Graves in *Royal Riviera* describes him (from the evidence of his works) as 'A cynic, a sadist and a Communist'. The grounds of his château are adorned today by an emaciated male nude with a deathshead in place of genitalia. He was also, apparently, capable of more delicate flights of fancy, since he stocked his gardens with white birds to which he attached miniature flutes. His wife had a complementary *penchant* for white peacocks, birds so ill-disciplined they strayed frequently on to the nearby

railway tracks, bringing the famous Train Bleu to a halt. Timetables
became so disrupted that an official complaint had to be made.
Tragedy soon overshadowed the carefully nurtured serenity of the
Rivieran pastoral. Scott Fitzgerald's deterioration into alcoholism
and creative inertia accelerated; Zelda suffered her first nervous
breakdown. The Murphys' son Patrick was found to be suffering
from tuberculosis. In 1927 Isadora Duncan died on the Promenade
des Anglais – extravagantly as she had lived – strangled by a long
scarf caught in the wheel of a car. In the following year Avery
Hopwood, an American playwright, walked into the sea at Antibes,
fully clothed, and drowned himself. The 'desperate bargain with the
gods' had been broken.

A series of wet summers at 'Trouville, Deauville and all the other
villes' brought 'sheer society' to the summer Riviera. In 1927 Grant
Richards was already complaining of traffic, speculative building and
overcrowding. According to Benjamin Ficklin Finney '1930 was the
last of the great years, after that the Riviera became too crowded'.
This was also the period of the Wall Street Crash, and although in
1930 there were more Americans on the Riviera than ever before
they rapidly lost their position of dominance and their role as social
arbiters of the new tourism. The introduction of the paid holiday in
France in 1936 brought a new influx of lower-class French holiday-
makers. In his Riviera novel *The Rock Pool*, Cyril Connolly sums up
this development in a remark about 'Parlez moi d'amour ousting the
stricter blues'. After 1930 it was no longer possible to maintain the
illusion that the summer Riviera was the exclusive pleasure reserve of
the beloved of the gods – those who were all distinguished by some
remarkable personal quality. The Murphys left Europe for good in
1933. Finney never returned to the Riviera after 1937. In 1935 Cyril
Connolly remarked of the expatriate colonies (in prose appropriately 'twenties-modish): 'The bars are closed, the hotel is empty, the
nymphs have departed.' If this was the end of the exclusive expatriate
cliques it was only the beginning of the summer Riviera. Quantity
naturally increased at the expense of quality. Beverly Nichols
remarked (in *All I Could Never Be*) of the 1930s Riviera: 'The people!
Ye Gods, – the people! Drunken, debauched, heartless, of an incredible vulgarity – swooping, screaming, racketing.'

The escape from disillusion had led to another, painful disillusionment. The discoverers of paradises either (as explorers) kill off the
unsuspecting noble savage with syphilis and the common cold, or

less dramatically (as tourists) ruin them and their paradisal environment with the rampant commercialisation that is 'the nemesis of élitist escapism.

The insights of creative writers frequently pre-empt those of sociologists and psychoanalysts by many years. This seems to be the case when we consider the development of the Pleasure Periphery in this century. As early as 1925 Aldous Huxley recognised its essential characteristics: 'Forty miles of Mediterranean coast have been turned into one vast pleasure resort . . . one vast shuffling suburb – the suburb of all Europe and the two Americas – punctuated here and there with urban nuclei.' In *The Rock Pool* Connolly observes its dubious effects on vulnerable host societies when he speaks of: 'elderly peasants and shopkeepers who seemed to have acquired an air of licentiousness from their customers . . .'. The romantically cadential Fitzgerald passage quoted as heading to this subsection has an ambiguous and (with hindsight) almost menacing undertone. The idealistic seeker of 'the world of pleasure' must (in the 1920s) look beyond the most immediately accessible Mediterranean regions of southern France and Italy to the 'Isles of Greece, the cloudy waters of unfamiliar ports'. By the late 1930s tourism's avant-garde had reached as far as Bali. According to *The Long Weekend* Bali 'became fashionable for its dances, music, clothes, climate and beautiful girls. Rich British and Americans flocked there and came back with gaily coloured Bali-esque prints . . . for the rich it had the advantage of being so far away from Europe that the middle-class tourist and the hungry painter could never afford to overrun it'. Bali was and still (barely) is the archetypal Eden/Paradise Isle, blessed by a luxuriant climate with inhabitants who all appear to be spontaneous musicians, painters and dancers. What had been imported earlier, for the delectation of Parisian intellectuals, could now be visited. Today Bali is in vogue once again; as a result it is experiencing serious social disruption and its whole complex and delicate culture is at risk (see Chapter 9).

In the later 1930s the structure of the Western European Pleasure Periphery was already established. Capri had been popularised by Norman Douglas' novel *South Wind*, the Balearics, more prosaically, by the lowness of the peseta. In both cases tourist development was temporarily halted by political factors, respectively the Mediterranean crisis and the Spanish Civil War. *The Long Weekend* states that:

More than ever in the 1930s middle-class people went abroad for
their holidays; either on cruises or on the cut-rate European tours
that the many travel agency services were offering: Scandinavia,
the Danube countries, Holland, Dalmatia, even North Africa were
added to the list of holiday countries.

Contemporaneously the North American Pleasure Periphery had
expanded from California into Mexico, and from Florida into Cuba.
The Second World War naturally caused a major hiatus in the development of international mass tourism, but it did not alter its essential characteristics. The post-war expansion is implicit in pre-war
tourism.

This continuity is clearly illustrated by Saint-Tropez's history as a
resort. In the 1920s it had attracted the painters Bonnard, Signac,
Braque and Dufy. In 1923 Colette was already complaining of overcrowding. After the Second World War, Saint-Tropez was in a
depressed condition, much as the traditional Rivieran resorts had
been after the Great War. The pre-war artists' colony had gone and
the place had a generally faded, nostalgic air. It was precisely this
atmosphere that persuaded Roger Vadim to choose Saint-Tropez as
the setting for his film *And God Created Woman*. The success of the
film promptly destroyed Saint-Tropez's special quality. It became the
preferred resort of such jet set and cinema luminaries as Brigitte
Bardot (the star of the film), Françoise Sagan, Claude Chabrol,
Sacha Distel and Annette Stroyberg. The village soon became a
'must' for anyone wishing to be thought fashionable. The life-style
that developed there represents another variation of the simple-life
theme – expressed in nudity, the ubiquitous faded denim and (most
recently and obscenely) the craze for ex-Vietnam uniforms with real
blood stains and bayonet tears. The Saint-Tropez set were probably
the inventors of that most persistent trait in the 'sixties and 'seventies
high fashion, described by Tom Wolfe as 'Funky Chic', whose
devotees indulge in a purely sartorial rejection of class; they adopt
versions of the characteristic dress of labourers, sailors, cowboys,
urban negroes or common soldiers – or more precisely, they adopt
what they conceive to be the characteristic dress of these non-
bourgeois groups. This conception derives largely from films and
novels, and bears little relation to the contemporary reality of
labourers or urban negroes. Anti-cultural tourism has spawned
anti-fashion, the latest descendant of the Murphys' 'functional' beach-
wear.

SIMPLICITY WITHOUT INNOCENCE

. . . the hidden aim of sublimation and the cultural process is the
progressive discovery of the lost body of childhood.

N. O. Brown, *Life Against Death*

I have spoken earlier (Chapter 1) of 'a flight from civilisation and progress in search of a world of pleasure'. The artistic and cosmopolitan élite that had popularised the Riviera as a summer resort was disillusioned with the idea of progress (which in Stein's words, 'had really nothing to do with civilisation'). It was also disillusioned with the traditional forms of Western civilisation, and at the same time, too closely attached to that civilisation to reject it utterly. The members of this élite wanted to escape from excessive sophistication and *ennui*. They wanted something new, something fresh, whether it was jazz or Dadaist manifestations. They also wanted to return to a life of the senses, to a lost innocence; if the Diver/Murphys' 'expensive simplicity' lacked innocence it was, nevertheless, *about* innocence. One of the means they used to regain this 'world lost' was tourism. They alternated between the complexity and sophistication of Paris and 'the incorruptible Mediterranean'. In the summer the Riviera was empty of the 'Society with its foolish cliché'. It was a classical landscape turned in upon itself, 'fixed inextricably in the past', imbued with 'the poise and the distress of the ancient world' with 'its simple and limited cycle of joy and sorrow'. This was not a fresh beginning as it may have seemed at the time; it was a distinctly Alexandrian simplicity, 'The last refuge of the complex'.

This most recognisably modern form of leisure and escapism arose, like the modern style in art, out of a clash between the over-sophisticated and the primitive. The refined style of its originators was fated to be vulgarised; their Greek restraint and elegance was bound to give way to Roman ostentation and excess. The outward forms of this lifestyle – the beach parties, sunbathing and matelot sweaters – were to be imitated all along the Mediterranean coasts, but the personal qualities that made it valuable were to be lost in the process of popularisation. The Murphys and their circle had perfected a style of elegant living that, unlike the pre-war aristocratic models, did not require titles and inherited fortunes; it was open to wide imitation on the part of the bourgeoisie. If the Villa America existed today it would be 'featured' lavishly on the pages of all the

glossy magazines. Just as aesthetic preference gives way to materialistic considerations of status and class, the Murphys' recognition of
the artificiality of their way of life gives way to 'mystification'.
Rivieran tourism becomes a technique for avoiding the recognition
of social realities, since the social reality of the tourist destination is
frequently one of grinding poverty and political oppression. What had
been a carefully preserved illusion is now taken for fact, in order that
the tourist may enjoy, undisturbed, his holiday.

LIDO LIBIDO

Happy those early days, when I
first shin'd in my Angel Infancy.
Henry Vaughan

Simplicity without innocence requires intelligence and personal distinction if it is not to sink to the level of mindless atavism. The
conscious seeker of the world of pleasure becomes the sun seeker of
the travel agent's brochures. The summer Riviera of the 1920s is the
direct ancestor of the 'costas' of the present day with their pre-
packed, simplistic formula of sun, sea, sand and sex. An élitist model
has been extended first to the bourgeois, and then to the petit
bourgeois and (in the days of the package tour) to the working classes.
This kind of tourism would seem to demand only a hotel, a beach, a
reliable amount of sunshine and the presence of a sufficient number
of other tourists, preferably of the same nationality. Its central figure
is the bronzed, bikinied, blonde, whose presence, as we have already
observed, frequently obliterates her surroundings.

Two things distinguish this tourism: its apparent simplicity and its
recent historical origin. Any simple formula that appeals to millions
of ordinary people must have a motivation deeply rooted in the
culture and psychology of those ordinary people. It is a tourism
stripped of the overt educational motivations of the Grand Tour:
since it seeks sameness and familiarity it does not belong to the pursuit of the exotic. It is related to, but also remote from, the sophisticated 'versions of pastoral' of the 'twenties Riviera. It is related in
that it is the final, mass expression of the flight to the South, and
escape from the metropolitan world which began to appear in the
tourism of the eighteenth century (growing in momentum with the
industrialised conurbations of the nineteenth and twentieth cen-

turies). It is related in so far as it seems to involve a rejection of the complexities of 'civilised progress'. It is remote in that it lacks self-awareness and is, in the final analysis, an implement of the general repression of individuality demanded by the 'civilised progress' of Western Capitalism. It is 'performance principle'* tourism.

Since it is based on illusion the tourist industry resists analysis, yet it proves to be highly susceptible to analysis in terms of neo-Freudian theory, specifically that of N. O. Brown. There is a scene in which the lost summers of childhood seem longer and hotter than those of adult experience. This is borne out by the fashionable acclaim accorded to such recent films as Joseph Losey's *The Go-Between*, Luchino Visconti's *Death in Venice* and Robert Mulligan's *Summer of '42*. In childhood the members of the North Atlantic middle classes enjoy a 'privileged irresponsibility' which 'permits and promotes an early blossoming of the essential desires of the human being without repression and under the sign of the pleasure principle'. These 'essential desires' are narcissistic and hedonistic. Innocence assumes that 'the world was made for the benefit of human beings, has a human shape and a human meaning and is a world in which providence, protection, communication with other beings including animals, and, in general, "mercy, pity, peace and love" have a genuine function'.[3] It is a world entirely centred on the child-narcissus. This outlook remains deeply embedded in the adult mind when this 'privileged irresponsibility' has to be surrendered to Reality and Experience (as against Pleasure and Innocence). The innocent vision of childhood:

> . . . having nowhere to go is driven underground into what we should call the subconscious where it takes an essentially sexual form. The original innocent vision becomes a melancholy dream of how man once possessed a happy garden but lost it forever. . . .[4]

– unless, like the Murphys, he was lucky enough to recapture it in the garden of the Villa America. Such partial recoveries of Paradise Lost are a possibility only for a privileged minority.

The adult also loses his sense of completeness and identification with a benevolent nature when it becomes necessary to engage in

---

* That social coercion and repression demanded by the particular freakish nature of our consumer society, which goes beyond what is strictly necessary for the preservation of an ordered society.

socially functional labour. This is especially the case with North Atlantic tourists of the 'fifties, 'sixties and 'seventies who, for most of each year, engage in a form of alienated labour that provides little opportunity for individual expression, or the gratification of essential desires. This potentially explosive situation changes if the adult is allowed to step outside his social/cultural setting into a temporary freedom from alienated labour and into a social/cultural setting towards which he feels no pressing responsibilities. Now, in an exact sense he is able to enjoy again this 'privileged irresponsibility' of childhood, and briefly his essential desires are allowed to blossom 'under the sign of the pleasure principle', insulated from his established reality principle by the simple device of distance and an exotic setting. The thinner the veneer of culture and education the more this will tend to emerge; the tourist's essential desires will manifest themselves as sun, sex and water (rather than sand). He will wear minimal clothing, indulge in idle sex (or at least flirtation), enjoy 'water play' and sunbathe, becoming the sun-tanned 'child of nature'. The Mediterranean environment allows him to entertain, once again, the childhood illusion that nature is benevolent. In this manner a sober citizen of Manchester or Düsseldorf can become a 'lord of misrule' for two weeks on a Spanish beach. Thoughts of social responsibilities or the evidence of high culture that may be around him will impinge very little. 'The nursery – like peace and goodwill, the emphasis on the simpler virtues' of the Divers/Murphys becomes simple infantilism. The tourist may become childlike, but he cannot become innocent for two weeks. This tourism is a parody of N. O. Brown's 'progressive discovery of the lost body of childhood' with sublimation at a very low level.

The tourist is the centre of his strictly circumscribed world. The package tourist visiting any of the Mediterranean rivieras or 'costas' is surrounded, furthermore, by surrogate parents; the travel agent, the courier, the guide, the hotel manager and his service staff all relieve the tourist of responsibility and protect him from harsh reality (a reality which in Spain, Southern Italy or the Caribbean is, indeed, often harsh). Their solicitude restricts his activities to the beach and a list of approved 'sights' (natural or historical); in a wider sense the package tourist's sensuality and aesthetic sense are as contained and restricted as they are in his home country. The protectiveness of this highly controlled form of tourism also prevents the tourist from realising the implications of his tourism. Consequently he can regard areas of great natural beauty and cultural interest as his sand-pit and swimming-pool.

This has been one of the principal means by which the tourist industry, since the Second World War, has offered its customers temporary release from the stringent demands of a highly developed consumer society. In this sense it seems a purely benevolent industry, tending to heal the psychic scars of metropolitan alienation and anxiety, but it only seems so if viewed in isolation. Although it is the industry of pleasure, tourism is not opposed to the official functional values of productivity, conformity and obedience to routine – it complements them. There is a middle ground between the sub-conscious desire to return to an egocentric world of infantile pleasure, and the conscious seeking of escape and relaxation through tourism. This middle ground consists of a body of generally accepted 'subter-ranean values' that are apparently opposed to the formal values of society; alongside acceptance of the deferred gratification necessary for productive labour is the pursuit of short-term hedonistic fulfil-ment; alongside conformity and submission to routine is a recogni-tion of the value of individual expressivity and new experience. To put it simply, it is a case of functional versus non-functional, work values versus the values of leisure. In an affluent and highly organised industrial society, work tends to lose its dignity and personal signi-ficance, and the individual seeks to discover his identity and sense of purpose in his leisure time. In the midst of affluence and high tech-nology this is an attitude which seems increasingly rational, and, without social restraints and controls, it could, potentially, threaten the hegemony of repressive, official values. The intervals of leisure in the working week would come to seem inadequate. The peaceful co-existence of the two value systems is ensured, however, by the provision of 'institutionalised periods in which the subterranean values are allowed to emerge and take precedence. Thus we have the world of leisure, of holidays, festivals and sports . . .'[5] The Mediter-ranean beach holiday of the north-west European is an obvious example of the contained expression of subterranean values. It is a form of officially sanctioned deviancy; the tourist is allowed to reject the formal work values to which he normally adheres but his pursuit of hedonism and expressivity takes place in a controlled, artificial environment, and in strict isolation from his home society. It is therefore doubly 'safe'.

The image of the Mediterranean 'world of pleasure' is kept before

the affluent producer-consumer, but it can only be attained by fulfilling society's demand for work and productivity. In this way the
principles of performance and productivity can encompass the world
of pleasure, and the promise of liberation becomes another instrument of repression.

6 The Pleasure Periphery

The Second World War marked a watershed. Before it, in the 'twenties and 'thirties, organised tourism was chiefly a matter of trains, boats or coaches. Post 1945, such travel was increasingly by aeroplane, thus allowing the Pleasure Periphery to expand into new, mass destinations like Spain, Greece, Bermuda, the Bahamas, Cuba and Hawaii.

Each decade has seen a massive increase in the importance of aircraft in this process until, today, we are on the verge of truly Global Tourism, in which the pleasure peripheries of the different continents are rapidly merging. Americans have been deserting the Caribbean as they find trips to Europe as cheap and interesting. The European vanguard has tired of the Mediterranean and is looking further afield to new destinations, including the Caribbean and, even, the United States themselves. The Japanese, meanwhile, are circling the globe in either direction, becoming the leading national group of tourists to the United States, ousting American Servicemen and Australians as leading holiday-makers in the Far East, and becoming increasingly important visitors to Europe.

An example of the growing competition between various tourist destinations has occurred just recently, when the Caribbeans suddenly realised that North American tourists were losing interest. Instead of redoubling their sales efforts in the Americas, they tried to encourage Europeans to come in increasing numbers, as a way of reducing the area's overdependence on its role as playground of the American East Coast. However, Europeans who can afford to fly to the Caribbean are equally capable of flying east to places like Kenya in East Africa, or the Indian Ocean's 'islands of love', the Seychelles. The Caribbean hoteliers association realised this and sent a delegation out to see what this competition was like. So the Caribbeans find themselves competing not only with the cathedrals and beaches of Europe for their traditional American clientèle, but also the lions in East Africa and the temples of India which are their rivals for Europe's travel budgets. Competition now comes from destinations half the globe away.

Although this world has significant continuities with pre-1939 tourism, it is built on a scale totally unknown to the Murphys, who were essentially dependent for mobility on ships, railways and, to a lesser extent, cars. However, as their charmed world in the Riviera of the 1920s crumbled before the harsh reality of the Great Slump, so was the structure growing of the new transport industry which would revolutionise tourism – that of the aeroplane. Originally the fledgeling airlines primarily served businessmen and government officials, but some of the routes, particularly those serving the needs of Empire, were attractive to rich tourists as well. Thus Bermuda, linked by flying-boat to New York in 1937, fitted nicely into the communications network developed for the British Empire. Similarly, Indonesian islands like Bali were only just off the main arteries of the Asian empires of the Dutch and ubiquitous British. However, it was the Mexican resort of Acapulco which can probably justifiably be claimed as the first international resort to have depended primarily on air-borne tourists.[1]

Mexico to the north had always attracted Americans. After all, the early Hollywood moguls chose Los Angeles for film-making, at least partly because the Mexican border was near enough to flee across if the legal wrath of New York competitors should catch up with them. Then, with prohibition, the seedy 'Boys' towns' mushroomed along the U.S.–Mexican border. Tijuana, Nuevo Laredo and Ciudad Juarez were places to which parched gringos came in their search for booze, broads, gambling or whatever turned them on. This 'tourism', however, had little to do with the real Mexico lying further south, accessible only by rail or air.

Acapulco, way down on Mexico's Pacific south-west coast, originally developed as a purely Mexican resort in the 1930s, slowly attracting a handful of adventurous travellers – and the very rich. In 1940 the oil multi-millionaire, J. Paul Getty, was told about it and took a look at Revolcadero Beach, exclaiming: 'I've seen every beach – wouldn't this make a wonderful home for mother?'[2] He immediately got his aides to work, telling them that this was 'heaven on earth', and proceeded to find ways of circumventing the Mexican law forbidding foreigners from purchasing land within fifty miles of the coast. Through his political contacts in Mexico, and some shrewd legal advice, he was able to enter a partnership with a wealthy Mexican citizen and bought 900 acres at 3 cents an acre. 'Heaven' came cheap.

In the meantime, the Second World War meant that non-combatant

Americans had nowhere exciting to go, so the rich and the fashionable took to flying down to Acapulco. The Hollywood stars attracted a wider clientèle and the resort exploded – almost literally, since its population zoomed from 10,000 to 150,000 in the course of a decade. If Acapulco was probably the first international tourist resort made possible by the development of passenger aircraft, then it was the Europeans who were really enthusiastic about marrying this new technology to mass tourism, in the way Thomas Cook had done with railways. In fact, even in 1938, the company that bore his name was running holidays in Nice, using chartered aircraft.[3] The war in Europe put a stop to further experiments along these lines, but was eventually responsible for stimulating a boom in 'package tourism' which might well have been developed somewhat later than it was, if the war had not happened at this particular time.

The war helped in some fairly intangible ways. It finally killed the Great Depression, ushering new eras of more or less Keynsian-inspired prosperity, without which the growth in tourism would have been impossible. It also bred a new degree of cosmopolitanism. The Italian boom of the late 1940s and early 1950s owed a great deal to GIs returning to the scene of their active service. Similarly even today, property operators in the Pacific are cashing in on nostalgic ex-GIs, now nearing retirement, who feel they might like to settle down in one of the exotic islands they fought over in the Pacific campaign.

Above all, the war left a world filled with planes and military airfields. The latter were often found in extremely remote locations, particularly on small islands which were difficult to supply by sea in the middle of hostilities. So, within Europe, as the era of post-war austerity eased, the tourist found himself with a choice of islands like Corsica, Sardinia, Majorca and Minorca in the Mediterranean, which were attractive, cheap and often already well equipped for taking planes.

Nineteen-forty-nine saw the first post-war attempt to build a package holiday around air transport, the model for most of today's global tourism. Vladimir Raitz (Russian émigré and educated at the London School of Economics) had the idea of selling a Corsican holiday camp to British tourists. A relative newcomer to the industry, he realised the only way he could cut the costs sufficiently was by chartering a plane at rates well below the standard fares. So he approached the British authorities who eventually let him go ahead, provided that the total cost of the holiday did not undercut the scheduled airline fares, and that he only dealt with specific groups such as teachers, nurses and students.

So, in 1950, he was advertising for such clients, flying these pioneers out to a life of shared tents and twice-daily meat dishes. His company was soon successful, and Horizon Holidays (one of Britain's Big Three up to 1973) went on to help develop Majorca and Sardinia as destinations. Then, in 1956, they started flying tourists down to the Spanish mainland, which had been ignored since the war.

The areas selected were to become two of the boom areas in Spain – the Costa Brava (north-east coast, up against the border with France) and Costa del Sol (the southern Mediterranean coast from Gibraltar to the east).

It was not until the early 1960s that Raitz's competitors all started using aircraft in a major way. A successful rival, Global, was still running coach 'packages' to places like Oberammergau and Rome, until its first use of aircraft in 1960.

Other countries followed suit. For instance, 1950 saw the first faltering steps of that French institution, Club Méditerranée, which, starting as a sports association, depended on its 2,500 members and a tent village in Majorca. Like many of its rivals, it had its money problems and in 1953 found it had no money to pay the next instalment of the tents. Despite appeals, the tent manufacturer gave them no extra time to pay, but that company's son and heir joined 'Club Méd' as a partner. The German situation was more complicated, starting somewhat late. By one of those quirks which shapes industries, travel agents were worried that, if they sold too many air trips, they would lose their concessions to sell rail tickets, which they saw as more profitable. So nothing much happened until the 1960s when mail-order companies like Neckermann started selling serial package holidays, using their stores as points of sale. Sweden, on the other hand, accepted package holidays from the start. The government took the line that such holidays were socially desirable, so tour operators should be free to sell as widely as possible and, by 1968, the Swedish figure for aerial package holidays was around 5 per thousand head of population, which was almost double the 2·7 per thousand of the British who are also strong clients of this kind of holiday.

The growing willingness of tourists to take to the air has produced three major phenomena since 1945. First, there has been the annual

ALPINE PERILS
Nineteenth-century alpinists (above)
Alpine resort of La Plagne (below)

TOPHATTED TO TOPLESS
Victorian bathers (above)
Copenhagen beach, 1972 (below)

flood of North Americans across the Atlantic to Europe – new imperialists visiting the fading cultures from which they once sprang. Then, there has been the growth of the Caribbean industry, where American tourists have stepped into the vacuum left by the political withdrawal of the old colonial powers. Finally, within Europe, there has been the spectacular explosion of the Mediterranean resorts, drawing heavily on sun-seekers from the colder parts of the continent; primarily, this has involved Italy and Spain – the former building its industry on its cultural heritage, while the latter has relied on providing cheap holidays in the sun.

In practice, however, more adventurous souls, like Hemingway, had been exploring Spain and its Balearic islands (Majorca, Minorca, Ibiza) well before 1937. The international outcry following Franco's victory, and his ambiguous role in the Second World War, killed these developments stone dead and it was not until the early 1950s that Spanish tourism started to revive.

Since statistics were first seriously gathered in 1951, the number of incoming tourists has been increasing on average by 15 per cent per annum, with virtually no setbacks. The result has meant that the 1·2 million visitors of 1951 are now 34·6 million (1973 figures), which means that of every six international tourists, one is visiting Spain. Even if the statistics need taking with a grain of salt, since they include French and Portuguese excursionists, there is now a tourist for every Spaniard, of whom one in twenty-five works directly in hotels or restaurants. Many others are involved in transport, construction, or agricultural work indirectly linked to tourism as well.[4] This explosion has had virtually nothing to do with traditional Spanish culture which, for most tourists, means merely Flamenco, bullfights and paella. What they are really looking for are the 'Four S's' (Sun, Sand, Sea and Sex) and, provided these are offered cheaply, preferably in a package in which waiters speak the tourists' language and offer familiar food and drink, the tourists are happy. So garlic is removed from the food, the lingua franca becomes English and German and English beer is as easy to find as Coca-Cola and the local wine.

Cheapness, a lengthy coastline, good weather and closeness to industrialised Europe have been the chief secrets of Spain's success. No one in their right mind has ever claimed that hastily erected resorts like Benidorm, Palma or Torremolinos have any of the intrinsic interests of places like Monte Carlo or Nice, but the cost of living for a tourist in Spain has always been at least half of that in France. So, though the early package tour operators were interested in France's Corsica, it was Spain's Balearic Islands which creamed off the bulk of this market.

The real driving force behind the Spanish boom has been the north European tour operators. At least a third of all tourists to Spain come on air-based inclusive tours, particularly from Britain and Germany. This is a trend which the Spanish government has encouraged by giving incentives for hotel building, whilst directly financing the construction of airports, roads, sewage treatment plants, etc., which have been crucial to the continued success of the industry. The result is that Spain is heavily dependent on the tastes of north Europe's working class (office employees and workers make up 47 per cent of all incoming tourists) and the growth of most resorts has been fuelled by investment coming directly from the operators, or by speculators who sign advance deals with the latter before a brick is laid.

The Spanish, however, are worried that their 'cheap' image may now be a liability. The average tourist to Spain spends relatively little by world standards and the competition is growing. On one hand, there are nearby countries like Portugal which are deliberately building their industry to cream off the upper-class tourists who might still be going to Spain. At the other end, her prices are under attack from new destinations like Yugoslavia, Greece and North Africa which can be just as cheap, provided airfares are not pushed up significantly by petrol shortages. Moreover, these latecomers should be able to avoid some of the mistakes stemming from the lack of planning which has accompanied much of Spanish development. Already, tour operators are starting to find some resistance from tourists when considering some of the older Spanish resorts.

What is particularly fascinating about Spain is that it has arrived at this mass-market position a mere twenty years or so after being a snob destination. Torremolinos, for instance, which is currently one of the top three or four resorts, was still a poverty-stricken village in 1955. A few foreigners had 'discovered' it – a mixture straight out of Hemingway, including artists, fringes of the film industry, retired colonials. The first formal tourists brought in by tour operators were relatively well-off – the sort of Britons who might have previously gone for holidays in places like Le Touquet and Deauville on the French northern coast. By the early 1960s it had become fashionable in a big way. Brigitte Bardot made a film near by and it became *the* cosmopolitan Spanish resort, to which the more liberated Spanish youth came to copy the latest fashions like the mini-skirt. The *Playboy* accolade was bestowed; it was, they said, '. . . home to movie stars and smugglers, heiresses and the disinherited, the eccentrics and the ephemera of 5 continents'.[5] James Michener further immortalised it in his bestselling book *The Drifters*, and the fashionable tide moved on. The artists moved east along the coast, the rich moved west toward an aristocratic enclave round Marbella; many simply moved on to new countries like Morocco, Yugoslavia or Greece. Today, then, if you visit this town, you find it bustling and rather proud of its moment in the eye of the fashionable world. It is, however, physically undistinguished and there are already signs that its only future is as an Atlantic City or Blackpool of southern Spain (the Costa del Sol).[6]

Torremolinos is thus an example of the rapid change in Spain's market status, which should be viewed as a warning to every government looking at tourism as an easy option. There is nothing unusual about the rapidity of this change. After all, products have a limited life and, at the end of it, the industrialists replace them with new ones. But the 'product' in tourism is not a car or a cough mixture, but towns or regions which cannot be junked when the tourists choose to move on. Admittedly, the industry in its air-borne phase is too new for definitive statements but one suspects that we have created a series of totally artificial towns whose ultimate fate must be to be dynamited into the sea once the tourists lose interest in them. Certainly, the tourists will move on. That is what the impact of air travel is all about.

Already, the demanding European is moving on, searching for newer, less crowded destinations. He increasingly passes over Italy which is one of the Mediterranean countries with the greatest tourist potential, combining a dazzling cultural heritage with sun and a long coastline. Unfortunately, it also possesses a polarised and slow-moving political system, which ensures that much of the crucial infrastructure lags behind the needs of a rapidly urbanising society. Tourists thus find monuments like the Colosseum closed because the money to repair it that was voted by parliament has not yet filtered through the Byzantine civil service. Venice, which is slowly sinking into the Adriatic as a result of nearby industrial development, is left for foreign campaigners to rescue. The 1973 cholera epidemic in

Naples (a disgrace for any modern state) was allowed to drag on as the relevant authorities took inadequate steps to counter it. Industrial pollution is allowed to ruin areas of considerable tourist appeal (Naples again, and parts of Sardinia) because no government is strong enough to keep rapacious industrialists under control.

The Italian industry, which was the largest on the Mediterranean after 1945, has lost its pride of place to Spain and is losing tourists to newcomers like Greece, Yugoslavia, Cyprus, Morocco and Tunisia – and this is ironic, since the Italian authorities in the 1950s were pioneers in their treatment of tourists, offering them special cheap petrol, and standardising tourists' meals so that less adventurous foreigners need not be frightened of eating out in Italian restaurants.

The richer, more adventurous traveller is now moving to quieter climes where distance and expense keep the masses away, and where overall economic development has not yet destroyed the quiet, attractive villages which so appeal to this type of tourist. So he drives along Yugoslavia's Dalmatian coast, visits the Greek islands or, even, goes as far as Turkey where Istanbul is an exotic attraction with few rivals. Some tourists, though, prefer North Africa which is, again, more exclusive and exciting than the Spanish heartland. So, instead of visiting Madrid or Granada, they are investigating the mysteries of Tangiers, Marrakech and Casablanca. These are places where one can still feel a thrill akin to that felt by great explorers of past centuries. One is, in practice, just a cog in a giant industry but, in these new destinations, this is not yet blindingly obvious. The new resorts are starting to rise, but they are not yet on a scale which dominates the rest of these societies.

What we are thus seeing is the rapid conversion of the whole of the Mediterranean coast into the Pleasure Periphery of Europe and, to a lesser extent, of oil-rich Arabs. Naturally, there are some impediments to this development. For instance, the travel industry finds the Arab–Israeli conflict infuriating. The Nile, Cairo, Beirut and, above all, Jerusalem appeal powerfully to many tourists, but until a settlement is reached on the Palestinian issue, tourism in this area will remain insecure. Tourist operators cannot invest too much effort into an area in which a war is always about to break out. Then there are the socialists in Algeria and the communists in Albania who are hostile to foreign investment and, in the case of Albania, try very hard to do without any tourists at all.

However, despite these localised problems, the growth of the

Mediterranean industry will continue inexorably. Informed predictions suggested that (before the energy crisis intervened) 100 million tourists would annually converge on this sea by 1980; most of them would arrive between May and September. The social and economic impact would naturally be shattering. In the words of travel writer John Bishop: 'It somehow seems impossible to believe that in the last twenty or so years the travel industry has been responsible for changing the way of life of the Mediterranean people in a way never equalled by Alexander the Great, Julius Caesar, the Greek philosophers, the Christian church, nor any single event during more than 2,000 years of history.'[7]

Unlike European tourists who seem primarily hedonistic, Americans appear, at first sight, to be true successors to the classic Grand Tourists. Until the Japanese and Germans challenged them in recent years, they were always glaringly conspicuous in the tourist traps of Europe. They would be standing in the Acropolis, talking through Mozart concerts in Salzburg, or shouting at one's travel agent that they 'want to go to Florence, not some goddamned place called "Firenze" '. Caricatured, despised, but wealthy, they were the prime participants on Europe's tourist-run from the Sistine Chapel in Rome, through Florence's Uffizi Gallery, to the Louvre in Paris, the Rembrandts in Amsterdam and the Changing of the Guard in London. Each city is reduced to four or five 'typical' attractions, and the tourist goes back home certain that he has 'done' Europe. Or, in the words of the film title, *If it's Tuesday, this must be Belgium.*

This picture of the American tourist seeking his roots in Europe is somehow misleading. Statistics are deceptive, making the trans-atlantic trip seem more important for Americans than it is, while grossly inflating the cosmopolitan holiday habits of Europeans. The distortions arise from the fact that Europe has a lot of national boundaries compared with North America. Thus it is in many ways ridiculous that a German travelling from Hamburg to Majorca counts as an international tourist while a cousin going from Pittsburgh to Miami is merely a statistic in American domestic tourism. If we take statistics too seriously, we overestimate the importance of the Mediterranean, forgetting the fact that its current boom is closely related to the development of u.s. domestic resorts in Florida and California.

A pattern thus emerges in which Americans find their sex/sun holidays primarily within the United States, with a certain amount of overflow into the Mexican border area. However, once they decide to go overseas, then in over 55 per cent of cases[8] they make the trans-atlantic flight to Europe, with the Caribbean and Central America coming a low second choice at under 30 per cent. Once in Europe they make for Italy, Germany, the United Kingdom, France, Switzerland and Spain, in that order.

The choice of Italy as the most popular country and the relatively low position of Spain suggest that they are coming for 'culture', rather than for mere beach holidays. This also squares with the fact that a significant number of them are students in their long vacations. The contemporary Grand Tour is alive and well.[9]

A further boom area has been the Caribbean whose tourist poten-tial has only really been unlocked by the arrival of the jet age, though planning for tourism goes back at least as far as the Second World War when Roosevelt and Churchill discussed, amongst all the other issues, the long-term economic future of the American and British islands. They considered tourism seriously, and an Anglo-American Commission was created, which the French and Dutch later joined. It ran a survey of what the islands could offer visitors and then organised a conference in 1946 which brought together tourist authorities from throughout the area. The Commission con-tinued its activities over the years, changing its name in the 1950s to how it is now known, the Caribbean Travel Association, which, in 1953, showed that it knew where the future lay by moving its head-quarters from Antigua to New York. The United States already dominated the scene.[10]

The boom started with Cuba's Batista who in the 1950s needed little persuasion by the Mafia's Meyer Lansky that gambling and tourism would cure the country's economic ills. A wave of Miami-inspired hotel building took place. The Havana Hilton was opened; the 22-storey Capri had its roof-top swimming-pool; the 30-storey Havana Riviera was raised by 'a group of North Americans appa-rently implicated in the murder of Chicago gangster, Anastasia'.[11] Stars like Eartha Kitt, Maurice Chevalier, Lena Horne and Nat King Cole flew in to perform in nightspots like the Tropicana, which was allegedly the world's largest nightclub. Casinos multiplied. The pornographic films available at the Shanghai cinema are still fondly recalled by this art form's *cognoscenti*. The rich thronged El Country Club, and the coast was dotted with famous yacht clubs and hotels with their private beaches. The boom's promise seemed infinite and the *Havana Post* somewhat misleadingly claimed that the city was bidding for the title 'Las Vegas of Latin America'. No one in Las Vegas envisaged the American authorities permitting so wide-open a town on U.S. soil. Havana was something else again.

The city portrayed so vividly in Graham Greene's *Our Man in Havana* died with Castro's overthrow of Batista late in 1958. It was almost inevitable in the circumstances that Castro should close the industry down, and Lansky fled on the final day with all the other key members of Batista's Cuba. The gambling interests still hoped for a comeback, linking up with the Bay of Pigs invasion, and discussing ways of eliminating Fidel, but even Lansky's million dollar price-tag on Castro's head was not enough. The Cuban tourist industry was dead, but one can argue that it had dug its own grave. Admittedly Castro's early character was formed by his experience with old-style American imperialism, in the form of United Fruit, which dominated the area where he was born, but at least part of the popular support for his struggle against Batista stemmed from revulsion against the excesses of the tourist industry – this latter-day, far more shadowy form of imperialism. One might also say that Fidel Castro is a political product of Caribbean tourism.

By the early 1960s jet travel had really started to open up the Caribbean to mass tourists who were diverted from traditional winter resorts like Bermuda, many miles to the north. This era also saw the start of the boom in the Bahamas which became the leading destination in the Caribbean. The story of its rise to prominence is as sordid as Cuba's history.

The Bahamas were always attractive through their closeness to Florida and, as far back as the 1920s, there were entrepreneurs seeking ways of linking these islands to the periodic property booms which sweep this state. One such attempt, for instance, died with the 1926 Florida land crash, but, even then, there was talk of a casino drawing its clientèle from the puritanical shores of the United States which was then unwilling to let its citizens slake their thirst, let alone darken the doors of gambling dens.

The late 1940s saw a hopelessly visionary project by the British holiday-camp pioneers, Butlins, who tried to create a vacation village on Grand Bahama, the island nearest Florida. Shares worth £2 million were issued in Britain, and the company built an airstrip, some conference halls and a dock, but the scheme flopped horribly, which was hardly surprising since, even today, tour operators are only just starting to sell Caribbean holidays to the British market in any significant numbers. What was left of the project was offered for sale to a group from Chicago, which was promptly exposed by the *New York Herald* as being connected with the dreaded Murder Incorporated. The deal thus fell through, but the would-be purchasers were again interested in opening gambling operations aimed at the American market.[12]

Although the Bahamas were officially a British colony, they were wide open to ambitious entrepreneurs, and Lansky needed a new gambling base to replace Havana. Actual power was in the hands of the notorious 'Bay Street Boys', a group of local politicos-cum-businessmen, led by Sir Stafford Sands who, though Minister of Finance and Development, managed to collect at least $1,800,000 in fees from Lansky, as the gambling interests moved in.

They made for Grand Bahama. To all intents and purposes, it was owned and controlled by one man, Wallace Groves, who had been gaoled in the 1940s for stock manipulation and had been involved in some of the early property deals in Key Bascayne (site of Nixon's Florida White House), and who then surfaced in the Bahamas where he engineered a deal of a generosity remarkable even by colonial standards. A company he controlled, called the Grand Bahama Port Authority, was given wide-ranging privileges in 1955 to administer Freeport, which was to become the island's main town. Groves then fronted a new company which came to control three major casinos in the Bahamas – the Freeport Casino, the Lucayan Beach Casino and Nassau's Bahamian Club. These were granted exemption from Bahama's gambling laws through the kind offices of Sir Stafford Sands, and the tourists started flocking in. But various official and unofficial investigations round 1967 made it clear that Groves was acting on behalf of Lansky who, according to *Life* magazine, took 30 per cent of the profits of the Lucayan Beach Casino, and 15 per cent of the gross from the Bahamian Club.

Once the casinos were opened, hotel building started apace, and tourist numbers increased from around 250,000 in the early 1960s (the kind of numbers going to Cuba in the mid 1950s) to over a million today. It has consistently taken over half of the total Caribbean market through the 1960s, despite the winning of independence from the British and a transition to black political power. This has caused some tensions, since the industry has always been white-dominated, and islands like Grand Bahama have virtually been states within states. The first black premier (Lyndon Pindling), for instance, was elected in 1967 and has demanded that the industry employ mostly black workers, thus frightening off a number of potential investors, but until 1974 he has not seriously tried to control the casinos which are the heart of the Bahamas' tourist industry. This is probably a tribute to the skill with which Lansky has played Bahamian politics, with *Forbes*[13] alleging that he backed Pindling in the 1967 election, and also citing a memo from a u.s. consul general to the State Department which claims that there is evidence that some of the new Bahamian leaders are getting finance from criminal sources.

However, the Mafia is not the first freebooting force to pose political problems for the government of these islands. Nassau was, after all, once the pirate capital of the western Atlantic under characters like Blackbeard, who were attracted by the isolation of the islands and by their reasonable proximity to North American trade routes (i.e., much the same things which attract tourists today). In the 1700s, the British regained control by sending troops in with the navy, but the plight of this new micro-state is more serious, since it has to exert sovereignty over too many underpopulated islands which grievously tempt North Americans searching for the kind of private fiefdom in the sun which Onassis has managed to create on the Greek island, Skorpios. These contemporary buccaneers will not be so easy to displace. For one thing they are normally rich enough to buy their way out of most trouble. Increasingly, though, they are looking for ways of winning total independence by secession. The Abacos islanders tried this gambit. They had long prided themselves on being different (i.e. lighter-skinned) than their titular leaders in Nassau, and they tried to persuade the British to keep this one island as a British colony, instead of including it in the newly independent state. The request was denied, but there is little doubt that commercial self-interest was the strongest motivation at work. There is also the fact that any small Caribbean island is now eyed hungrily by numbers of North American businessmen. Trying to take advantage of this, without losing political control over such islands, is probably the hardest task facing many of the new Caribbean states.[14]

It is all too easy to forget that North Americans, West Europeans, and the Japanese are not the only people who take holidays. For instance, there are the Arabs who, between Middle Eastern crises, are a significant force in the industries of Egypt, Iraq and, particularly, the Lebanon. These three countries have large cosmopolitan cities (like Cairo and Beirut) and cultural legacies even richer than those of Italy and Greece. The Lebanon, though small, could easily become one of the great playgrounds of the world if domestic politics and Middle Eastern crises would permit it. It is again based on a rich archaeological heritage, is part Islamic and part Christian, and has a cosmopolitan ambience found nowhere else in this area. Beirut in particular has a worldly reputation which particularly appeals to Arabs from countries where there is a heavy puritan streak of Islam. It has gambling in the form of the famous Casino du Liban, and prostitution, but is also close to spectacular mountains where skiing is possible in the winter months. Thus it is particularly attractive to oil sheikhs, and has the sort of attraction for the region that Las Vegas has for Middle America.

Then, there are the East Europeans who have developed tourism round the Black Sea, making what is virtually a self-contained, parallel industry to the West's. Just like West Europeans, they surge, lemming-like, down south to the sun and the sea of the Crimea, the coasts of Romania and Bulgaria, and the Adriatic coast of Yugoslavia (should that country be in political favour at any particular moment). They do so, moreover, in numbers sufficient to make Bulgaria a more important tourist destination than Greece, which is immediately to the south. Being dedicated to planning, the authorities have created a series of resorts like Romania's Mamaia and Bulgaria's Golden Sands which are as much tourist ghettos as anything found in Spain. Some of the newer resorts like Vulkan and Neptune in Romania are physically more impressive than the newer Spanish resorts – kinds of restrained Disneyland on the Black Sea, where West Europeans can find relatively cheap beach holidays among Russians, Czechoslovaks and East Germans who are not allowed to experience the less disciplined attractions of Spain and Greece.

Elsewhere in the world, regional international tourism has developed for the richer élites. Argentinians and Brazilians will, for instance, meet in the fashionable Uruguayan resort of Punta del Este (off which the *Graf von Spee* was sunk in 1939). To the north, oil-rich Venezuelans are important visitors to Colombia. On the whole, though, the élites of the Third World are not too interested in their own resorts. Given the chance, they take a neo-colonial Grand Tour back to the true roots of their bastardised culture – Europe and

North America. It is a little known (but tragic) fact that Latin Americans in Europe are the biggest per caput spenders of all visitors to that continent. This phenomenon is a sad reflection on the inequality of wealth in Latin America, but it is also an illuminating index of the depth of cultural brain-washing which has taken place in the Third World.

The growth of the Pleasure Periphery has been made possible by the development of a massive supporting industry – the Hiltons, Avis's, Club Méditerranées and Neckermanns of this world. The dynamics of this industry have been extensively analysed elsewhere,[15] so we are not, in this book, going to go into the intricacies of the battles between the charter (or supplemental) airlines and their scheduled competitors which has been waged around the world. Nor will we look too deeply at the technology of the industry which has led to the post-1945 DC-3 being replaced by jets like the Jumbos, which can fly about four times as far at about the half the cost per seat-mile. We will not chronicle the growth of the great chains of 'accommodation racks' like Hiltons and Holiday Inns, which have replaced those genuinely evocative hotels of the inter-war era like Shepheards of Cairo or the Raffles of Singapore. The intricacies of traveller's cheques, travel agencies and tour operators will be left for others to describe.

Let it suffice to say that the heart of the industry is people-processing. Just as the great meat-packing companies take live cattle into their slaughter-houses and find a profitable use of every part of the resultant carcass – be it bones, hooves or meat – so do the great tourist conglomerates try to control as many stages as possible as their clients are separated from their money in the course of a holiday. Thus the airlines want to own hotels; banks want to own tour operators as a way of increasing their hold on the traveller's cheque business; well-integrated tour operators will try to bypass travel agents by selling direct to the public; others will own charter airlines, cruise liners and their own hotels. Until the passenger leaves his hotel and ventures into local restaurants, all his money may have been going to but a single company. That is Integration at its clearest.

People-processing is now a science taught at business schools and, sadly, much of the innocence and fun has now gone out of the industry. Older entrepreneurs who started fledgeling businesses in those seat-of-one's-pants days of the late 1940s are retiring and being replaced by financial specialists whose hearts might just as well be computers. It is sad listening to the old-timers complaining that their successors don't drink, don't sleep with their female employees, and might just as well be manufacturing egg-timers. Somehow the industry is just not fun any more. The accountants do their sums, downgrading the importance of flair, excitement and the discovery of unique, new destinations. Far more important to the money men are the break-even points. Charter flights have to fly at least 90 per cent full to be profitable; scheduled airlines at 60 per cent; hotels at 50 per cent and railways at 40 per cent. If some other company is doing their sums better than you are, it does not matter how much fun you may be having, your company goes bankrupt.[16]

The people-processors hate individual tourists, especially those with quirks and idiosyncrasies (though computers are helping the industry handle such non-conformists). The individual needs almost as much attention as a flock of mass tourists, so he offers disappointing returns. As a Vice-President of the Common Market Travel Association once put it: 'The individual traveller could be described as "the idiot who has not moulded himself into groups".' Quite so.[17]

An example of what is happening is the story of the Club Méditerranée. On the surface, 'Club Méd' is a fresh, invigorating organisation. It has been consciously built around a philosophy which stresses that people who live and work in cities need holidays in totally different surroundings. So the atmosphere of the hundred-odd holiday villages which they operate round the world is kept as informal as possible. Telephones, radios, newspapers and TV are banned unless there is an emergency. Wallets and other valuables are locked away at the beginning of one's stay. Instead of money one uses poppet beads which can be worn anywhere as bracelets, necklaces, etc. The Club's staff are called G.O.s (gentils organisateurs), who are chiefly educated young people who live on an equal basis with the holiday-makers. Accommodation in the basic villages is in thatched huts with minimal furnishings and no electricity or plumbing (there are communal washing areas). The easy mixing of guests is encouraged by the banning of advance booking of tables in camp restaurants so one rarely finds oneself sitting with the same group twice. Each village has a wide range of free sporting facilities like water-skiing and yoga classes. The Club is happy with its image of sexual freedom, which it certainly does nothing to discourage.

Despite its informal image, it now ranks third in the world in terms of available bed-space, after Holiday Inns and the Hilton Organisation, with 60,000 beds at the end of 1972. It has thus come a long way from 1950 when it started with 2,500 members and a tent village in Majorca.

The original entrepreneurs had to call in outside help in the 1960s, when its expansion into skiing led them into liquidity problems. They were rescued by the Edmond de Rothschild group, which later brought in American Express as an investor. In 1973, the Club Méd formula was franchised to C. Itoh, the giant Japanese trading company which, with American Express and eight other Japanese companies, has launched the (geographically horrifically titled) Mediterranean Club Japan. Capitalised at $40 million it will expand the holiday village idea through the Pacific: first in Hawaii, later in the Caroline and Mariana Islands. In addition to this venture, the parent company has diversified both geographically and in the type of holiday it sells. It has developed English-speaking villages in the Caribbean's Guadaloupe and Martinique. Other villages can be found as far afield as the Philippines, Mauritius, Malaysia and the Ivory Coast. They are investigating Bali and Brazil as well. It has spawned a ranch in France and a successful Paris hotel. In addition, it has triggered imitators like the Valtur chain in Italy, which is backed by companies like Fiat, Esso, Alitalia and the London merchant bank of Warburg.

Above all, it has become a glamour stock on the Paris Bourse, since it is such a wonderfully simple money-making idea. Originally, it required next to no investment, and had built up this wonderful image of fun and adult relaxation. Unlike the ventures of Walt Disney and Hilton, it caters for the world's swingers – for the young-in-heart, the liberated and the romantic. However, no one should forget that it is as much a commercial enterprise built round a simple formula as Holiday Inns or Colonel Sanders' Kentucky Fried Chicken. The Gallic atmosphere is diluted as the company sets up English-speaking clubs aimed at the Americans, South Africans and British. Soon there will be a German-speaking village, while around the globe there will be the chain of *villages nipponaises*. Slowly the atmosphere is changing. Articles in the financial press still extol its profit record, but a note of caution creeps in as the journalists note that villages which first cost some $50,000 to create, now need $6 million investment. Such articles tell one about the Club's computer. Some of the newer villages are now staffed by *gentils organisateurs* of a noticeably lower dedication than in earlier years; one finds clients complaining that they have been cheated over the value of their poppet beads. So innocence perishes. That is the way of the Travel Industry.[18]

The world's biggest hotel chain would not really approve of the upstart Club Méd. For one thing, the three men who built Holiday Inns into a chain of 1,670 hotels and 260,000 rooms are deeply religious, displaying the Ten Commandments prominently on their office walls, alongside pictures of the Pope, Pat Boone and Billy Graham. Most of their Inns have a chaplain, and each room has a bible which is opened and turned to a new page by a chambermaid. Unlike Club Méd, they do not approve of free and easy sex. Many a time, they believe, a faithless spouse has been saved from sexual abandon by a timely glimpse of the Good Book. As vice-chairman William Johnson told one reporter: 'I find that a man who has been to a tomcattin' party knows he's wrong. When the sun is down, and he has sobered up, he'll say: "I wish I had the principles of Holiday Inns." '[19]

The chain was started by Kemmon Williams, a former popcorn vendor, who in 1951 could not find a moderately priced hotel on the way to Washington with his family. He thus borrowed £125,000 and built one in Memphis, Tennessee. His chain now processes a quarter of a million people daily. Within the next ten years, they hope to double the size of their operations to 3,000 hotels, which will include luxury ones in places like Monte Carlo, and others with first, second and third class ratings, in addition to their bread-and-butter motels.

Their secret is the secret behind many a u.s.-based leisure industry. Franchising. Just as Coca-Cola and Pepsi are bottled in many parts of the world by closely supervised, locally owned companies, so Holiday Inns are basically a chain of hotels built with other people's money and run by other people's management. All this, however, must be to the specification of the Holiday Inns' headquarters.

The construction of the hotels must be to specified designs which include the positioning of light switches (to the right of the door), and the open bible in every room. Professional inspectors check standards every three months and if they slip beneath the approved level, then the right to call the hotel 'Holiday Inn' may be summarily withdrawn.

The franchiser pays Holiday Inns some 6 per cent of his turnover and, in return, every Holiday Inn is linked to a Memphis-based computer centre (by satellite if necessary). They claim this is the world's largest private communications network, and, through it, one can book airline tickets, hire cars, as well as book oneself into yet another Holiday Inn. The franchiser also gets a company manual which tells him everything from how to run the desk and control the algae in the swimming-pool, to how often the lubricating oil should be changed in the motel's washing machines. The franchisees even get access to the recently opened Holiday Inn University, which will service more than 3,000 employee students a year, thus making it one of the biggest industry-operated training schools in the world.

This, then, is the quintessence of today's Mass Tourist Industry. Everything is standardised, since standardisation allows one to control costs. Everything is linked by computer, since computer reservation systems allow one to increase the utilisation of rooms. Nothing is left to chance, since uncertainty makes calls on management time.

However, even if the tourists are willing to accept a certain amount of uniformity to keep the price of their accommodation down, there are some signs that they are becoming tired of destinations offering little more than beaches, restaurants, bars and cinemas which one can get anywhere round the Pleasure Periphery. The search is on for man-made attractions which can rival the best natural and historic 'draws', and the State of Florida shows how the simple beach holiday is being replaced by a high-technology product.

Florida is an example of how a tourist destination can become ruined by slack planning. Miami Beach, for instance, no longer boasts of good beaches since many of the bigger hotels were built too close to the sea, thus leading to advanced erosion of the sand in front of them. The Everglades, which are the State's supreme natural attraction, are slowly drying up as coastal developments tap the water which has kept them as swamps. The Florida Keys have been ruined by unchecked property speculation. The city of Miami has become a massive urban sprawl without the slightest architectural redemption.

To compensate for this rape of a state, the size and quality of the man-made attractions has been rising. Today, one goes there less for the beaches and Everglades and more for attractions like the lion country safari, the advance circus showcase of Ringling Bros. and Barnum and Bailey, the various seaquariums, the parrot and orchid 'jungles', the Old West frontier town and, of course, that half-a-billion-dollar 'Magic Kingdom', Walt Disney World.

The story of this contemporary Xanadu-for-the-masses is by now well known. It was the brain-child of Walt Disney, who not only wanted to improve on Disneyland on the West Coast, but also wanted to ensure that, this time, the bulk of the related commercial developments would still be under the control of Walt Disney Inc. So, his company bought up 27,400 acres in mid-Florida, invested at least $500 million in fantasy, created employment for 'over 10,000' and car parks for 12,000 cars. In return, it has been rewarded with over 22 million visitors in its first two years of opening, a rate which is over four times the number of tourists who visit Greece. In some ways, this is an unfair comparison, since visitors to Greece will spend far more on such a holiday than visitors to Disney World. On the other hand, one suspects that for many tourists the Acropolis has little to offer which can compare with the mythical appeal of 'Cinderella Castle', 'Adventureland' or 'Main Street USA'. The Acropolis was never one of the Seven Wonders of the World, but there can be no doubt that, for the tourist industry, Disney World is. The era in which a tourist destination could rely on historic ruins or its beaches are dying. Tomorrow it must possess major man-made attractions, be they casinos, sporting facilities, nightclubs, large-scale animal reserves or fantasy parks. In an era of growing competition between destinations, the 'leisure domes' of Las Vegas and Florida point to the way mass tourism will go.

7 The Dismal Science

The economics of tourism are totally deceptive. At one level, most people cannot believe how vast it is, yet, in 1974, international tourist receipts stood at approximately $29 billion, or roughly 6 per cent of total international trade. It has very nearly been the largest single item in world trade;[1] it is larger than world trade in raw materials, iron and steel, and ores and minerals; it is roughly as big as world trade in textiles; only trade in motor vehicles, chemicals and fuel surpass it in size. Since 1960 it has grown at slightly over 10 per cent per annum, about double the rate for trade in agricultural products, and only slightly behind annual growth of trade in manufactured goods.[2]

At the same time, it all looks so easy. Third World countries see that they are actually increasing their share of world tourism.[3] They think of their abundance of sun, sea and beaches. Surely these poverty-stricken states merely have to build some hotels and an airport for the tourists and that precious foreign exchange to come rolling in? What easier or more profitable industry could there be? It all looks too good to be true . . . and it is.

Tourism is not called an industry by accident. Like steel or computers, it needs management, capital investment, manpower training and all the other activities associated with a major, competitive industry. It only looks easy because it is still relatively new, and the days when individuals or countries could start from scratch and almost overnight become major forces in the world industry are still close enough to be remembered vividly. However, this mythology is dangerous. Even before the 1974 energy crisis, the industry was maturing, and mature industries are prone to vicious competition and falling rates of profit. The early seat-of-their-pants entrepreneurs give way to professional managers; the weak go to the wall; and the successful become even stronger, reinvesting heavily to maintain their lead. In most industries, such competition is normally just between companies; in tourism we are dealing with rivalry between nations. Tourism is becoming as cut-throat as any other commodity. The days of virtually automatic profits are over.

On the surface, one can certainly make a good economic case for tourism. It brings in valuable foreign exchange, helps countries' balance of payments and creates employment both directly and indirectly. One can even argue that it corrects regional imbalances, since it normally requires investment in just those unfavoured areas well away from the cities.

It is, for instance, an extremely important component in many countries' balance of payments. Both Spain and Italy have positive travel balance of payments of over $1 billion; Mexico has a balance of around $750 million; Austria, France, Portugal, Switzerland, Greece and Yugoslavia all had balances of over $100 million in 1970. In a number of countries, tourism is the most important export: this included Kenya, Tunisia, Morocco, Spain and Greece in 1970.[4]

These sums cannot easily be dismissed. Developing countries find foreign exchange particularly precious. It allows them to import goods to overcome major bottlenecks. It is often argued that Mexico, in particular, has been enabled to avoid the stagnation which is endemic in the rest of Latin America, due to the buoyancy of its tourist sector, which has allowed them relative freedom in importing goods needed for continued industrial growth. The same is true of Spain. By the end of the 1940s, she was just starting on industrialisation but had little foreign currency for imports. What she did have came from agricultural products and mining, both of which were subject to market fluctuations. Then came tourism, the industry which saved Spain's balance of payments. One Spanish paper summed the situation up like this: 'Just as in previous years the European economy was saved by the 16,000 million dollars of the Marshall Plan, so was the Spanish economy saved by the phenomenon of tourism. Tourism brought 11,000 million dollars to Spain – and 11,000 million dollars exactly were invested by Spain in industrial equipment.'[5]

It goes without saying that hotels, bars and taxis also employ local citizens. In various Caribbean islands well over a third of the labour force may be employed in the tourist sector; in the Bahamas, the proportion had risen to 65 per cent by the late 1960s.[6] It has also been estimated that Yugoslavia, Spain, Switzerland and Italy each employ over 100,000 people in the industry, while British analysts claim that British holiday expenditure abroad may be supporting between 200,000 and 400,000 jobs in foreign resorts.[7]

As a rough rule of thumb, each new hotel will directly employ about one person for each room, but employment has also been created by their construction. One example of this is Walt Disney Inc.'s vast Disney World complex in Florida. It directly employs between 10,000 and 12,000 people, and led to the immediate construction of at least 17,000 motel and hotel rooms. Another 8,000 were under construction within six months of its opening, with another 14,000 on the drawing boards. The boom created was so great that people were commuting seventy-five miles a day to work, and even neighbouring states found themselves stripped of workers.

There are also other indirect employment effects. Someone has to grow the food for the tourists and make the souvenirs for them to buy; tourist employees have to spend the money they earn. However, there is considerable debate among the specialists as to what the spin-off or 'multiplier' effect actually is for this industry. Their estimates vary widely. On balance, though, it looks as though the more recent, highly detailed studies in areas like the Caribbean are less convincing that tourism has anything but a minor impact on the rest of the economy. Later in this chapter, we suggest reasons why this may be so.[8]

On the surface, the economic case appears particularly strong for Third World countries. As a World Bank report puts it, they are normally faced with dubious world market prospects for primary products, and strict limits to the amount of manufactured exports which the industrialised nations are willing to accept. Tourism is thus one of the few viable industries available to them and, in the report's words: '. . . it provides for many a useful element in diversifying their sources of foreign exchange earnings and, for some, one of the few export opportunities available.'[9]

Examples from the Caribbean show the sort of dilemma they are thinking of. The larger islands like Jamaica (population 1·9 million) can support an agricultural sector on a national scale, which remains still the most important economic activity. In the smaller islands with populations of between 50,000 to 100,000 (Antigua, Dominica, Grenada, etc.), tourism has roughly eclipsed traditional agricultural activities. In the really tiny islands with between 8,000 and 20,000 population (Monserrat, Cayman, the Virgins) tourism is by far the most important industry, although it hardly existed some fifteen years back. Carleen O'Loughlin, a Caribbean researcher, who puts forward such comparisons, has also compared the effect on the per caput income of islands which are heavily dependent on tourism.

'. . . There is a strong suggestion that islands which have benefit from tourism have also obtained the fastest income increase.'[10]

It all looks very, very convincing. Here is an industry which will save a lot of the Third World from poverty . . . so why are some economists becoming increasingly sceptical about its overall value?

A number of illusions about the economics of tourism need exploding. First, just because a tourist spends a dollar in a country there is no guarantee that it is going to stay there. In large parts of the tourist world, many of the hotels and restaurants are foreign owned, so part of the tourist dollar flows out inevitably in the form of profits or dividends; many of the top managers are expatriates who, as well as being paid more than local employees, will tend to bank a good part of their salary out of the country; much of the food and drink may have to be imported to meet the conservative tourist palate, thus eating further into that precious foreign exchange; likewise, the tourists demand expensive machinery like air conditioning, lifts, speed boats and cars, all of which will have to be imported by all but the most sophisticated host countries. Even the World Bank accepts the fact that in many of the smaller, less developed destinations (just the ones so hopeful about tourism) the outflow can be as much as 55 cents for every dollar spent, though, as destinations become larger and more self-sufficient, the leakages diminish, and more of the tourist money sticks with the hosts.[11] Some would put such leakages even higher. Newspaper reports suggest that between 60 and 80 per cent of tourist receipts in Jamaica flow out again immediately.[12] A detailed study of smaller, more dependent Antigua suggests that about 42 per cent of this income was flowing out again in the early 1960s. Kenya has a leakage of at least 40 per cent; the Bahamas 43 per cent.[13]

There is a second illusion which the official statistics tend to disguise since they do not take fares into account; a goodly proportion of the total money spent by tourists on a holiday will never reach the host country in the first place. It goes instead on transport to and from the destination, and the former part of the holiday is firmly controlled by airlines, car-hire and bus companies which are overwhelmingly owned in the tourist generating nations. This means that destinations like the Indian Ocean's Mauritius will only hold on to 10 per cent of the total cost of an incoming package holiday.[14] This suggests that the ultimate winners from such long-haul tourism are the tour operators and airlines. Moreover, the growing tendency for the same company to own both an airline and hotels opens up yet a further channel for ensuring that the minimum amount of money sticks with the host countries. Such companies will be tempted to manipulate their internal book-keeping so that the profits are made on their transport activities rather than in their hotels. If the latter appear unprofitable on paper, the overall company can escape taxation and get round exchange regulations which they may wish to avoid.[15]

The next illusion is that tourism is an easy and cheap industry to enter – that a small investment immediately creates a lot of employment and guarantees quick returns. This is only true if one ignores the very heavy expenditure[16] that host governments have to make in infrastructure purely for the benefit of tourists. In the Caribbean, there is a general rule of thumb that for every dollar invested in the private sector, governments will have to match it dollar-for-dollar with investments on public sector projects. Most of this expenditure is for the primary benefit of the tourists and of limited use to local citizens, yet there are few cases where tourists are paying enough to cover the cost of the public investments they have made necessary.

At the same time, the sheer scale of tourist projects is increasing steadily. As a result, the coordination of private and public investment becomes more and more essential; and, as the size of risks grows, what was once quite an easy industry is now becoming decidedly dangerous.

The key first investment for new entrants to the Pleasure Periphery is an *airport*, preferably capable of taking anything up to the size of Jumbo jets. The Greeks, for instance, are planning further new international airports as a way of opening up Kos, Rhodes, and Corfu; another fifteen islands will be connected by light aircraft. The Spaniards are now at the stage of upgrading their existing airports; the one at Malaga, which serves Torremolinos and Marbella, was rebuilt in 1969, and then again to take its first Jumbo jet in 1972. The fashionable Seychelles Islands owe their entry into the long-haul tourist stakes entirely to the opening of their international airport in 1971.

A lot of money, however, can be thrown away if governments get their calculations wrong. The Thais, for instance, were at one stage planning to attract more tourists by spending $200 million on a second international airport serving Bangkok (this plan was eventually seen to be a waste of money and dropped). The Tanzanians poured £6 million into Kilimanjaro airport, hoping to attract tourists from neighbouring Kenya. Unfortunately, it is so close to the established regional airport at Nairobi, that they have had no success in persuading airlines to put the airport on their routes. They have even had difficulty in getting East African Airways, in which they have an official stake, to switch. Even European countries have these difficulties. West Germany's Kassel-Calden airport was given a $10 million modernisation, but found that tour operators refused to put it on the international holiday network, thus making the investment a total waste of money. Antigua reinforces the lesson. It has the only international airport within its neighbouring Caribbean Islands. It has a good chance of becoming a destination for mass tourism, but only has four hotels with more than fifty beds, and the prices are horrendous. Antigua is not an island which can afford to throw money away, but its airport is grossly under-used.[17]

Other kinds of activity also need considerable government expenditure:

Sewage disposal. This has posed major problems, particularly around the Mediterranean. The Spanish have been forced to spend some 1,490 million pesetas (£11 million) on this for the Costa del Sol alone.

Water. Many destinations have totally inadequate water supplies. In Antigua, water was more expensive than rum until they built a dam and desalination plant. The Canary Islands are turning to desalination plants as well, though there were reports in 1972 of an enterprising Swedish company which was trying to export bottled water to them. In Cyprus, tourism and traditional agriculture compete for inadequate supplies; in early 1973, there were plans for desalination plants, cloud seeding and, possibly, an underwater pipeline from a continental neighbour. Kenya is finding water shortages a major barrier to the development of her coastal strip.

Roads. Most major resorts are plagued with traffic jams. Tourist authorities tend to pander to the tourists by building bypasses, motorways, etc., instead of developing public transport systems and telling the tourists to use them.

Sand-trapping. Sandy beaches are a selling point and can be created. In 1973, the Maltese authorities were considering ways of extending three beaches by trapping sand brought in during storms. A similar system is used in Israel. Other resorts dredge sand from the sea, or rob inaccessible beaches to replenish others which are being denuded. Apart from the immediate cost, one worries about the local ecological effects.

Housing. Local authorities will probably have to build temporary accommodation for construction workers in the early stages of a tourist development. In large cities like London, there is an increasing need for subsidised housing for hotel and catering employees who cannot afford to live near the city centre and work odd hours when there is no public transport to bring them from the suburbs. If migrant workers are used to staff hotels as happens in much of Europe, there will be added social costs to be considered.

Telecommunications. This is particularly important if a country is going after business and convention travel in a serious way. The Lebanon is having to invest heavily in improving its telecommunications with Europe with this market in mind.

Education. Special tourism schools will be needed as the industry expands, though students can be sent abroad to schools in places like Switzerland (very expensive). Countries like Mexico now teach tourist-related skills at secondary school level.

Airlines. Earlier we mentioned how much tourist money never reached the host countries because they do not control the airlines on which the tourists arrive. It is therefore tempting to create a national airline, which is then given a protected share of the tourist traffic. At their best, like El Al, national airlines can be money-spinners and of strategic importance. At their worst, they can be extremely expensive and can lose money very fast. Malta has just created one, arguing that it needs to encourage tourists from new countries like Germany; at the time of creation, Germans could only reach Malta by a three-leg journey; with her own airline, Malta can fly them direct.

All such projects are expensive, and one cannot truly assess the benefits of tourism without fully putting them in the equations. Certainly the local inhabitants can do with things like sewage disposal and water supplies, but much of this money is spent primarily on tourist needs. Much of it is also spent in parts of the country bearing little relevance to the day-to-day needs of the vast bulk of the local citizens. Almost by definition, the tourists want to get away from the slums and urban, industrialised sprawls in which many of them will live.

It is thus all too easy to underestimate the true costs which are directly attributable to tourism. The authorities in Hawaii looked into this problem in 1968. They worked out the daily cost of public services provided for the tourists. They found the total daily variable cost was $0·688, which broke down as $0·189 for highways, $0·249 for airports (indicating how expensive these are), $0·058 for police protection, $0·032 for fire protection, $0·049 for sewage and $0·111 for local parks and recreational facilities. They also costed how much the public purse had to invest when settling an immigrant family of four; this came to $3,041, suggesting that even permanent tourists can be expensive in the initial stages.[18]

It is difficult to tell whether income and tax generated by tourists generally recompense governments for all the incidental costs they incur. One is struck however by how little tourists are taxed round the world, and how often they are encouraged by subsidies at every stage of their holiday. This starts with the *aircraft* in which they fly ('subsidized engines . . . in subsidized airframes . . . operated by sub- sidized airlines, who don't want the wretched things anyway'),[19] and runs to *airport charges* (generally not enough to cover interest on capital employed, let alone operating costs) and *airlines* (run seem- ingly for national prestige rather than profit). *Hotel building* and operating attracts direct subsidies (the British government offered £1,000 per hotel bedroom built before spring 1973), the waiving of import duties, special loans and tax holidays (a high proportion of Caribbean hotels change hands at the end of tax holiday periods).[20]

Wherever one looks round the world, official subsidies for tourism come crawling out of the woodwork. The Greeks put aside £1 million for improving private houses which could be developed as tourist lodgings. The Belgian government was offering a £6 million loan to the overall cost of an Inter-Continental hotel, before the whole deal fell through. The regional government in Sicily offers a package to tour operators, including a refund of up to 30 per cent of the tour costs, provided the savings are passed back to the clients. That African home of Free Enterprise, the Ivory Coast, offers any tourist or hotel company registering with the government tax exemptions on necessary materials' imports and industrial and commercial profits, plus ten years' exemption from land taxes and five years' exemption from licence taxes. By the time all the concessions are added up, there is obviously virtually nothing left for the government.[21]

Bodies like the World Bank are aware of such practices, arguing that they can be justified in certain circumstances, but adding cau- tiously that 'the case for incentives of wide applicability is not proven'.[22] George Young has no such inhibitions: 'Economic logic has been left far behind, and the Gilbertian situation is being approached whereby it will pay everyone to be a tourist because of the subsidies to which he is entitled; and it will pay no one to be a resident because of the high levels of taxation needed to subsidize the tourist industry.'[23]

There is a further tendency to argue that any job created is a 'good' one, but this is to ignore the fact that different industries have different employment structures; some of these will be of greater long-term benefit to an economy than others. In this respect, tourism is out of place for industrialised economies, though of some importance in Third World ones.

It is argued that tourism is a distinct improvement over old plantation economies. Sugar cultivation, for instance, produces a large number of low-paid, unskilled jobs and a few highly paid, managerial ones, with virtually nothing in between. Tourism, it is argued, produces a range of 'lower-middle' occupations like taxi-operation, cooks, relatively senior service and office jobs in hotels, entertainers, boat operators, skilled craftsmen and artists. This wider range of jobs gives greater opportunities for training and promotion. It should lead to less polarised societies by creating the chances for small businessmen to find a niche. At its most uncompromising, the argument runs that: 'The lower paid or the less ambitious find even the most menial jobs in hotels somewhat preferable and better rewarded than weeding canes or breaking stones in the hot sun.'[24]

This is quite convincing, except for the fact that in the Third World the bulk of the top jobs in hotels and catering still go to expatriates, who also get disproportionately paid. Within the hotel sector, which is where most of the permanent jobs are created, the bulk of them are still semi-skilled at best. There is the further problem that the industry is a seasonal one in most parts of the world, with the result that seasonal unemployment is still high.

However, although the job structure of tourism may be a distinct improvement on subsistence agriculture in the Third World, it is not at all certain that tourism is really suited to industrialised economies which are basically short of labour. The last thing they need is an industry creating low-skilled, low-paid jobs, but that is what tourism does. We have already seen elsewhere how migrant workers are being called on in much of Europe to keep much of the industry

going. This causes some social problems, but there are other implications. Florida, for instance, is having distinct second thoughts
about the runaway success of Disney World. This has certainly
created employment; the unemployment ratio for Greater Orlando,
where it is located, went down from 4 per cent in 1971 to 1·8 per cent
in 1973. However, most of these have been service jobs, and Florida
is becoming concerned by the fact that only 12 per cent of the state's
employment is in relatively well-paid manufacturing, compared with
28 per cent nationally. This absence of high-income jobs is putting a
strain on their tax-base, which now relies heavily on sales and gaso-
line taxes. In an age where economic growth comes from increasing
the productivity of working citizens, hotels and restaurants are a
distinctly unpromising sector to encourage – particularly when the
status of jobs in the industry is so low.[25]

Much of the argument about tourism's impact in the Third World
turns on what indigenous industries it replaces. Some argue that
much of the income from tourists merely goes into creating the infrastructure necessary to keep them returning; there might be other,
less fashionable industries which would respond as well to the
management talent and investment poured into the tourist sector.

These questions tend to be ignored. It is argued, for instance, that
'many of the scenic areas of the United States are precisely those
areas that cannot be farmed and that have existing underemployment
because resource-oriented industries such as mining or lumbering
have declined in importance'.[26] Similarly, it is tempting to see
tourism as the saviour of West Indian islands with their 'remittance'
villages – societies kept going by postal orders sent back by their sons
working over the oceans. It is even argued that tourism stimulates
local agriculture as seems to have happened in parts of Spain like the
Costa Brava.[27]

In general tourism kills local agriculture stone dead. It does
this by luring away the labour force, and by turning farmers into
property speculators. Particularly sad are the ghost villages springing
up round the world, created by rich city dwellers buying second
homes in picturesque farms and villages, paying sums which the
local rural population cannot afford. Absentee landlordism is introduced and whole agricultural communities have all their vitality
knocked out of them. As one observer puts it about the Alps:
'Tourism, however, is no less an industry than steel manufacture and
its introduction into Alpine valleys has been no less destructive of

total population patterns and traditional culture than if each hotel had been a blast furnace.'[28]

This is particularly noticeable among the smaller islands of the Caribbean where tourism has been presented as the only hope – another illusion. John Bryden, who has carried out one of the best analyses of the economics of tourism, points out that it kills both export-oriented and domestic agriculture. Imports of everything (including food) are increased and traditional agricultural exports decline. There is little evidence that the unskilled and semi-skilled jobs created in hotels are any better paid than in the fields. After analysing alternative strategies, he finds that the returns on investment in hotels are close to minimal, the result depending on the extent of foreign ownership, how many expatriates are employed and where the money has been raised. He points to the unsettling social fact that peasant farmers are displaced, inflation rises as local sources of food are replaced by imports, property values soar beyond the reach of local citizens, and increased import duties hit low-income citizens in particular.

It may seem odd that tourism, this brash modern industry, can be economically valueless (or even disadvantageous) to economies based even on virtual subsistence-level agriculture. But it can be true. Tourism depends on resorts, which are built for the benefit of foreigners, and are of no intrinsic value to local inhabitants. However, because the industry is modern and glamorous, and there are some jobs which pay better than traditional ones, everyone drops tools and rushes to serve the foreigners. The locals build the resorts and serve in them which, if fully controlled by foreigners, will contain few really worthwhile jobs. In the meantime, the fields return to weeds; the locals lose their traditional skills; they lose their ability to produce anything of direct practical use to themselves. While they've been building the resorts, they haven't been building the schools, the irrigation systems or the textile factories which would help educate, feed or clothe them. They have to rely on ever more expensive imports; the grip of the tourists on their best land grows; they incur ever more serious foreign debts which they will still have to pay, even if they never receive another tourist. So, for the sake of this industry, they can lose their land, their jobs and their way of life – for what? A life of helping satisfy the whims of rich foreigners? If they are not careful, that is all they will get out of the tourist sector.

Despite some claims to the contrary, tourism has been a pretty stable industry. Since the Second World War, it grew handsomely each year. Some countries suffered because of political tensions; the Lebanon and Jordan were badly hurt by Middle Eastern troubles; Ireland paid for the Ulster killings; the Bahamas ran into trouble in the late 1960s when its citizens got the reputation for surliness; Monaco became unfashionable and went through a twenty-year slump. However, these were exceptional cases and, even then, it was rare for them to drop more than 20 per cent of their tourist business.

By the standards of traditional commodities like coffee or rubber, it was thus extremely stable. Until 1974, it suffered none of the massive price fluctuations which make it impossible for planners to know what their earnings will be from one year to the next. Notably, tourism has been one of the few commodities where the Third World has been consistently increasing its share of the world market. However, it looks as though the situation has just changed.

As we write, it is clear that the energy crisis has led to a quantum jump in the price of airline fuels and the industry's first overall decline for over twenty years. Airlines are attempting to merge or rationalise their route structures; tour operators are going bank-rupt; hotels are starting to close, never to open again. It will take a couple of years before the industry really starts to pick up again. However, even before this, there were those who were arguing that the industry was starting to mature; that the days when tourism was an élite activity were over, and that it was now becoming a mass production industry like making cars and toothpaste, or running supermarkets. The arrival of Jumbo jets and giant hotels was inevitably leading to declining profit margins, desperate international competition and losses.[29]

There is little that can be done to restrain competition, since entry into the industry is all too easy (though getting more expensive). If any country with an airport and some hotels can join, then profit margins will always be squeezed as prices are kept down to the levels of the newer, more efficient units. The widening of the Pleasure Periphery also means that distant locations will compete, like the Caribbean and the Seychelles; it is getting much more difficult for one country to keep its prices significantly above those of other countries offering similar attractions. Simultaneously, the scale of necessary investments is moving sharply upwards. Nowadays, a few hotels are not enough; instead, whole new towns need building from scratch. For instance, one of the latest creations of the Mexican tourist authorities is Cancun, which was planned from the start to have 40,000 beds. The giant French scheme for Languedoc–Roussillon on the Mediterranean was planned to include six resorts for a total investment of something like £350 million. Even a simple indicator like the average size of hotels points in the same direction; at least nine countries now have hotels which average 100 or more rooms each; most of these are relatively new destinations – Bulgaria, Hungary, Monaco, Portugal, Romania, Turkey, Puerto Rico, the Philippines and Thailand. Again, clear evidence that the size of the stakes is increasing.[30]

The picture is now clear. We are moving into the age of the downmarket, mass tourist. We can expect the average profit per tourist to fall. Thus the British are finding that the expenditure of the average American tourist is static, if not falling. The Greeks found the average spending per head by visitors declined during the 1960s from $126·5 per head in 1961 to $120·3 in 1970, even though the average length of stay actually increased slightly.[31]

Of course, quality high-margin tourism will survive, but countries cannot guarantee to hold on to such tourists for more than a decade. After that, the mass tourists will move in, driving out the pioneers and reducing the average profit margins. In this era, which may well include too many tourist resorts round the world, only the very efficient and well-placed industries will make money; the rest will lose it.

So, one further illusion about the industry is removed. Tourism is very far from being the easy industry which most people think it is. If anything, it is the hardest industry that Third World countries could choose. It is not like making cheap toys for the industrialised world, which does not demand much investment, and where poor quality can be disguised by low prices. The mass tourist is not interested in the problems faced by the host country. He has invested a lot of money into his holiday and he does not want to experience bureaucratic red tape, unfamiliar food, inadequate nightlife, badly designed hotels or untrained waiters. The destination countries have therefore to get all these aspects of a holiday very quickly right, if their resorts are going to survive in the increasingly competitive world of international tourism. It means the planners have got to know the tourists very well and must have the ability to orchestrate a whole range of disparate activities from hotel design and construction to food production or running an airline – the totality of operations which go to make up a successful holiday. Bad planning will be punished; the tourists will not come back and those expensive, empty resorts might just as well be dynamited into the ocean.

So the economic benefits from much of tourism may well be totally illusory. All that planning and construction could be for nothing. There are too many countries planning to expand into the industry too fast. There are too many powerful airlines and tour operators waiting to prey on the weaker tourist destinations. As the sheer scale of the necessary investment rises, so do the risks grow. Countries will be tempted to cut prices to fill hotels or, even, whole resorts.

Even before the events of October 1973, one suspected that the unquestioning enthusiasm about the economic benefits of tourism would disappear. In its place would come the cold realisation that tourism, for all its glamour, is just one more industry, with particularly complex economic and social side effects. It is no longer possible to believe that it is an easy or a cheap industry – or a profitable one.

SECTION TWO: CULTURE

8 The Barbarian and the Tourist

... as I examine the Travellers-of-the-Future I get the eeriest flash
– Déjà Vu. There is something antique about the scope and scale of
these huge, expected peregrinations, mass movements such as have
hardly been seen since the obscurer Dark Ages when tribes would
shuffle grimly over the landscape just a nose ahead of War, Plague,
Famine and Death, obliterating cultures as they moved.
Anthony Haden-Guest, *Down the Programmed Rabbit Hole*

Tourism is an invasion outwards from the highly developed metropolitan centres into the 'uncivilised' peripheries. It destroys uncomprehendingly and unintentionally, since one cannot impute malice to
millions of people or even to thousands of businessmen and entrepreneurs. In the past, mass movements of people have always been
regarded with dread. The nomadism of barbarians was a direct
threat to the continuity of urban cultures and settled agricultural
systems. Both the barbarian and the tourist are motivated by the
desire to escape – the first from hardship (overpopulation, scarcity
of pasture and the pressure of hostile neighbouring tribes), the
second from affluence (high technology, overcrowded conurbations
and environmental deterioration). Both the barbarian and the tourist
escape in the direction of something beyond their customary experience. The barbarian coming from forest or steppes, or some semi-
civilised region of feudal barons and squalid towns stands before the
(to him) unimaginable fabrication of the great city; here is wealth,
fine living and an ordered existence. From the vantage of a camp
outside the walls the city is miraculous and beautiful, but once inside
the walls he is unable to regard it as anything but loot and booty; he
subjects it to the inevitable 'sack, pillage and rape'. Once this is
complete he may look up puzzled at what he has done, he has
entered the dream and destroyed it. He may then strive to adopt what
is left of the culture on which he has so violently intruded, its regalia
and titles and established religion. He may listen to its scholars and
philosophers and patronise its artists. The city may revive or it may
relapse into barbarism and decadence, becoming a parody of its
former self.

As a mass movement of peoples tourism deserves to be regarded
with suspicion and disquiet, if not outright dread. The tourist comes
from a highly developed urban culture, and therefore seeks its

opposites. We have already defined this as an escape from uniformity and complexity in search of the exotic and the simple. The pursuit of the exotic is directed towards other cultures (distant in time or space). The pursuit of the simple is directed towards other cultures in so far as they are seen to be more *primitive* than the home culture, but in its most common form it is anti-cultural, directed towards the encapsulated world of the Mediterranean or tropical beach where the tourist can forget the high cultures of the past and present as well as the social and environmental realities of the country he is visiting. The tourist travels from his metropolitan home to the world of antiquity, to picturesque, pre-industrial cultures and to the unspoilt animal kingdoms of African game reserves. In relation to culture we may redefine touristic goals as the antique, the ethnic and the pristine. From the distance of the metropoles the remaining aspects of these ideals seem immensely precious and desirable – survivors in a world of increasing cultural uniformity and high technological complexity. But the individual who visits the havens of the antique, the ethnic and the pristine is, unwittingly, instrumental to the expansion of high technology and the uniformity it imposes.

A scene in Fellini's film *Roma* provides a striking analogy. A tunnel is being excavated beneath the city. The workers inadvertently break in upon a long-buried and perfectly preserved villa of Imperial Rome. Its walls are covered with brilliant frescoes but as the air of the modern city rushes in they fade and crumble. The act of discovery has led directly to the destruction of something fragile and irreplaceable. Peripheral cultures only retain their air of antiquity and their ethnic individuality by virtue of their isolation from the dominant and expanding cultures of the metropoles. This is especially true of the remote island cultures of Bali and the South Pacific. Once distance has been contracted by the building of an airport capable of taking jets, the antique, the ethnic and the pristine in their cultural and environmental aspects are immediately threatened. The tourist demands uniform standards of accommodation, food, and so on, and thus requires the installation of high technology infrastructure. Although he may have been motivated by the desire to escape from his home society, the tourist soon imposes its values on the society he is visiting. The single, most effective agent in this process is the tourist's money. The tourist's superior economic wealth rapidly erodes the sensuous and aesthetic wealth of cultures that have developed in isolation from the western world. There is no need to look to 'the Travellers-of-the-Future' – the tourism of the present has already begun the work of 'obliterating cultures'. Perhaps we can best show our respect for other cultures by staying away. The student of tourism is confronted with the melancholy and 'irresoluble' paradox of anthropology:

> the less one culture communicates with another, the less likely they are to be corrupted, one by the other; but on the other hand, the less likely it is, in such conditions, that the respective emissaries of these cultures will be able to seize the richness and significance of their diversity. . . .[1]

ACCELERATION AND NOSTALGIA

Technological advances both make the expansion of the Pleasure Periphery possible in practical terms, and help to create its psychological basis. It is these advances that have produced the immense acceleration from the recent past, the lost 'long, hot summers' of the English and the 'organic community' of pre-industrial societies. So the tourist driven by an obscure desire to get back wishes to escape from the fast pace and alienation of his home society to somewhere hot, stress-free and 'olde worlde', by means of the advanced technology that, itself, makes this escape necessary.

It is the 'olde worlde' which concerns us here. Western culture is a culture dominated by the past, with its clinical museums and its concert halls dedicated largely to the music of the past. (It is, perhaps, in the field of music that the backward-looking nature of bourgeois culture is most clearly evident; the average 'classical music lover' is entirely out of touch with the development of music since 1910.) With the acceleration from the past the process of nostalgia has also accelerated. Pre-1914 Europe already seems a remote lost world, a world of lost certainties, of the security and stability attendant on imperialist, hierarchic structures. Since the 1960s, the 1920s, 'thirties, 'forties and even the 'fifties successively have been the objects of nostalgic sentimentalism and idealisation. Already the 1960s are coming to seem quaint and loveable: nostalgia threatens to overtake itself. Thus metropolitan culture tints its fashionable aura with aspects of its own recent past.

The world of fashion is closely linked to tourism, and since the 'sixties there has been a growing tendency for western fashion to adopt the decorative elements of Third World cultures; one thinks of the proliferation of Afghan kaftans, bandanas, Mexican smocks. We do not look to the present reality of North Africa or India, but to their most traditional elements, in items of dress, or *genuine primitive* artefacts. All this implies a distorted view of the world, a world which revolves around the neuroses, fads and fashions of the metropolitan centres. It is decorated in primary colours; it is the world of the nursery.

The North Atlantic Community's veneration for the past is not shared by other societies. Studies of tourism in south-east Asia have shown that few Asian tourists trouble to visit the great medieval ruins of Pagan (in Burma), Angkor (in Cambodia)* or Borabodur (in Java). Modern Italy is notorious for its wilful neglect of its cultural heritage; the Roman Forum was recently closed because its monuments had been allowed to deteriorate to such an extent that they were a danger to visitors. The Italian attitude to antiquities is often not merely negligent but positively aggressive; in Milan vandals attack medieval frescoes, and in Ferrara a baroque church has been converted into a car wash. Modern Italy is, perhaps, irritated by the continued emphasis that foreigners place on its past – since foreign adulteration of Italian cultural heritage is a centuries-old tradition. Furthermore the country's artistic wealth is so enormous that it is taken for granted, and it seems a matter of small consequence if some of it is lost; thus the ordinary Italian is not unduly disturbed to see *yet another* Roman bas-relief obscured by advertisements for Campari and Appiacola.

The fact that our veneration for the artistic achievements of the past is not a universal attitude should not lead us to think it merely a neurotic symptom. Such a veneration implies a high level of civilisation, in which a considerable degree of leisure is available to a large part of the population. Our interest in antiquities also plays an important conservationist role. This is particularly evident in Turkey, a country that is probably richer in historical monuments than any other. A high proportion of these monuments, however, are not strictly Turkish, but Greco-Roman and Byzantine. Religious dictates had caused the plastering over of Byzantine mosaic decorations when churches were converted into mosques. Ruins were regarded

* Political conditions now make it impossible for any tourists to visit Angkor.

as convenient piles of ready-made building blocks.* In her book *Ionia*, Freya Stark recounts how she vainly pleaded with Turkish peasants who were felling the last remaining column of an obscure Aeolian-Greek town. In the 1920s some monuments (notably the Church of the Virgin in Nicaea) were deliberately destroyed because they were associated with the Greeks with whom Turkey was then at war. Even today it is probably still true that educated Turks value the thirteenth-century Seljuk mosques and medrasses more highly than Greco-Roman cities or Byzantine mosaics, and they must feel some resentment of cultured visitors whose attention is directed principally towards Troy, Ephesus and Aghia Sophia – visitors for whom the Islamic heritage is a dispensable 'extra'. Nevertheless western influence has been felt, and to good effect; for example, churches that had been converted into mosques have been secularised and opened as museums. This has made possible the discovery of some magnificent mosaics beneath the layers of plaster and whitewash. The part tourism has played in this reassessment of Turkey's artistic heritage is, admittedly, small. Most of the credit must go to Ataturk's insistence on westernisation, improved standards of education in Turkey and the efforts of various western cultural foundations. Nevertheless, tourism has played its part. Tourism is the most immediately evident demonstration of our concern for the past. In Turkey, the arrival of increasing numbers of westerners who had come to tour the Greco-Roman cities (especially Pergamum, Ephesus and Priene on the west coast) must have made the local inhabitants aware that the ruins were highly valued by others (even if for reasons they could not understand). The most popular sites soon acquired an economic value and it became more profitable to act as guides, sell souvenirs or work for archaeological expeditions, than to demolish potential tourist attractions piecemeal. The entrance money paid by tourists to enter archaeological sites, or to visit museums on the sites, also contributes to their preservation and upkeep.

There are drawbacks of course. It is arguable that the conversion of 'historical monuments' and 'artistic treasures' into tourist sights, robs them of their magic. It is certainly unfortunate that the desire to attract more tourists sometimes leads to injudicious reconstructions; for example, we have observed crude reconstructions in garish red

* In more remote areas this may still be the case.

brick and concrete at Ephesus and Side respectively. Such reconstructions are of small interest or use to archaeologists or historians,
they simply pander to the tourist's lack of imagination. Where
government supervision and control is inadequate, the realisation
that western tourists are attracted to antiquities had led local entrepreneurs and hoteliers to encroach on those antiquities. This is
happening on Turkey's south coast. Side is a Greco-Roman city in a
spectacular state of preservation built on a promontory between two
crescents of sand. This conjunction of attractions has been its
undoing; a barrack-like hotel and a number of makeshift shacks
have appeared on one of its beaches. The Turkish village, built
picturesquely in among the ruins, is now full of signs advertising
PENSION and DISCOTHEQUES. Similar atrocities are in progress at the
equally beautiful site of Corycos, further east along the same coast.
This kind of destructive development is avoidable; the controlled
development of the Yugoslavian coast has demonstrated that places
of unusual historical interest and natural beauty can operate as
tourist attractions without being ruined.

The most common complaints against historical/cultural tourism
are largely subjective, indeed, romantic and poetic. The mere presence
of tourists in the hallowed sites of antiquity is felt by some to be a
desecration. The presence of large parties of 'mass tourists' inhibits
the meditations on fallen grandeur of the romantic and putative poet.
The crassness of tourists confronted with the monuments of the
glorious past is proverbial. The reactions of middle-Americans
patrolling the Athenian acropolis, cameras at the ready, constitute
the basis of innumerable tired jokes and humorous anecdotes. For
the record, the present author's favourite example of this genre
involves a sensitive American girl who was visiting the Acropolis in
a state of rapt communion with the past, when her reverie (a stroll
perhaps with Socrates or Sophocles) was rudely shattered by an
abrasive shriek of: 'Say, Harry! Come an' take a look at this WRECK!'
No one is easier to caricature than the tourist confronted with *real
culture*. The joke usually depends on a complacent sense of superiority to the mass of tourists. Nothing annoys some tourists more than
the presence of other tourists, and the most pretentious and snobbish
will not admit to being tourists at all. They will compete with each
other to demonstrate their extreme sensitivity to any trace of 'commercialisation'. A stall selling soft drinks adjacent to an archaeological
site will be loudly condemned as a symptom of this universal blight,

even though the critic will gratefully imbibe its Coca Cola after he has 'done' the site.

It seems safe to say that as long as the capitalist system lasts, it will continue to impose a commercial value on art and antiquities. Since we cannot generally expect governments and bureaucrats to act according to the dictates of pure aesthetics, it is probably as well that tourism can make the preservation and upkeep of art and antiquities a viable investment. This would seem to be one of the few considerations that can spur the Italians to take steps to prevent the total disintegration of their artistic heritage. Disintegration is not too strong a word, since Italy must be the only country in the world where churches are adorned with public notices reading: DANGER! FALLING ANGELS. The continued pressure of world opinion is also vital to the survival of Venice, and the more tourists visit the city the stronger the pressure is likely to be.

There is another, less direct, way in which tourism helps to conserve antiquities. The intrusions of the cultured hordes of the mass democracies may offend romantic antiquarians and irritate archaeologists but the alternatives are much worse. Artistic pillaging has been a prominent feature of western culture since the Renaissance. The Roman cardinals and popes of the Renaissance pillaged Hadrian's villa at Tivoli; the English 'milords' of the eighteenth century bought up any Italian art treasures that came on the market; in the nineteenth century Lord Elgin removed sections of the Parthenon frieze. When large numbers of tourists can travel easily to view antiquities *in situ*, there is no longer any need to cart them away in sections. Some of the motivation is removed, and, if a work of art is well known to art experts and the public, it will be difficult to sell, even if it can be stolen. Tourism in itself cannot be considered sufficient deterrent of course, and in Italy, with its vast number of relatively obscure, uncatalogued, but highly marketable art treasures, 'devastating pillage' continues. When an ancient culture is too remote to be accessible to the touring art lover large-scale pillaging continues with twentieth-century efficiency. Organised gangs are at present busy in the jungles of Central America, hacking up the sculptures of the Mayan ceremonial complexes, and shipping them to the private collections and museums of the North Atlantic Community; they are frequently badly damaged in transit. In this way our greedy fascination with the exotic and the ancient impedes the serious work of archaeologists and anthropologists. With each stela removed from the Maya sites, the possibility of solving the many enigmas of the culture becomes increasingly remote. Yet our rich art-fanciers and our museums – the supposed custodians of the world's artistic heritage – continue to buy from sources at best dubious and often frankly illegal. With such attitudes prevalent among the culturati, what can we reasonably expect from the average tourist in the way of understanding or respect for past cultures?

The tourist may well be nervous and insecure in a foreign country and consequently only too willing to leave the organisation and selection of his cultural experiences to a tour operator. His education does not equip him to understand these experiences. The modern tourist in Italy or Greece, imbibing culture along with the Coca Cola, is playing his part in the final democratisation of the aristocratic grand tour. In the seventeenth and eighteenth centuries the viewing of antiquities was an extension of a classical-biased educational curriculum. The tour was culturally *integral* since the tourist belonged to a culture that constantly looked to the 'correct' classical models for inspiration. In this century the 'classics' have been displaced from their central position in the western educational system. They now constitute a specialist subject and most of us grow up largely ignorant of Greek myth, literature, history and philosophy. This has occurred in a period when more Americans and northwest Europeans are visiting Greece than ever before. This in itself suggests that cultural tourism is not fulfilling its educational potential.

For the middle-class tourist a token veneration of the ancient is an automatic reflex; 'It's old therefore it must be beautiful, interesting, *improving*'. The educational tour still exists but the tourist is more like an obedient child than a discriminating and knowledgeable observer. His experience is strictly regimented in accordance with a particular view of culture. He is fed with simple statistical information – the monument's age and dimensions, etc. – and *humanised* statistics – how many people worked on its construction and the number of years it took them, how many people could stand on the capital of a single column. No attempt at critical appreciation is encouraged; great age forbids personal opinion. It is not possible to observe that there are ancient architectural monstrosities, just as there are modern ones. Such an observation might distress or provoke the disapproval of fellow tourists. It is, of course, difficult to conceive of an interval of thousands of years in human terms, and the monument threatens to become empty and meaningless. This void is filled with easily palatable deodorised versions of 'Life in Ancient Times'. The tourist in the organised party is told that, despite the unimaginable interval of time, the ancients were 'just like you and me'; they were born, they married, they died and were buried beneath sentimental inscriptions; they had theatres, public baths and libraries; they kept pets. In fact, the ancients are presented as good bourgeois. Nowadays it is also permissible to point out the ruins of the brothel to the tourist party, but the phallic sculptures that originally served as adornment and trade-signs will usually have been placed discreetly out of sight. A retrospective pruriency is imposed on pagan mores, just as middle-class 'good taste' is imposed on Greek aesthetics. Our conventional idea of a Greek temple is a vision of sun-bleached marble, all purity and proportion; but in fact the marble was originally gilded, stuccoed, and painted in brilliant reds and blues, the height of 'bad taste'!

We should not be surprised if a tourist from the American midwest finds that the most interesting thing about the Athenian acropolis is the view of the Hilton. The institutionalisation of cultural tourism began in the eighteenth century; as we have seen (Chapter 2) the visiting of antiquities had become a matter of routine, something undertaken because it was the 'done thing'. The list of 'sights' visited was evidence of the tourist's cultural credentials. Consequently the list would often be run through as quickly as possible. The organised coach tour has greatly facilitated this kind of tourism. Landscape and peoples become a blur seen from a coach window, as the tourist speeds from one antiquity to the next – isolated even from prevailing climatic conditions by air-conditioning. Delphi or Olympia become places where you stop to look at some more broken columns and have another drink. Sheer speed prevents any real contact with history or culture.

The most frequented sites/sights acquire a curious unreality. The monuments are viewed in anaesthetised isolation; they are cut off from the surrounding landscape and community by the fence surrounding the site, the turnstile by which it is entered, the glass of the coach window. There is a feeling that the place has been stared at so repeatedly and so uncomprehendingly by so many people that it has become a ghost of its former self. Every detail of the site is so familiar from professional and amateur photography that it seems to be a *genuine, life-size reproduction of the original*. Perhaps this is the inevitable fate of monuments whose only remaining function is to be tramped round and stared at, carefully preserved, hygienically maintained for that purpose. Mass tourism may help to conserve antiquities, but it is arguable that sites that have become institutionalised 'tourist sights' are no longer worth seeing.

The unreality of the established tourist sight is perhaps accounted for by the development of an attitude which we have traced back to the second half of the eighteenth century (see Chapter 2); that is: 'the suppression of the human life of a country to the exclusive benefit of its monuments'.[2] This achieves its ultimate expression in the cultural coach tour, moving as quickly as possible from one ancient monument to the next. An even more extreme expression of this attitude may prove to be the 'Venice Preserved' of the late 'seventies and the 'eighties. We have already suggested that tourism can play an important part in rescuing the city from the combined attacks of a rising sea level, Italian industrialisation and Italian bureaucracy. This may be achieved at a high cost. In an article in *The Sunday Telegraph*,[3] Allen Andrews suggests that one of the factors which could save Venice would be 'the development of the Grand Hotels conception of Venice as an all-year-round visitors resort to compete with Monaco in its prime'. Obviously this would cater to our nostalgia for a lost aristocratic style of tourism, a nostalgia which recently gained definitive expression in Visconti's film of *Death in Venice*. The Grand Hotels scheme also involves 'congress halls, and discothèques, covered pools and tennis courts, and English-style pubs . . .'. Such development can only divert attention from one of the city's central problems, that is, depopulation. Native Venetians are, understandably, deserting their sinking city for its industrial satellites of Mestre and Marghanera. A city largely inhabited by a shifting population of tourists is no substitute for a vital community. Foreign concern for Venice is entirely focused on the historic and the nostalgic, in the words of Joan Fitzgerald, a sculptress working in Venice: 'Artistic vitality in Venice depends on the encouragement of the artisans; and the great funds will spend one hundred thousand dollars on a church floor but nothing on helping a woodcarver to retain his lodgings.' The Managing Director of the Campagnia Italiana dei Grandi Alberghi which owns six of the top hotels in Venice and the Lido has said: 'We want more than a cleaned, dead monument; we want a living Venice.' But what the Grand Hotel scheme offers is a Venice entirely given over to satiating the tourist's thirst for the historic and nostalgic, punctuated with the reassurance of disco-thèques and 'English-style pubs' – a pseudo city.

DEEP-FROZEN FOLKLORE: CULTURE AS COMMODITY

Tourism as cultural improvement fails in one very obvious respect. A tourist standing in front of the pyramids is quite likely to say: 'The place would be marvellous *if it wasn't for the Arabs*' (substitute Greeks/Italians/Spaniards as required). Between sights the arche-typal culture vulture complains of the lack of hygiene, greasy food, and above all, the idleness and dishonesty of the natives who are not seen as connected to the Glorious Past. The centres of the great cultures of antiquity are not to be found in north-west Europe or North America. They are located in Mediterranean Europe and the Third World – those areas left behind by Modern Progress. The fact that they have fallen behind *must* be the result of the idleness and dishonesty of the people. Centuries of foreign domination, followed in the twentieth century by the economic imperialism of the North Atlantic Community are not taken into account. Any admission of even a part of the truth questions all the tourist's presuppositions, brings the collapse of his complacency. He will not enjoy his holiday if he allows himself to become distressed at the plight of the natives. Consequently, even when his tourism is directly concerned with culture and history, the tourist is not encouraged to develop any real sense of history. Nor is he encouraged to view a foreign culture as a *totality* (of people and environment, art and religion, past and present). The touristic view of culture is necessarily schizoid and fragmented.

One cannot expect a tourist to be interested in the problematic realities of an underdeveloped nation, struggling to come to terms with the twentieth century, when he has come to relax, and when the resorts of the underdeveloped nation have been sold to him (by the travel trade and the government tourist boards) as appropriate places in which to relax. In so far as he takes an interest in life beyond the hotel and the swimming-pool or beach, he is interested in the surviving aspects of the antique, the ethnic and the primitive. These may well be those traditional and regressive elements of indigenous culture which the national government is desperately trying to reform (or forget).

The staff of the hotel may or may not be local people, but in any case doormen, waiters, porters and barmen tend to be regarded as an international breed with little or no identity. Outside the hotel the local inhabitants are expected to be living replicas of the national costume dolls on sale in the airport. They are expected to have picturesque rituals, colourful habits, archaic technology – in fact anything other than the international style of the western bourgeoisie; in practice this means that the natives must be (relatively) poor, ignorant and superstitious. Traditional customs soon take on the status of a sideshow. There will be prearranged 'spontaneous' outbreaks of singing and dancing. Patrick Rivers has cited the example of Tunisia where traditional wedding ceremonies have proved so successful with tourists that they are now staged on demand. In the same way the inhabitants of North America's Indian Reservations go through their tired routine of ritual dances for the benefit of tourist parties. The tourist's illusion that the life of the country visited is a pageant arranged for his benefit becomes a reality; the touristic pseudo-event is born.[4]

The tourist buys his holiday as a package, he also buys culture as a package. Thus foreign cultures, however ancient and complex they may be, are reduced to a few instantly recognisable characteristics. Their culture becomes a commodity. The more desperate a country's economic position the less it can afford to quibble over selling its birthright. This syndrome is inevitably at its worst in Third World tourist destinations, but it is also to be found in the most long-established and affluent destinations. The Director of the Swiss National Tourist Office said recently: 'Strangers to this country may immediately conjure up such typically Swiss symbols as Alpine horns, chalets, cuckoo clocks, yodelling and cheese making, but Switzerland, of course, has far more to offer than "deep-frozen folklore".'[5] The reader will be able to compile similar lists of emblematic artefacts and customs for Spain, Greece, the Caribbean, Hawaii, the U.K. and so on. Unless there is a radical alteration in the tourist industry there is no reason why the average tourist should realise that any of these places 'has far more to offer'.

The commercialisation of culture is most immediately evident in the souvenir industry. The mass-produced souvenir is the twentieth-century equivalent of the artistic loot of the Grand Tourist – a placebo for the acquisitive instinct. In one sense this is a substitution we should welcome, since it means the real art treasures stay in the country: if the tourist expects it to be there, it generally stays there. Tourism apologists also claim that the touristic demand for souvenirs, and more generally the demand for the quaint and traditional, provide a stimulus to local arts and crafts. This is doubtful; the World Bank's 1970s survey states that tourism 'often leads to a serious deterioration in the standards of local arts and crafts'. Carleen O'Loughlin has said of the Caribbean: 'Tourism provides financial incentive to the practice of the arts, particularly those connected with entertainments or the making of handicrafts. But does this patronage have any strings attached? The adoption of West Indian artistic forms of expression in dance, steel bands and carving, to cater to tourists can lead not only to the loss of the tradition but also to a distortion of the original meaning which may in fact be unidentifiable to later research workers. . . .' The only flaw in this argument is the author's apparent assumption that the inhabitants of the Caribbean live and die for 'later research workers'.

It is difficult to make unchallengeable general statements concerning aesthetic values, since they cannot be anatomised in the objective, statistical terms beloved of our research institutes; but it seems safe to say that when the indigenous artist or craftsman comes to value his work chiefly in terms of whether it will sell to tourists, then ancient artistic formulae lose their meaning and vitality. The best selling lines are simply reproduced in an increasingly diluted and westernised form. Even in New Guinea the carvers of ceremonial masks have started to produce masks specifically for sale to western art dealers and tourists. Far from being dilutions these masks employ extreme distortions of form, but the result is the same since these stylistic distortions are quite meaningless in terms of native ritual and symbol. Western art-fanciers, however, find them excitingly bizarre, reminiscent, perhaps, of our own dear Picasso. (In this case things have turned full circle, since the great innovators of twentieth-century art were inspired, originally, by the strict stylisations of 'primitive' art.)

There are occasions when tourism seems to serve a conservationist role (and, even, a revivalist role). In Isfahan the Shah Abbas Caravanserai has been converted into an hotel. The conversion caused an outcry since the caravanserai stood on religious property, adjacent to a mosque and a theological school; as an hotel it would have to serve alcohol. Despite the outrage caused to fundamentalist Moslems, the conversion did save an old and very beautiful structure from further decay. Furthermore the restoration of the caravanserai, carried out by the few practitioners of the traditional arts and crafts still living, led to a whole scheme for the restoration of the Safavid buildings of Isfahan, executed by the same craftsmen. Tourism cannot be blamed for the fact that local artistic standards have declined sharply since the golden age of Shah Abbas and the Safavids. A rather less substantial example is cited by J. Forster,[6] concerning Hawaiian handicrafts. Here the tourist demand has led to a revival of grass skirt and mat weaving when the art was on the point of dying out. He does point out, however, that the profits from this revival went largely to Honolulu retailers: 'A hat . . . which took two days' work would be sold by the manufacturer for 50 to 75 cents and might retail in Honolulu in 1957 for five to six dollars.' This might suggest that in those cases, where tourist preferences cause a deterioration of aesthetic standards, this loss is not always adequately compensated by increased local prosperity, even assuming that an aesthetic loss *can* be compensated by material gain.

Most readers will be able to bring personal experience to bear on this question. One's chances of purchasing an 'art object' of some real value, at a reasonable price, increase in ratio to one's distance from established tourist centres. This is strikingly apparent in Turkey where the ceramics, rugs and jewellery to be found on the west coast are both more expensive and poorer in quality than those to be found further east. In general our preoccupation with antiquity leads to mass-produced 'Nefertiti heads' and crudely literal imitations of 'Grecian urns' while the authentic indigenous styles that may have grown up in the intervening historical period often fall into decay. What we end up with is the emptiest kind of neo-classicism – unimaginative and technically crude reproductions of long-dead styles. This is cultural sterility since imaginative invention and individuality are not required. The imagery of antiquity is debased by its mass production, becoming kitsch and cliché. It thus becomes increasingly inaccessible to serious contemporary artists as vital source material. In this more subtle sense, also, tourism alienates people from their heritage. The souvenir industry helps to perpetuate an entirely nostalgic view of art; the souvenir of the past, and the souvenir from 'abroad' become indistinguishable; the weight of the past suffocates the creativity of the present. Tourism is only one element in this process but an important one, since it has considerable financial weight.

These symptoms are not only found in the more distant tourist destinations of the Mediterranean and the Third World. The Western European nations are also victims of tourism's mythologising. 'Yodelling and cheesemaking' may not be the total reality of Switzerland, similarly the thatched-cottage–stately-home–mock-Tudor England of tourist mythology may not be recognisable to many of the English themselves. Despite this the myth of quaint Britain has been assiduously cultivated since the conclusion of the First World War. It must be admitted immediately that this campaign is directed at the indigenous middle class as much as foreign tourists; polystyrene oak beams and Georgian bow windows (with 'bottle glass') proliferate throughout the nation's suburbs. In this manner has Britain accepted its post-imperial status. It is a patriotic campaign. On every level, from poetry to pub décor, we promote the idea of Quaint Britain, the olde worlde of North America and the colonies, the poor cousin of north-west Europe.

Our reserve and politeness are national institutions; they are reflected in our typical landscape – that of Oxfordshire and Warwickshire. The tourist 'milk run' (to use the parlance of the trade) goes from London thro' Oxford to Stratford (the unofficial capital of Quaint Britain). The whole tour can be completed in a day. It need hardly be said that the intensely cultivated, park-like landscape of Oxfordshire and Warwickshire is *not* characteristic of Britain as a whole, any more than London is representative of British cities. Yet many of the 8 million tourists who visited England in 1973 regarded this as typical; this was the Britain that tallied with impressions gained in the classroom. (It is arguable that Britain is holding one of its greatest tourist assets in reserve. As the source of the Industrial Revolution Lancashire and Yorkshire have great nostalgic potential. It seems likely that Jumbo-jet tourists will become increasingly attracted to industrial archaeology, the primitive origins of the technological sophistication that makes their tourism possible.)

London remains the hub of the tourist's Britain and the capital of a defunct Empire. Under the banner of 'Swinging London', Britain has been promoting its decadence for some time. This may seem the opposite of Quaint Britain, but it is equally unreal and works (as a lure) in tandem with Historic London. Motorised guides enable the affluent visitor to 'do' London in a day, without expending much energy: Buckingham Palace, Trafalgar Square, the City, St Paul's, the Tower, A Typical English Pub, and so on. If the tourist does not insist on getting out of the car and actually *visiting* these places (with the exception of the pub), there will even be time for the more recondite pleasures of Highgate Cemetery, Hampstead or Chelsea. We even know of one tourist who asked to be shown 'something really different' and ended up visiting Battersea Dogs' Home.

In London the tourist can enjoy metropolitan decadence without the viciousness of New York, or the irascibility of Paris. During the summer months it becomes a pleasure metropolis (as does Amsterdam). There are Georgian terraces adjacent to the chic of the King's Road, and Royal Parks adjacent to the burgeoning hotels of Kensington. In Biba, one of the most emphatically stylish emporia in the world, a kind of permanent (though constantly changing) exhibition of the Interior Decorative Arts, suffused with Art Deco gloom, London has a unique tourist attraction. London's double role as a still vigorous metropolis and international tourist resort unfortunately creates real inconvenience for local inhabitants and national tourists. At the height of the season the most popular tourist sights become so overcrowded that it is no longer possible to gain any real pleasure from them.[7] Referring to the publicity given to Quaint Britain in 1963, Brigid Brophy remarked: 'Such publicity is not, of course, intended for foreigners, who, should they take it literally enough actually to come here, quickly discover that we have no provision for them.' That situation has changed in London, at least. In the last three years the government has allowed scandalous tax-exemptions and subsidies for hotel builders. The results are, to say the least, interesting.

Externally these new hotels are conventional exercises in 'Airport Moderne' – massive, crudely detailed, brilliant with glass and steel. This international airport-hotel style deserves some analysis. It is the Imperial style of the twentieth century, it imposes cultural uniformity, it proclaims the superiority of western technology and design, it emphasises the superior wealth of the foreign visitor. It perhaps serves something of the same symbolic purpose as the elaborate and pompous, stylistically identical public buildings of Roman or British Empire-builders. It presents a kind of deadening, modern, pseudo-classicism. Its most sophisticated exponents are Hilton International. Reflecting that there would be 'Hiltons for Kenya, Kuala Lumpur, Kensington, Melbourne, Okinawa, Quebec, Stratford-on-Avon and

Sydney' and that further possibilities (for the late 'seventies) were 'Bali, Bahrein, Djakarta, Dubai, Kano, Lahore, Lisbon and Vienna', Anthony Haden-Guest[8] was put in mind of a science-fiction scenario: the World menaced by a Thing that spontaneously reproduces, 'The scientist-hero is wrestling against time to find How It Does It, – Air-blown spores? Telekinesis? A kink in the space/time warp? Still the blobs keep appearing and they grow until . . . There it is! Another Thing – and just like the first. . . .' A good number of the Hilton 'Things' that Haden-Guest listed have since materialised, but the metaphor is, perhaps, unsuitably *Organic*. There is nothing blob-like about the international hotel circuit, it is more like some vast glittering machine with a mind of its own, its arteries and cells filled with the sibilance of air-conditioning.

The cultural arrogance implicit in the style becomes most clearly apparent in Third World countries. The international hotel builder automatically assumes that conventional western architecture is 'ideally suited for all parts of the world, because it is technically the most advanced and the most sophisticated style of building'.[9] The architect will frequently have 'no local experience or knowledge of the climate or the social traditions of the people'. A luxury hotel is invariably the last thing the local people need in material terms, it is also the last thing they need in cultural terms. The uncompromising modernity and alien style of the hotel does not suggest the possibility of any smooth transition from traditional to modern. On a simpler level the hotel is almost exclusively for the use of foreigners; its prices will be prohibitive for all but the country's ruling élite. This admission and exclusion graphically demonstrates the alienation of the national bourgeoisie from the mass of the population. For that bourgeoisie the new hotel is a status symbol, with it their country has entered *the Modern World*! For some intellectuals and the less prosperous majority of the population the hotel may soon become the focus of resentment and anger.

There have been attempts to relate hotel architecture to indigenous culture, notably in Tunisia and East Africa. In Tunisia most of the new hotels are low and spreading, built around courtyards in the manner of the traditional Islamic caravanserai. Such architecture does not destroy the rhythms of the Tunisian landscape in the way that more conventional development would have done. Unfortunately recent reports suggest that this style is not popular with package tourists, who apparently prefer the reassurance of high-rise, neo-functionalist, neo-brutalist, pseudo-classicism. One way of avoiding the problem of developing a hotel style appropriate to the local environment (and without resorting to quaint archaism) is to convert existing buildings. As we have seen this has happened in Isfahan; on the Yugoslavian coast an entire village has been converted into a hotel complex without any alteration of its external aspect; in Java the palaces of sultans have been similarly converted. This would seem the best solution were it not for the fact that it is also the most direct way of alienating the indigenous population from their cultural heritage. There is also a growing tendency to make hotels less *obtrusive* even where no attempt has been made to link them to local styles; the catch-phrase is: 'No higher than the tallest palm tree.' This is not an entirely adequate response to the problem but it must be welcomed, nevertheless. For many resorts, however, such innovations come too late. At Famagusta, Cyprus, one of the most beautiful beaches in the Mediterranean has been converted into a kind of poor man's Miami. Local environmental conditions have been ignored so completely that for most of the afternoon the beach is in the shadow of its fringing high-rise apartment blocks and hotels.

Conrad Hilton is perfectly clear about the meaning of the Hilton style; he has said: 'Each of our hotels is a little America.' In these circumstances the Stratford Hilton is as much a statement of cultural arrogance as a Katmandu or Bali Hilton. Even in the metropolitan centres hotel architecture frequently ignores the style and scale of surrounding buildings. *The Architectural Review* has complained that in London the new hotels of 'these last catastrophic three years' have arrogated 'a civic importance which belongs by right only to public buildings'. The London Hilton, a structure entirely lacking in any architectural distinction, now terminates the long vistas of Kensington Gardens and the Serpentine.

The most interesting feature of the new London hotels, however, is the style of their interior décor: '. . . you enter the lobby. Before you stretches a hall. Cool and distant and almost white. Crystal chandeliers bathe the marble floors and columns in soft white light. There are people but it is rather quiet. Not sombre though. Composed perhaps. And elegant. This is the Churchill.' This scrupulously unctuous description[10] is taken from the Churchill Hotel's brochure. The exterior of the Churchill may be functional-modern, its interior is pseudo-Adam down to the air-conditioning and lighting fixtures.

Similarly, the lounge of the Elizabetta Hotel is rouched and draped in velvet and brocade; corinthian columns purport to hold up the corniced and coffered ceiling; the furniture is drowned in a luxuriant froth of pseudo-rococo scrolls. It suggests nothing so much as the interior of one of the more conservative Parisian Houses of Fashion. From the application of 'period charm' these interiors take off into the realms of pure fantasy; spiral staircases illumined by 'sun-burst' lights, 'gothic-inspired chesterfield chair groups'; a ceiling covered with *70,000 real magnolia leaves* dyed crimson; a renaissance bar with gothic arches and a reproduction of the Laughing Cavalier next to the exit sign. . . . The possibilities are infinite, cultural blends and clashes previously undreamt of, a whole new High Camp rhetoric of interior décor. This is, unquestionably, the way of the future.

Charles Jenks describes these hotels as 'self-contained cities which have so many amenities and historical frills that the tourist needn't leave to see London at all'. This is a touristic breakthrough and Hilton International have been among its most energetic exponents. Wherever the Hilton is it is likely to resemble 'a Los Angeles Insurance office' from the outside, but inside 'interior decorators have gone to appalling pains to incorporate local motifs'. Perhaps Hilton International are a little nervous of the possible indelicacy of Conrad Hilton's exuberant patriotism. They describe the Nairobi Hilton as 'A uniquely circular, 17-storey guest-room tower, inspired by tribal legends that life is a perpetual circle'. Its interior is adorned with 'Dramatic murals of majestic Masai warriors . . . imaginative, Afro-modern sculpture, ancient tribal symbols on wood, splashes of safari colors and zebra skins. Everywhere brilliant masses of exotic flowers accentuate the beauty.' The folkloristic climax to this diverse ensemble is the Amboseli Grill, 'stunningly designed to represent the interior of a huge native hut'.

Haden-Guest's comment on this phenomenon deserves to be quoted in full:

> Not for nothing do gastronomes, folk-lorists and other travellers to antique lands look forward – with mingled emotions, to a day when cultural cross-communications will have become so free and easy that in the entire terrestrial blandscape only the Hiltons will stand a proud and determined guardian of native manners and mores. It will be the Hilton interior-decorators who will be a repository of the artistic motifs of times gone by and it will be Hilton Tours who will furnish an audience for colourful local ways.

Traditional craftsmen will ply their archaic trades by courtesy of
Hilton Gift Shops, swords will be beaten into ashtrays and dying
customs will live forever on Polaroid. In the Hilton coffee shops,
skilled food technologists will find ways of preparing local delicacies which you can eat in perfect safety and they will be brought to
the table by waiters sporting, perhaps, a touch of authentic cos-
tumary . . . in the last genuine Greek tabernas, Suki-Yaki houses,
Nordic Smörgasbords and Old London Pubs in the whole wide
world.

The prospect before us, fellow tourists, is a World of Kitsch – the
apotheoses of the pseudo. The folkloristic, *indigenised* interior décor
of the new international hotels does not contradict their standardised
Airport Moderne exteriors – it complements them. The essential
formula is *'local delicacies which you can eat in perfect safety'*, or 'the
best of the olde worlde and the best modern plumbing'. The standardised, the formalised have absorbed the requisite elements of the
historic and the ethnic – they can all be found behind the Los
Angeles-insurance-office-façade. There is no need to go outside the
hotel if the waiters, doormen, porters are wearing national costume.
Your steak is served by a Malay warrior, a Bedouin tribesman, or a
Tahitian Wahine.

This is the *reductio ad absurdum* of cultural-educational tourism.
There is no longer any need for the real thing; the all-embracing
mythology and machinery of international tourism everywhere sub-
stitutes highly-coloured, hygienic, approximations, paraphrases and
reproductions. In Fiji in 1970 a Major C. F. A. Wagstaff had plans
to build an English inn: 'We would like a fine replica of an Elizabethan Inn with a timbered front.' No doubt anxious to export
Quaint Britain, the British Tourist Authority has sent him 'blue-
prints of The Anchor on London's Bankside'.[11] A Spanish hotel
consortium has gone further. It has purchased a group of uninhabited Pacific islands, the Pearl Islands, and intends to endow each
with different instant national characteristics: 'One island will be
turned into an Arab town; another will be Chinese; others Polynesian and Spanish, while one will become a "pirate stronghold".'[12]

9 Lotus Eating

No occupation; all men idle all;
And women too but innocent and pure.
Shakespeare, *The Tempest*

Tourism's preoccupation with the cultural is, generally, superficial. Nevertheless, cultural/antiquarian tourism still has its positive elements; it is ostensibly concerned to understand and appreciate and is not mere romantic-fallacious escapism. It still has the potential to educate, since, in its highest form, it seeks to view and understand the origins and development of cultures. Anecdotes of tourists' crassness are numerous but there are also tourists who *do* experience new feelings – who come to some new realisation of their relation to history when visiting cultures other than their own, or observing the monuments of past cultures. A new awareness of the complexities and troubles of past or foreign cultures may conceivably turn the tourist's thoughts back to the complexities and troubles of his own culture. The more highly industrialised forms of tourism may militate against this, but it is still a possible aspect of holiday travel.

The cultivation of the ethnic and the pristine (whether in the form of idyllic tropical cultures, the unpeopled wastes of Iceland or the Animal Kingdoms of Africa) belongs to a negative mythology. Few urban dwellers would truly relish a life of archaism and agriculture, yet we frequently cite the supposed harmonious simplicity of more primitive cultures as a desirable alternative to our own urban culture. We (our sociologists, physicians, psychologists, philosophers and anthropologists)* talk endlessly of the stress, alienation and deteriorating environment of our cities. We claim the right to therapeutic escape, but do we sufficiently consider the possible stresses resulting from the claustrophobia and isolation of small, primitive communities? Our cities may well be in crisis, but the city is not *essentially* corrupt, decadent and polluted. Perhaps if we responded to townscapes as much as we respond (or claim to respond) to landscapes, our cities might not be in such a mess. The more we flee (imaginatively and physically) in the direction of Nature and Simplicity, the more this crisis will worsen;

* And, perforce, the authors of this book.

Our cities run to squalor and our machines run amok because our citizens' minds are not on the job of mastering the machines and using them to make the cities efficient and beautiful . . .[1]

The general standard of civic design in nineteenth- and twentieth-century Europe and America has been appalling. The eighteenth century, by contrast, cultivated the city as an art form. This was the corollary of imposing formality on nature.

Seventeenth and eighteenth-century landscape painting (particularly the work of the French painters Poussin, Claude and Watteau) is usually landscape with figures, landscape with ruins—landscape given human scale and meaning. The exaggerated distaste with which Alpine 'wildernesses' were regarded may seem absurd, but the adoration of the wild and the savage that superseded it is more than absurd, it is a surrender of rationality and a negation of civilisation (specifically of the achievements of the eighteenth-century Enlightenment). In Wordsworth's poem *Michael*, Nature (the *wild, mountainous* nature of the Lake District) is identified as the exclusive abode of Virtue and Wisdom, the city as the origin of all human evil. This myth proved highly addictive, almost the opium of the bourgeoisie. The industrial revolution had created problems that could not be solved within Europe's existing social/political framework, and after the traumatic experience of the French Revolution, social revolution was an option the bourgeoisie and the aristocracy could not afford to consider. Consequently the city is no longer regarded as an art form but as an unpleasant necessity. The middle classes move away from the city centres to ever more far-flung suburbs (thereby encroaching on the nature they venerate). Their suburban architecture is a fantasy architecture – pseudo-gothic-Tudor-rustic – the predecessor of Hilton's folkloristic interior décor.

The Cult of Nature is a way of avoiding responsibility; our frayed, alienated psyches cannot support the weight of a civilisation, which (it is implied) *we have inherited through no fault of our own*. In the 'seventies it requires a combined effort of imagination and intellect to see the city once again as 'one of the great indispensible devices of civilisation' and to see that civilisation as 'a device for centralising beauty and transmitting it as heritage'.[2] This is an effort we do not need to make since the tourist industry indulges all our fantasies of returning to 'a communal country childhood that never existed and to a 'natural state' that never existed. Tourism is the industrialisation of a delusory mythology and the effects of this on tourist generating centres and host countries alike are equally ambivalent.

The most potent images of man's former-idyllic-natural state are located in islands: the homelands of the noble savage, the original sites of the Garden of Eden. These are, invariably, Mediterranean or tropical islands and the mythology which surrounds them is predominantly sexual. Ulysses encountered sirens on Thasos, and on other islands (which cannot be conclusively identified) – the enchantress Circe and the nymph Calypso. His time with Calypso was an idyll; his time with Circe involved sexual degradation symbolised by the transformation of his comrades into pigs. On the Island of the Lotus Eaters he encountered the original Flower People. The Lotus Eaters were addicted to their peculiar diet and lived in a permanent state of blissful drowsiness; those members of Ulysses' crew who ate the Lotus had to be forced to leave the island. In *The Odyssey* this is only a brief episode, but Tennyson expanded this into a lengthy poetic idyll of serene melancholy and languorous enervation, set in a land where 'it seemed always afternoon'. In a 'Choric Song', Ulysses' crew forget the outside world; they forget their duty to family and state and their minds return to childhood to 'live again in memory / With those old faces of our infancy'. 'The Lotus Eaters' remains one of the most popular of English nineteenth-century poems, and it is now possible, to some extent, to *enact* the idyll – though with rather more sun-bathing and less 'exquisite melancholy'. The island of the Lotus Eaters is now popularly and quite plausibly identified as Djerba – an island close to the coast of Tunisia which is firmly established as an essential part of the North African tourist circuit. No doubt there are tourists who, like the members of Ulysses' crew, find it difficult to leave Djerba's placid landscape of palm groves and virgin beaches. (It is just as likely that some tourists will find themselves profoundly bored by this realisation of the ideal – of which, more later).

Djerba's promoters have been quick to exploit the Lotus Eaters' legend – it would be difficult to find advertising copy writers more prestigious than Homer and Tennyson. Similarly Seychellois tourist authorities have enthusiastically endorsed General Gordon's suggestion that their islands are the site of the Garden of Eden – no matter that the Bible does not mention a sea voyage in its account of the expulsion from Eden. The Caribbean islands are uniformly 'Paradises', if we believe the tourist literature. Bali, the Seychelles and the South Pacific islands are all 'islands of love'; the alleged 'promiscuity'

or 'permissiveness' of their inhabitants has become a major selling
point – tacitly countenanced by officialdom. The language of their
advertising is openly sexual; tourists are invited to allow themselves
to be *seduced*; they are invited to enjoy the islands' 'unspoilt beauty'
'with a special possessive pleasure'. The tropical islands of the world
are thus offered as a playground for the affluent, western male
chauvinist. No doubt there are many frustrated western males who
would like to imitate the heroic example of one Alexander Hare
who, in the nineteenth century, occupied the uninhabited atoll of
Cocos Keeling, taking with him his personal harem of forty women.
There were no rival males within a thousand miles; his harem he
referred to as 'my flower garden'.

The 'flower gardens' offered by the tourist industry are in general
conventionally heterosexual. There are, however, some islands with
more exotic sexual mythologies. The legendary debaucheries of the
ageing Tiberius have unquestionably enhanced Capri's touristic
image. In David Divine's words:[3] 'On the superb contrasts of sex,
sadism and sunshine 150 years of whispering campaigns have built
an edifice of delicious and titillating scandal for the modern tourist.'
Capri is the place where, according to Tacitus, 'new names for types
of perversion were invented', and according to Suetonius, the place
where 'adepts in unnatural practices' were gathered from all parts of
the Empire. Capri's tradition of debauchery and perversion was
enthusiastically revived in the early years of this century by the
Krupps and the favourites of Kaiser Wilhelm II. More recently, an
historic tradition of vice and corruption has been exploited touristi-
cally in Haiti. The promoters of the Habitation Leclerc, a luxury
tourist complex above Port-au-Prince, openly proclaim that it is
intended to be 'the most extraordinarily lascivious and decadent
place on earth'. Lotus-eating has, here, become orchid-eating.

The Habitation (which we will consider further in Chapter 11) is
still exceptional; the image with the widest appeal is the simplest.
This is still, very much, the ideal of an isolated island life – that is, free
from want (because of the fertility of the natural environment) and
free from sexual guilt. This is prelapsarian tourism. The people are
innocent, uninhibited, ignorant of sexual vices, ignorant of money or
politics; they are Rousseau's 'noble savages'. Their society is, above
all, a society without neuroses. The profound attraction of this mythology is strikingly revealed by the success of the Club Méditerranée,
which attempts to encapsulate this innocent, Golden Age, existence

for the modern tourist; the clients sleep in huts, eat communally in the open air – the atmosphere is gregarious and sexually permissive, and, most significantly, money is replaced by beads. It is money that is the real serpent in the twentieth-century Eden – and the Club Méditerranée beads are an obvious attempt at exorcism without loss of profit. The artificial idyll of the Club Méditerranée is isolated by its surrounding fencing. The isolation of the proto-typical Eden isles of the Indian and Pacific Oceans is being rapidly ended by air travel. As soon as the international airport has been built (on Bali, Fiji or Tahiti, there follows the rapid introduction of some of the most volatile elements of metropolitan culture into societies that have only survived into the present century by virtue of their isolation.

FORBIDDEN FRUIT

It seems mythologically appropriate to begin our survey of island tourism in the Seychelles – the erstwhile Garden of Eden. This myth centres on the vast seed of the female coco-de-mer palm – which, as often remarked, bears an extraordinary resemblance to the female pelvis, or, in General Gordon's words, 'the belly and the thighs'. It is not surprising that a Victorian military man should conclude that this was the original Forbidden Fruit, and the coco-de-mer consequently the Tree of Knowledge. The breadfruit tree he considered the Tree of Life and the Seychelles' oceanic isolation he accounted for by reference to the biblical flood. As Douglas Alexander remarks: 'The fact that Eve would have had to make a steeplejack climb to pick the nut . . . and would have wrecked her teeth biting through the 7 to 10 cm. husk, did not discourage the General in his views.'[4]

It would seem that the Seychellois live up to the (somewhat gross) suggestion of the coco-de-mer. Alec Waugh has said: 'Nowhere in the world, except Tahiti, are amatory emotions less restrained, and nowhere, not even in Tahiti, is there such an accessible variety of young girls.' An American journalist anatomised the charm of the Seychellois girls: 'They're French enough to have good shapes, English enough to have good manners, Asian enough to have a touch of the exotic about them and African enough to have the call

of the wild in them.' As is evident from this exuberant passage of
racial stereotyping the Seychellois' girls are seen very much as fruit
to be plucked; according to Alexander: 'An elderly islander be-
moaning the Seychelles' precarious agricultural economy, recently
remarked: "There's one crop that comes up with unfailing regularity:
women, thank God." '

It is curious that next to the portrait of Queen Elizabeth II on the
Seychelles 50-rupee note there stands a group of palms whose fronds
spell out, unmistakably, the word SEX. The Seychellois' attitude to
sexuality would appear to be happily amoral; the conventional
western regimentation of sexual relations does not apply. Illegitimacy
is common, causes little scandal and paternity is usually acknow-
ledged. If marriages break up the partners form new relationships
without bothering to go through the process of divorce. Thus far the
prospects for the roving male chauvinist would seem to be good, but,
unfortunately, the Seychelles also harbour some of the world's most
virulent strains of venereal disease (see Chapter 14). The visitor who
takes the 'Islands of Love' promotion too literally may leave with an
unwanted souvenir that he will find difficult to discard. We might
also question the ethics of this promotion from the point of view of
the Seychellois women themselves – since it has turned them into an
economic commodity. Nothing could be more destructive of liberated sexual mores than the imposition of a commercial valuation.
One wonders how long it will be (if it has not happened already) before
the Seychellois themselves adopt this valuation of their sexuality,
and begin to sell their advertised charms to tourists. There is already
some evidence to suggest that the Seychellois are coming to regard
their tourism industry as degrading and exploitative. In February
1972 a bomb exploded, damaging one of the islands' newest tourist
hotels. *The Financial Times* commented: 'The bombings, the most
serious in the Seychelles to date, are thought to be the work of
political extremists who have recently called for the expulsion of
foreign interests and demanded an end to the tourist industry. . . .'
A report, appearing in the *Travel Trade Gazette* at the same time,
painted a glowing picture of tourism's prospects in the Seychelles
and made no mention of the bombings.

The Seychelles authorities see tourism as a solution to the islands'
chronic balance of payments problem, but they are aware of some
of the problems involved. Governor Sir Bruce Greatbatch has said:
'We are trying to avoid the mistakes that have been made in the rest

of the world. What we want is a controlled and gradual development which will make the islands self-sufficient.' It is, of course, absurd to suggest that an industry dependent on visiting foreigners and foreign business interests can create 'self-sufficiency'. Government and travel trade are colluding to perpetuate an image of untroubled tropical bliss that places unsuspecting tourists at risk and directly threatens indigenous life-styles.

The erotic status of the Seychelles recently received a new boost when the 1974 Pirelli calendar was photographed in the islands. The models are not Seychellois, nor does the Seychelles' landscape appear very prominently, being limited (almost) to the reflection of palm fronds in the sun-glasses of one of the European models. Inevitably the calendar's introductory blurb mentions the 'amazing' fruit of the coco-de-mer.

A DELICATE BALANCE

In Bali the gap between myth and reality is much greater. Bali is called an 'Island of Love' yet Balinese society has been described (by Alex Frater) as having 'much in common with Italian society – both are deeply conservative, religious and bound by strong family ties which are difficult, if not impossible, to penetrate'. Unmarried girls are closely guarded; public displays of affection are considered indecent. There is considerable sexual freedom among married Balinese, but discretion and delicacy of behaviour must always be strictly maintained. One of the most attractive features of Balinese sexuality is the lack of emphasis on 'role-playing' as this is understood in the West. Women play an equal role in most areas of life and sexual differentiation is very much played down: 'From religion to politics, to economics, to kinship, to dress, Bali is a rather "unisex" society, a fact both its customs and its symbolism clearly express.'[5]

For the visiting Don Juan, Bali presents few opportunities. Its culture has developed in comparative isolation from the rest of the world and has a hierarchic class structure based on a combination of Hindu caste systems and Polynesian rank titles. The outsider who wishes to form a liaison with a Balinese girl must possess infinite patience and ingenuity, and an athleticism which may well be tested

in areas other than the sexual. Alexander Frater recounts the experience of one European:

> I was put in touch with this chap and after several meetings during
> which I had to give him my entire curriculum vitae, not to mention
> my income, religion, cultural tastes and political beliefs, he said
> okay, he would fix it. He would write me a letter. Finally the letter
> came. It contained a detailed plan of the house I was to go to, with
> notes as to who lives in each room. And I was told to go at midday
> precisely, because then the house would be empty but for an old
> aunt, whose room was outlined in red. 'This woman like young
> men' the letter warned. 'Go past on tiptoe and when in girl's room
> push wardrobe against door to stop her getting in. Bed stands with
> head near window giving clear view of road. While lying with girl
> look out as her father and uncles soon coming home for lunch. If
> you seen, jump from window, (2 metres) run through bamboos,
> over stream and up hill to temple. Priest is friend of mine. Give him
> cigarettes and he will hide you. . . .

Even this degree of contact would have been exceptional since
Balinese women generally regard European men with something
approaching total physical revulsion as 'gross, hirsute and evil
smelling'.

As even the tourist brochures agree there is more to Bali than
palms, beaches and beautiful girls. It has a culture that, at first
glance, seems impeccably idyllic, exotic and picturesque. The island
is 'a marvellous synthesis of man and nature', a place of 'grace,
elegance and form, an enchanted garden painstakingly landscaped
over the centuries by a race of artists'. Its sculpture, painting, drama,
music and dance have retained a remarkable purity and individuality
of form. As we have already observed in Chapter 3 it has long
fascinated European intellectuals. It has become a favourite field of
study for anthropologists, Gregory Bateson and Margaret Mead
visiting in the late 1930s (the period of Bali's first tourist boom).
Consequently western academic knowledge of Balinese society and
culture is extensive.

This does not prevent popular misconceptions from persisting.
Exotic, picturesque Bali *does* exist – the Balinese themselves have a
highly developed sense of the picturesque (if we may apply that very
European term to so alien a culture). But the refined aesthetics and
ceremonious poise of the Balinese are achieved at a high cost in
psychic terms. Their insistence on grace and elegance is an expression
of their revulsion against animality in all forms:

Babies are not allowed to crawl for that reason. . . . Most demons
are represented in sculpture, dance, ritual, myth, in some real or
fantastic animal form. . . . Not only defecating but eating is regarded
as a disgusting almost obscene activity to be conducted hurriedly
and privately, because of its association with animality. Even falling
down or any form of clumsiness is considered to be bad for those
reasons. . . . The Balinese are aversive to animals and treat their
large numbers of dogs not merely callously but with a phobic
cruelty.[6]

It is not surprising, in these circumstances, that sexuality is subject to
scrupulous social controls, and that Balinese find the average western
male ludicrous or repugnant.

This suppression of human animality can also lead to appalling
outbreaks of mass hysteria, when the numerous animal demons that
people the Balinese imagination assume control. It is one such outbreak that has been partly responsible for the delay in the revival of
tourism in Bali, after the Second World War. When President
Sukarno of Indonesia fell from power in 1965, the right wing PNI
party embarked on a systematic extermination of Bali's communists.
This political motivation soon became incidental and the killings
became indiscriminate. 'Trance killings' began: 'Individuals and
groups, which often included small boys, went out in a self-induced
and murderous trance, usually cutting the throats of their victims or
splitting their skulls with clubs.' In the final phase of the massacres
the army joined in with a series of mass executions. In early 1966 the
horror ended as suddenly as it had begun; the demons, well satiated,
returned to their niches in the Balinese psyche. Something between
40,000 and 100,000 people had been killed. After a stunned pause the
bullet holes were plastered over, the Bali Beach Hotel was opened
and the tourists began to arrive.

In 1972 forty tourists a day were arriving in Bali, and there were
plans to raise the number to 400 a day. Western liberal opinion has
concentrated its attention on the threat to Balinese culture that this
poses. The World Bank Report (1972) stressed the importance of the
'environmental and cultural impact of tourism' in Bali 'where one of
the principal tourist attractions is the rich cultural life of the population. Here it is critically important that tourist accommodation and
other facilities should be located appropriately and tourist flows
regulated so as to minimise the disruptive impact on the daily life of
the people.'[7] Alexander Frater has remarked on 'a deterioration
already evident in painting and carving once intended for temples

and now aimed at the trippers'. We would respectfully suggest that
tourist sensibilities are also at some risk in Bali. The tourist is led to
expect an idyllic and friendly culture, but one can well imagine, for
example, the average English tourist's reaction to a people who treat
their dogs with 'phobic cruelty'. The promoters of Bali's 'Islands of
Love' image might also care to remember that the Balinese are prone
to a form of temporary insanity, called 'latah' that is induced, specifically, by 'obscene dreams, rapacious, explicit and violent'.

We do not suggest, however, that the World Bank's sense of concern is not well justified; there are already signs that tourism is
'disrupting the daily life of the people', in areas more fundamental
than aesthetic values. It is impossible to discuss tourism's social and
cultural impact without reference to economics (although our main
discussion of tourism economics is to be found in Chapter 7). In Bali
and the Pacific Islands (especially Hawaii, Tahiti and Guam) the
boom in tourism has produced rapid inflation with a consequent
sharp increase in land prices, and the retail prices of most essential
commodities. It may be taken as a general rule that, when this kind
of inflation occurs in largely agricultural Third World countries, the
established business men and land owners may profit but the poorer
sections of the population will inevitably suffer. To cope with rising
prices, the Balinese farmer has been forced to sell his cash crops early,
which has resulted in a glutted market and falling prices. He must
then attempt to sell his most nutritious (and therefore higher priced)
crops to tourist hotels while his family has to subsist on maize and
cassava. Patrick Rivers commented:

> In the poorer uplands of the country, such as Bangli, malnutrition
> is increasing and with it the attendant diseases. Bali is now in the
> throes of a major appraisal for massive tourist development:
> anxious not to frighten investors away, both the government and
> the local press deny the problem. Yet the same process has been
> reported in less developed Java.[8]

There are clear signs that the Indonesian government is worried
about the over-promotion of Bali. In February 1973 the government
withdrew Cathay Pacific Airways' landing rights at Bali's Denpasar
airport, and was threatening Thai International, Qantas and Pan
American with similar action.[9] The Djakarta government has also
put out an advert, declaring (of Indonesia as a whole): 'THERE'S
MORE TO IT THAN BALI'. Above this pronouncement is a picture of
cheerful Indonesian villagers (not, of course, the ones suffering from

malnutrition) who are described in the copy as 'known the world over for their natural charm and spontaneous warmth'. The tourist is encouraged to let himself 'be spoiled for a lifetime by the most unspoiled people anywhere'. We need hardly add, at this stage, that such bogus promotional prose is one of the fastest ways of removing the 'natural' and 'spontaneous' from 'charm' and 'warmth'.

These moves are motivated partly by a desire to increase the tourist receipts of Java, Sumatra and Sulawesi, but there would also seem to be a real desire to stop Bali being overrun with tourists. Excepting economic factors, which are largely beyond their control, the Balinese seem to be coping well with their tourists: they have displayed characteristic subtlety and indirection. It might even be said that Balinese culture has built-in defence mechanisms against the tourist invasion: a foreigner arriving in a Balinese village is *not* an object of curiosity (if curiosity is felt, it is disguised). As far as the foreigner is concerned the villager is, in Bateson and Mead's phrase, 'away'. According to Clifford Geertz the Balinese have a highly developed talent for looking through people, intruders are 'nonpersons, spectres, invisible men'. Perhaps the best way to preserve cultural integrity and authenticity *is* simply to behave as if the tourists are not there; but few Third World cultures have retained the degree of cohesion and strength necessary for such a subtle, collective exercise in social control. The Balinese 'Art of Being Away' would certainly seem a better technique than mixtures of open hostility and forced smile campaigns that characterise some Caribbean tourist destinations. There is no hostility in the Balinese attitude, nor is there friendliness; but the foreigner with patience, tact and a sincere interest in Balinese culture and society can gain acceptance. Eventually the indefinable moral-metaphysical barrier will be crossed, and the Balinese will become charming, responsive and even intimate.[10] It is only the casual, voyeuristic intruder who is automatically excluded.

Many aspects of Balinese culture and art are so bewilderingly complex and alien to western modes that they do not lend themselves readily to the process of over-simplification and mass-production that converts indigenous art forms into touristic kitsch. From the point of view of culture we may perhaps regard the future of tourism with qualified optimism, especially if the World Bank's advice is taken, and efforts are made to minimise its disruptive impact. Yet one cannot help regarding with some disquiet the possible long-term effects of the growing number of affluent foreign intruders in a culture so delicately balanced between aesthetic order and demoniac anarchy.

TAHITI WILL NEVER BE HAWAII

Tahiti is special. The Tahitians make sure it will always be so. They want their island to be truly Polynesian. They go to such lengths as to forbid constructions above the height of a coconut tree. They won't worry if Tahiti gets less tourists than Hawaii. They rather reserve Tahiti for the connoisseurs. Connoisseurs who will enjoy their wide sandy beaches and lagoons, their 'Tiare' and frangipani, their lush green mountains and their 'joie de vivre' with a special, possessive pleasure. Discover it with UTA.

UTA advertisement

The Pacific islands present a microcosm of Pleasure Periphery development. They all share the same idyllic, sexual, primitive mythology but every conceivable stage of development is illustrated among the various island groups – from overcrowded, polluted Hawaii to the still relatively untouched societies of Samoa and the Marqueses, with Tahiti and Fiji lying somewhere between these two extremes. The process of tourism development was already underway in the mid 1920s when Gabriel Kron visited Fiji. He had arrived from Samoa and was disappointed to find the inhabitants of Suva (the Fijian capital) unfriendly and commercial-minded compared to the Samoans. He was told by a British trader that 'these natives around Suva are pretty well spoiled by excursionists from Australia. Many rich Australians spend their vacation here, just as wealthy Americans spend theirs in Hawaii. The visitors have barrels of money and scatter it right and left to the natives as tips, allowing themselves to be photographed, or for souvenirs. . . .'

Tourism in Hawaii is already approaching a crisis stage. The pleasure peripheries of North America and Japan overlap in the archipelago. In the geographically limited environment of an island the cultural/social and ecological impact of tourism is more than usually direct and fast moving. Waikiki inspired Joni Mitchell to sing (in the song 'Big Yellow Taxi'):

> They paved paradise
> And they put up a parking lot,
> With a pink hotel, a boutique
> And a swinging hot-spot.
> Don't it always seem to go
> That you don't know what you've got
> Till it's gone.

SAFARI SHOTS
Lion hunting at night (left)
Safari Park, Kenya (below)

IMPERIAL ACCOMMODATION TO 'ACCOMMODATION RACKS'
Raffles Hotel, Singapore (above)
Royal Tehran Hilton (below)

The hula girls at Honolulu airport greet tourists with plastic garlands; a dense cloud of Los Angeles-style smog frequently shrouds the sunshine resort; the polluted coastal water displays a whole spectrum of colours other than the advertised azure. The proprietors of the Waikiki Hilton, while claiming that the seawater is perfectly safe (as safe as Miami's no doubt), will also admit that guests seem to prefer the swimming-pool. 'Behind the *Death-in-Venice* mystification', Charles Foley[11] found the fact of Honolulu's appallingly primitive sewage disposal system. This consists of a single pipe that each day deposits 60 million gallons of untreated sewage into waters within immediate proximity to Waikiki and Diamond Head. It was only a vociferous conservation lobby that prevented Diamond Head itself disappearing under high-rise apartment blocks.

These developments (or *overdevelopments*) are the result of a gradual erosion of Hawaiian culture and environment which began with Captain Cook. Our stereotyped conception of the Hawaiian is one more variant of the Lotus Eater–Noble Savage–Child of Nature theme – incarnated as 'bronzed, pidgin-speaking natives, laughing men and women with flowered muu-muus split up the side'.[12] In such American television series as *Hawaiian Eye* we have seen them serving drinks (with broad Polynesian grins), surfing spectacularly or doing the hula (grass skirts a-go-go). We should remember that the original population of the archipelago was decimated by syphilis and tuberculosis in the eighteenth and nineteenth centuries (see Chapter 14). Today there are a few thousand pure-blood Hawaiians left, and perhaps 100,000 of mixed Hawaiian blood. The rest of the population is Caucasian, Chinese, Japanese or Filipino. The remaining Hawaiians occupy the bottom of the social scale; when not occupied in being picturesque figures for the tourist, they are 'relegated to clapboard ghettos behind the floral curtain'. They have been dispossessed, in every sense of the word, they and their ancient folk culture have been institutionalised and industrialised. The tourist literature continues to depict the Hawaiian 'physical and social setting in romanticised and sentimental language with major emphasis on the native Hawaiians as a simple, child-like, lovable and uninhibited people'.[13] Their culture is reduced to two principal aspects – 'hula' and 'aloha'. Hula is not simply a question of swaying hips, flower garlands and grass skirts. It is (or was before tourism) a highly expressive combination of dance and dramatic gesture, based on traditional but highly flexible formulae passed down from one

generation of teachers to the next. The tourists' demand for hula
rapidly outpaced its natural occurrence within the Hawaiian cultural
context. As Thomas Hale Hamilton, a former president of the
Hawaiian Visitors Bureau, has confessed: 'Since real cultural events
do not always occur on schedule, we invented pseudo-events for the
tour operators who must have a dance of the vestal virgins precisely
at 10.00 a.m. every Wednesday.'

The exploitation of the aloha concept is more insidious, cutting
more deeply into the traditions of the native Hawaiian community.
In Lind's words: 'The aloha spirit of freely giving for the pleasure of
giving without thought of return is peculiarly identified with the
ancient Hawaiian folk culture in which property rights were to a
considerable degree communally held and therefore readily shared.'
In Hawaii, as in many of the Pacific islands, a culture of communal
living and free generosity clashes with capitalist business ethics (or
non-ethics), and the latter are overwhelmingly the stronger. The
business community and the state administration have been quick to
see the commercial potential of aloha. As Lind observes: 'In the
commercial setting of Waikiki, where thousands of tourists flock
each year the aloha Spirit is distributed much like S & H Green
Stamps . . . the Hawaiian Visitors Board constantly trumpets the
need for more and more aloha, the Chamber of Commerce urges its
perpetuation through the schools. . . .' Institutionalised aloha is a
slogan not a 'reciprocally operating force', and those native Hawaiians whose conduct is still governed by traditions of hospitality and
openness to strangers increasingly find themselves abused. Their
generosity is taken for naïveté and is 'sometimes repaid by a departure with an unpaid bill or the abuse of the host's property or sensibilities'. Inevitably disillusionment and resentment are the results:
aloha has become a bad joke.

One of the most attractive features of Hawaiian society is its lack
of racial prejudice; it is the only one of the fifty American states to
have a genuinely integrated multi-racial society. Some commentators
see tourism as a threat to this unusual degree of harmony. Paul
Jacobs, a mainland American journalist, has remarked: 'Hawaii,
committed to the phoney policy of tourism cannot escape the consequences of the mistakes it is making . . . I foresee the day when
racial tensions which tear mainland cities will envelop Hawaii.'
Lind comments more moderately that, 'the sheer numbers [of
tourists] involved, far exceeding the resident population at present,

would seem to offer the possibility of transforming the equality of race relations within the islands in a short space of time'. As it is estimated that Hawaii will be receiving 5 million visitors a year by 1980 this does not seem an over-pessimistic conclusion.

Lind also comments on 'one of the paradoxical aspects of tourism' – apparently, it is often those 'individuals who are most careful to preserve the conventionally defined distances between themselves and other ethnic or racial groups at home' who 'become most enamoured with persons of these same or other out-groups in the permissive atmosphere of Hawaii'. The credit for this does not really belong to Hawaii's permissive atmosphere but to the touristic mythology of the picturesque and the exotic. In Hawaii the normally racist middle-American can afford to lower the barriers; here, oppressed racial minorities do not seem to threaten his privileged position and he can afford to indulge in the quasi-aristocratic emotions of condescension to the poor. The simple (by implication *simple-minded*), grass-skirted, surfing Hawaiian does not provoke paranoid-aggressive reactions because his humanity and his culture are never truly recognised.

At present touristic over-development is largely confined to Oahu, the island of Honolulu and Waikiki, but this situation cannot last long. Massive development schemes are planned for the islands of Maui, Lanai, Kauai and Hawaii. Amfac Inc., Hilton and Sheraton are all involved in projects for Maui; among other developments a £300 million 'City of Flowers' involving '10,000 more hotel units along two miles of lovely coastline'[14] is planned for the island. The 'Waikikification' of the outer islands seems inevitable. It is unlikely that the powerful companies concerned will agree with the Hawaiian environmentalist who declared: 'We can't eat and drink dollars. If you destroy the earth in your hunt for money you end up with nothing. This state has to face up to telling the tourists that they can't come or that they must wait their turn.' Hawaiian businessmen are determined 'to keep on selling Hawaii'. Instant aloha and the plastic garland will reign supreme throughout the archipelago.

It will be apparent that there are many good reasons why Tahiti *must* never be Hawaii. Compared with Hawaii, even Tahiti or Fiji is still relatively unspoilt. What makes these islands so attractive to the metropolitan tourist is their lack of sophistication, their reputation as societies based on communal living, extended families and 'free-love' – still uncontaminated by the commercial values of the West. The erotic-idyllic view of the South Pacific islands had as its advocate

Paul Gauguin, one of the greatest post-impressionist painters, reproductions of whose works now adorn many middle-class homes. Samoa was also the subject of one of the classic works of modern anthropology, Margaret Mead's *Coming of Age in Samoa*. In a recent series of articles in *The Sunday Mirror*, the Marquesas Islands were described as 'paradises of sex'. Hiva Oa, the island on which Gauguin died, was described as 'a place of plenty where an ancient sex culture continues . . . home for 1,000 fun-loving, happy people'. Polynesian and Melanesian sexual relations are, by all accounts, blessedly free of guilt and jealousy. Sexuality does not become confused with property rights since these generally do not exist. In striking contrast to western customs, sexual technique is considered an essential part of every girl's education. She is taught how to increase her own pleasure, not merely how to accommodate a male partner, and female sexuality is not shrouded in mystique and mystification.

In this case it would seem that the conventionalised image promoted by the tourist industry is reasonably close to the truth; however, it is only possible to entertain, with equanimity, the idea of escaping to a Pacific Paradise by ignoring certain inevitable contradictions. The UTA advertisement quoted at the beginning of this section was coupled with a photograph of a garlanded, handclapping 'wahine'; it was juxtaposed in *The Far Eastern Economic Review* with an article which paints a picture of Tahiti that is very remote from an untroubled world of lagoons, frangipani and *joie de vivre*. '. . . The old days of free and natural love are over, the arrival of thousands of hungry French males, from naval cadets to members of the foreign legion, accompanying the technicians preparing to explode their bombs on Mururoa, have given the wahine a western idea of their value. Now love, or sex, is something to be paid for, with money, jewellery, an automobile or even a marriage certificate. . . .' If the French nuclear tests had not brought about this erosion of traditional mores, it is safe to assume that the increasing number of tourists visiting Tahiti would have produced the same result in the long run. Prostitution, both male and female, is becoming common in Papeeti, the Tahitian capital.

The question of tourism's cultural impact on the South Pacific is inseparable from the question of economic impact. Money and private property are concepts largely alien to the traditional societies of the area. Wherever it intrudes, organised tourism involves a display of conspicuous consumption. This is exaggerated in the South

Pacific because of the region's distance from the principal tourist generating centres. Tourists in the area will tend to be unusually wealthy; a 'Pacific Paradise Tour' of Tahiti, Mourea, Bora Bora, Samoa, Tonga and Fiji costs in the region of £1,000.[15] When this kind of leisure expenditure occurs within societies whose traditional structures are non-monetary the results can only be disastrous. The dollar, the pound and the yen could turn out to be, in their different ways, quite as destructive as the syphilis and the tuberculosis that decimated the region's population in the eighteenth century. The opening paragraph of an article in *Business Week*[16] is, in these circumstances, somewhat horrifying:

> If you crave the lazy Pacific life but are tired of the crowds on Hawaii's Waikiki Beach, how about a quiet plot of palm trees in the Fiji Islands? Such jet-setters as Juan Carlos, pretender to the Spanish throne and Crown Prince Emmanuel of Savoy have already signed up and the developer is eagerly looking for 5,998 other buyers.

Is Fiji to become a refuge for the surviving remnants of Europe's *ancien régime*? In Tahiti tourism unquestionably works hand in hand with French colonialism. The new influx of visitors in the 'sixties (following the building of an international airport) produced an economic expansion that 'so increased Tahiti's dependence on France that the old independence demands were no longer viable'.[17]

Providing we do not make the basic mistake of confusing innocence with sexual ignorance it is not an exaggeration to see tourism in the Pacific as a corrupter of innocence. Wherever it intrudes tourism converts the moral nexus into a cash nexus – particularly with regard to sexual mores and traditions of hospitality. The cliché that 'money is the root of all evil' acquires new force in societies where money was not an important feature of community relations before the advent of tourism. It is the very openness and lack of sophistication of Pacific societies that places them at such risk; they have none of the cultural defence mechanisms of more complex 'exotic' societies, such as Bali's.

The World Council of Churches has recently expressed concern at the social strains created by tourism in small, unsophisticated communities. It also advocates accurate information in publicity material, increased concern for employees and the deliberate provision of 'meet the people' programmes. Chief Tamasese of Western Samoa has stated that his country is not ready for intensive tourism development: 'The impact would destroy our communal family system.' In 1963 at Fiji's annual tourist conference the acting Colonial Secretary told delegates that there must be no 'prostitution of Fijian traditional ceremonial to serve the purposes of tourist entertainment. . . . There is need to ensure that the social problem which a large influx of tourists brings with it is recognised and that action is taken to ensure that it does not get out of hand'. He cited the example of the 'remote little port of Savusavu' which had become popular with cruise liners. In their attempts to emulate Suva the people of Savusavu had introduced public address systems and duty-free shopping facilities. They were told to stop. Despite this concern to preserve Fiji's unique qualities a recent arts festival was designed very much 'as a shop window attraction, aimed at letting the rest of the world come in and enjoy itself on the beaches'.[18] Organisation was left to foreign professionals familiar with the world of tourism, advertising and entertainment; the cultural needs of the islanders was evidently a secondary consideration.

Since the island cultures of the Pacific have not left great architectural monuments, their colourful people occupy an unusually important place in the list of tourist attractions. This results in the creation of synthetic natives; many of Hawaii's hula dancers have no Hawaiian blood at all, the demand for the ethnic has exceeded the available supply and consequently 'natives' must be manufactured from whatever human material is to hand. J. Forster comments: 'Within a very short time after a tourist influx the natives cease to be natives in dress, speech, habits and attitudes – that is assuming they were natives in the first place. . . .' They soon replace their picturesque costumes with cheap imitations of the metropolitan tourist's dress (T-shirts and jeans), while tourists adorn themselves with expensive imitations of native costumes (playing pastoral). The most common alteration in the characteristic dress of the Pacific islands that tourism has brought about is the adoption of the bikini top, an item of clothing that is neither very functional in the tropics, nor particularly decorative; it represents a capitulation to the prurient standards of the West. In general, it can be said that the things which make Pacific islands valuable and unique are precisely those things that are most easily altered or destroyed by tourism.

Charles Stinson, Fiji's finance minister, has said: 'I don't want to see the country of my birth ruined by millions of visitors running over it. But neither do I want to live in a poverty stricken country.'

The second priority would seem to be the dominant one since many of the big names in tourism and property development are already involved in Fiji, among them Slater Walker, Jardine and Matheson, Trust House Forte, P & O and Travelodge of Australia. In 1972 Inter-Continental Hotels, Holiday Inns, and Club Méditerranée were all negotiating for land. At least one massive development project is nearing completion. This is the Pacific Harbour Development which will eventually contain a man-made lake, an eighteen-hole golf course and 6,000 single family homes. According to a report in *Business Week* many Fijians 'fear that the project could turn into a rich, white ghetto and create an abrasive social situation'. Pacific Harbour will certainly be 'a rich, white ghetto', whether 'an abrasive social situation' will develop depends on the (unreliable) tact of the visitors, the forbearance of the Fijians and the foresight of their government. It is significant that in those areas of Fiji already immediately affected by mass tourism, prostitution and petty crime have increased sharply.

Ultimately it is not only the natives who will cease to be charming and picturesque, but the natural environment. According to Sue Tuckwell of *The New Internationalist*, the Pacific Harbour Development has already 'involved diverting the river and dredging canals to create miles of waterways, and bulldozing hundreds of acres of virgin bush. The resulting devastation of fish-breeding grounds – the chief source of Fijian protein, and of bird life has been casually discounted.' In 1972 the Fijian Prime Minister described Pacific Harbour Project as 'an experiment', and one only approved with reservations. The Government seems anxious to keep the island a resort without much 'action'; a casino has been considered but without much enthusiasm. It is to be hoped that the reluctance and ambivalence of the Fijian administration will keep development in check; they have only to look at Waikiki or the more highly developed Caribbean resorts to see what they must avoid.

BLISS IN ACTION

The trouble with paradise is that it soon becomes boring. Established religions have never satisfactorily answered the question, 'What do people *do* in Heaven?' The disembodied spirituality of the Christian

Heaven and the interminable group sex of the Islamic paradise are enervating prospects for all but confirmed quietist mystics or inexhaustible satyrs. The human mind seems unable to conceive of any purely pleasurable activity (or blissful inactivity) that would not eventually pall. We should not expect the tourist industry to have solved the problem that has defeated the world's theologians – even if it does claim to offer us a variety of paradises to suit every pocket.

If the urbanite tourist does succeed in finding some remote palm-fringed* beach, unspoilt, save for the unobtrusive 'no-higher-than-the-tallest-palm-tree' hotel in which he is staying, he must frequently find that sun, sand and palm-fronds *are not enough*. He has been conditioned to assume that the purity of nature is necessarily relaxing and restorative, yet before long he may start wishing that his particular bit of nature were a little less unspoilt; he will long for some oasis of noise, overcrowding, frenzied activity and rabidly commercial values: a discothèque where he can be happily deafened by the music of Detroit, London or Paris; or a casino, simmering with the barely suppressed tensions attendant on continual profit and loss. If the tourist comes in sufficient numbers he will not have to wait long before these necessary modifications to the idyll are made.

Such contradictions do not shake the general belief in the universal appeal of Lotus Eating, nor the concomitant belief that islands are the ideal sites for such pursuits (or non-pursuits). As one of the present authors knows from personal experience, the tourist who arrives on a Greek island and lets it be known to his fellow tourists that he does not swim and finds sun-bathing not only uninteresting but injurious to his health is likely to be regarded as a crank and heretic: Why in that case has he come? There are, of course, many personal reasons for pleasure-travel not covered by the stereotyped imagery and language of the industry. On a Greek island one might point to a rich hinterland of classical ruins, medieval churches, mountains, forests and beautiful villages inhabited by people whose traditions of hospitality to strangers are unaffected by tourism. The island will invariably have some literary or mythic associations. Lesbos has Sappho, Paros has the tomb of the poet Alcman, Naxos has Ariadne, Chios and Ios both claim to be Homer's burial place and Santorini is thought to be the original Atlantis. But for the majority of tourists an Aegean island consists of a couple of beaches, some cafés and,

---

* The palm tree would appear to be indispensable to tourism's paradisal mythology.

occasionally, a discothèque; their tourism is quite literally *peripheral*. On the larger islands this limited outlook ensures that their hinterlands will remain relatively untouched. On a small and sparsely inhabited island like Ios, however, tourism is inevitably more concentrated, and in the summer the island is virtually taken over by beach-fanatic tourists. Ios has only one village (of about 500 people) that is a perfect example of Cycladian architecture. The landscape is austerely beautiful adorned with strategically placed white churches and the beaches are magnificent. In summer 1967 it had few tourists, no roads and no electricity. Since then electrification has arrived, a discothèque has opened (playing Tom Jones interminably) and the tourists have multiplied. It is now being advertised in such magazines as *Melody Maker* and *Time Out* as an exclusive resort for the young and self-consciously 'groovy'. This hardly seems a suitable fate for the reputed burial place of Homer.

Many of the Aegean islands are still comparatively inaccessible (although Lesbos now has an airport), and very few have much in the way of tourist infrastructure. Tourism in these islands tends to be tourism for the young, the rich, the artistic and the eccentric. A number of islands have resident or semi-resident artists' colonies: Lesbos has Mithymna (where, appropriately, Orpheus' head was washed ashore still singing); Hydra and Skiathos have long been fashionable (for a time the Beatles were rumoured to be buying an islet off the coast of Skiathos). We have met novelists and poets on Paros, painters and poets on Ios, and so on. All this has a familiar ring; it was in much the same way that tourism began on the summer Riviera, and in other, now highly developed areas of the Mediterranean. The Aegean islands have everything that is necessary for the pursuit of the simple life and, for intellectuals, they present a classical landscape rich in literary and historical associations. All the signs indicate a massive increase in Aegean tourism before the end of the century; the Greek government is planning for 10 million tourists for Greece as a whole by 1980. Unless a fresh reactionary government* has a renewed spasm of nervousness concerning long hair and the other modes of dress and behaviour that it associates with 'hippy' depravity, a significant percentage of the tourists will be young – students and the readers of *Melody Maker* and *Time Out*. Speaking from personal experience it would seem that many of the younger

* A reactionary government is, for a variety of reasons, usually favourable to the development of tourism.

tourists in the Aegean area are blithely indifferent to and ignorant of the cultural significance of its coasts and islands. The same can be said of similar tourists (drifters, hippies) in Afghanistan, India and Nepal; as we shall see in Chapter 16, the semi-educated youth of the western world now play an important role as tourism's pioneers.

There are those for whom both the 'classical simplicity' of the Greek islands and the 'innocence' of Polynesia are not enough. Perhaps the real avant-garde of 1970s tourism are those who seek the *genuine primitive* – who seek barbarity and, in Barthes's phrase, 'everything that is contrary to the bliss of travel'. In 1971 Cook's organised a touristic expedition to climb Mount Everest to a height of 19,000 feet. In 1972 many of the members of that expedition joined a 'tribal tour' of New Guinea. In this tour the tourist has arrogated the role of the explorer and the anthropologist. The discomforts of tropical exploration are deliberately sought out. The tour involved walking for 100 miles through difficult terrain, including dense jungle *in the rainy season*. Also included were visits to tribes who have had little or no previous contact with white people – among them the Biami, a cannibal tribe with a war-like reputation. To the average holiday-maker such an extreme rejection of their air-conditioned comfort and security of mass tourism must seem perverse, yet the twenty people involved seem to have been perfectly ordinary Britons who, nevertheless, chose to spend approximately £800 of hard-earned savings in this bizarre manner. Mr and Mrs Cyril Rayment were among the party; Mrs Rayment remarked: 'We could have bought a new car with the money, but we would not have had the memories.' Mr Rayment, a 48-year-old tool-maker with a computer firm, explained that they were going on the (optional extra) cannibal excursion because the Biami 'might be *a little more interesting*'.[19] Miss A. Scargill, of Wetherby, Yorkshire, considered that the dangers of encounter with the Biami had been grossly exaggerated since, in her own words: 'The last recorded killing of a white man was last Xmas.' The tour begins to take on a surrealist hilarity, worthy of absurdist theatre. We can only hope that 'real cannibal feasts' will not become the next fashionable pseudo-event.

Instead of the conventional idyll with charming and friendly natives Cook's have offered a return to a violent and barbaric Stone Age and found a ready market. This would suggest a decadent and voyeuristic attitude on the part of their clients, recalling the Roman fascination with Barbarians and violence; it is, perhaps, a case of the bourgeoisie in search of 'The Other'. The tour also relates more simply to certain specifically British obsessions; it is an efflorescence of British heartiness and delight in overcoming adversities (even if the adversities have to be sought out). The tribal tourists in their khaki and sensible boots also evoke memories of the heyday of British colonialism, when natives were natives, their inferiority to the white man sufficiently demonstrated by their primitive superstitions and nasty habits.

Papua is receiving growing numbers of tourists from Australia and there are already signs that the local inhabitants find their new role as tourist attractions confusing. A bizarre incident occurred at a New Guinea arts festival in 1972. When the warriors of Okapa discovered they had not been awarded the first prize for their singing and dancing they responded by firing their bows into the audience of jet-tourists. The attendants, who were riot police in disguise, retaliated but made little headway until the tourists joined in the fight. The combined efforts of tourists and police eventually drove the Okapa warriors back into their jungle. This incident may be absurd but its implications are serious. Primitive, tribal societies are utterly unable to come to terms with an industry such as tourism – the motivations of which they cannot possibly understand. In a letter to *The Times*,[20] John Hemming of 'Survival International' described the Cook's tour as 'a shameless violation of the privacy of others. Their victims are tribal societies faced with enormous problems of survival. They have to adapt their tribal cultures to our aggressive western way of life and this task is greatly aggravated if they are to become tourist bait.' There is a certain amount of sentimentalism in this since, in place of 'our aggressive western way of life', the New Guinea tribes have their own aggressive non-western way of life. But the point is valid and is a useful corrective to the imperialist assumption implicit in much tourism, that primitive peoples can only benefit from increased contact with the western way.

Cook's New Guinea tour would suggest that nowhere (and no one) is safe from tourist intrusion. However remote the place, difficult the terrain, inclement the weather, barbaric the people, there will still be tourists willing to pay to go there in search of something 'a little more interesting'. One thinks with horror of the prospect of Xingu tours or Pygmic tours – tours of 'people reserves' just as we have tours of 'game reserves': 'See life in the Stone Age, TODAY'.

THE PEACEABLE KINGDOM

> The wolf also shall dwell with the lamb, and the leopard shall lie
> down with the kid; and the calf and the young lion and the fattling
> together; and a little child shall lead them.
>
> *Book of Isaiah* (11:6)

For the seasoned tourist, satiated with colourful peoples, antiquities
and beach idylls, who does not yet wish to cultivate discomfort in
the manner of Cook's New Guinea tour, there remains one further
escapist goal: the Animal Kingdom. Since the Second World War
our interest in exotic animals has become something of an obsession.
We have always hunted them and worn their skins; now, increasingly,
we want just to look at them. The tendency is away from hunting
safaris, real leopard-skin coats and cages, to photographic safaris,
mock leopard-skin and safari parks. It would seem that our relationship to animals is no longer exploitative, but benevolent and appreciative. The safari parks of Europe and North America are, of course,
a substitute catering for those who cannot afford the time or money
to visit the game reserves of East Africa. These now constitute the
principal tourist attractions of Kenya and Tanzania. A quarter of a
million tourists yearly visit Kenya 'to gape at the animals of the
Pleistocene age'. The East African reserves are expected to receive
1 million tourists by 1980.

On one level the attraction of the non-violent safari is obvious; in
the game reserves the tourist can see a greater number and variety of
free animals set against breathtakingly beautiful landscapes. We
should beware of taking too much for granted; an intense popular
interest in wild animals is no more natural to the human race than an
intense popular interest in antiquities, wild scenery or quaint people.
To many native Africans the western desire to look at and photograph animals must seem slightly mad. Traditionally they have
regarded animals as a source of food or a threat to their crops.

In a finely written essay of remarkable insight Francine de Plessix
Gray[21] speculates on the psychology of the photographic safari. She
refers to an obsessive imagery to which we have frequently returned
during the course of this book. She speaks of: 'An impulse to restore
innocence on the planet we have despoiled, a fantasy of returning to
some non-violent state of nature', and relates the appeal of the game
reserves and safari parks to 'the peaceable kingdom of Adam and
Eve in Eden'. The animals of the game reserves have no memory of

human aggression, they gaze without fear at the tourists in their minibuses: 'the walls of our nursery come alive . . .', or, in the words of the prophet, 'a little child shall lead them'.

The viewing safari presents us with one of those paradoxes in which tourism is so rich. The safari tourists' movements are more than usually restricted, and their experiences more than usually selected by others. They cannot leave their hotels except in minibuses in which they 'parade their captivity before the disinterested eyes of the free beasts'. The more expensive safaris reject the zebra-striped minibuses and luxurious hotels of the cheaper mass tours in favour of Land Rovers and tents. This is another variation on 'Funky Chic', getting as close as possible to the myth of the Great White Hunter. The Greek shipping magnate, Niarchos, has invented his own 'improvisations on the new primitivism', when he is on safari 'two large swimming-pools are immediately dug out, wherever he pitches camp, one for himself and another for his entourage'.

Safari tourism is not all sentimentalism and sophisticated primitivism, it is also voyeuristic:

> I think that people are travelling to Africa, not only to bathe in nature's innocence but also to witness nature's violence. To see predators on a kill is considered to be the great moment of a safari, a new outlet for the blood lust once channelled into hunting. It is the corrida of the 70's, with animals doing all the blood letting.[22]

It is not only the corrida of the 'seventies but the Roman amphitheatre of the 'seventies. It is a difference of degree only; our superior transport technology enables us to satiate our blood lust, while freeing us from guilt.

It might be argued that, however dubious the sentimental/voyeuristic motivations of safari tourism, its effects are still beneficial. Our veneration of the animal kingdom of Africa helps to preserve them inviolate; our tourism contributes towards the cost of the game reserves, and lends economic incentive to the preservation of threatened species. But even here, where our tourism seems most benevolent, we threaten, collectively, to destroy what we admire. Since it is entirely selfish, our sentimentalism does not recognise the rights of animals. We see them as figures in a fantasy of the pristine. We do not respect their privacy; lion cubs are starving from too close observation, and cheetahs, pursued by tourist vehicles, have been dying of heart attacks. While on safari Plessix Gray did not see a kill

but she did see a 'grimly instructive' near miss. Twenty-one minibuses gathered in a clearing to watch three cheetahs stalking a herd
of impalas:

> After we have watched them for some 20 minutes the cheetahs
> have approached to about 130 yards of their prey coming close to
> the distance from which they make their famous 60 m.p.h. dash for
> the kill. But as they reach the critical moment minibuses start
> crashing about them; tourists leaning on the open rooftops of their
> vehicles, cameras poised, urge their drivers to get the closest
> possible view of the kill. Startled by the commotion the impalas
> race about in circles and cough out their warning message. . . . The
> cheetahs must know better than we that they have lost their chance
> for dinner but they go on stalking for a few minutes, as if to finish
> their pose. And then, amid the clicking of some 50 cameras the
> lead scout turns away from the impalas. The 3 slink off into the
> plain. Their fragile rib cages seem terribly thin in the dusk, the
> black markings of their cheeks – like rivulets of black tears – seem
> to express their frustrated hunger.

We may have replaced the gun-shot with the photographic shot
but our interest is still a threat. Hordes of snap-shot hunters threaten
to disrupt the natural patterns of animal life far more drastically than
the traditional hunting safari. The deliberate killing of animals for
pleasure is certainly abhorrent – and the East African tradition of the
Great White Hunter is not an attractive one, since it is inseparable
from colonialism, racism and the more puerile kind of 'virility myth'.
There are still Americans who will pay vast sums for the privilege of
living out their Hemingway fantasies; for them, the kill is an affirma-
tion of their masculinity, and thus magnificent animals die to assuage
the sexual insecurities of the western male. For all this, it is arguable
that the traditional hunting safari involved a more genuine respect
for the animal-victim; it had certain in-built restraints derived from
an aristocratic etiquette (hunting as the 'Sport of Kings'). This was
a code 'based on the ambivalent feelings of loving and respecting
what you kill, in the precept that you shoot while also safeguarding
the species' young and females, that you attempt to perpetuate the
species abundantly for future generations of sportsmen'. This is not
intended as a vindication of the tradition of killing as a leisure
activity, but at least the Great White Hunter could not deny that the
animal was his victim, whereas the minibus tourist is blissfully
unaware of the damage he is doing. (Such an awareness can only be
demonstrated by a decision to boycott safari tourism in its present

form.) When Plessix Gray was on safari her guide was a White Hunter of the old school. When the tourist minibuses prevented the cheetahs from making their kill he remarked: 'It's so bloody rude to the animals.'

In general it would seem that the African guides and drivers show less discretion and respect than Europeans of the old colonial school. It is Africans who chase the cheetahs and crowd their minibuses in for the kill. They are restrained neither by the etiquette of Big Game Hunting nor by any sentimental regard for the animals. They should be restrained by the rules of the game reserves but they are encouraged by the tourists to break them. In the words of David Babeau, the game warden of the Serengeti:

> The heart of the problem is the poverty of my African brothers and the terrible wealth of the tourists. African drivers are constantly being tipped by tourists to break the rules of our parks and chase their animals. What can you do – our people are poor, it is easy for them to be corrupted.

Once again we discover that tourism's disruptive impact has a strictly (and crudely) economic basis.

In Kenya, native Africans see very little of the profits from the safari trade. Of more than sixty safari firms in Nairobi only one is wholly African owned; the industry is entirely dominated by old school colonials – petty monsters of bigotry, whose only concession to African independence is to call themselves 'professional hunters' rather than 'White Hunters'. For the rest they are openly contemptuous of all things African ('poor bastards, they don't know the first thing about land'), horrified at the thought of European women having drinks with their African guides, and aggressively hostile to Tanzania's socialism ('bloody Maoists'). Their detailed knowledge of African game is balanced by their enormous ignorance of African people. As Plessix Gray states, a safari in the company of such guides must be 'dehumanizing to anyone sympathetic to democratic principles'. Reputedly, most tourists find capitalistic, neo-colonial Kenya more congenial than moderate, socialist Tanzania, and as Kenya's white-owned safari firms are doing a roaring trade one cannot help concluding that the majority of their clients have no particular sympathy for democratic principles. A tourism industry such as Kenya's, with its perpetuation of the myth of the White Hunter, can only reinforce colonial values, and inhibit the process of Africanisation.

Albert Mongi, the deputy director of Tanzania's national parks, told Plessix Gray that the Kenyans were 'having more trouble acting like Africans, they are more dependent on the white man and the white image'. He also told her that although Tanzania welcomed tourists it was not prepared to alter its character to suit tourism.

There is one way in which the game reserves could be made to serve the interests of the poorer Africans, that is, if they became a source of meat. This would involve a policy of restricted 'cash-cropping' of certain species. This is not a new idea, but no doubt there are idealistic animal lovers who will continue to be appalled by it. Their sentimentalism gains intellectual respectability in the arguments of purist conservationists who maintain that nature has its own ways of coping with animal overpopulation and its attendant ills. There is not the space here to summarise the complex problems of wild-life conservation, but it is estimated that in 1970 'enough wildebeests and zebra died of overpopulation hunger to feed 50,000 Africans as much meat as they usually eat in one year'. Similarly cropping could have prevented the disaster in Kenya's Tsavo Park in the same year. During a drought 3,000 elephants starved slowly to death. Norman Myers – author of *The Long African Day* – estimates that cropping in anticipation of this disaster 'would not only have provided Africans with hundreds of thousands of pounds of edible protein but would have averted the deaths of some rhinoceros who died from the drastic foliage destruction caused by starving elephants'.

Controlled cash-cropping would justify the game reserves in the eyes of local Africans; they would come to seem something more than just the latest madness imposed on Africa by its former overlords. Most tourists, preoccupied with the pleasures of animal viewing, do not take into account the needs of East Africa's human inhabitants; indeed one suspects that they are hardly aware that much of East Africa is inhabited at all. As they speed through the bush from one luxurious hotel to the next they only encounter Africans as guides, drivers or waiters. Apart from the intrusion of such essential facilities as hotels and minibuses they like to think of the reserves and parks as pristine wilderness, *untouched by man*. Such an attitude militates against rational assessment and a solution to the problem of the reserves; a policy such as cash-cropping is interpreted as unjustified interference in the balance of nature. But the creation of the reserves themselves has already upset this balance; they are not pristine but more like vast zoos, with clearly defined boundaries which prevent the animals from migrating freely and thus deprive them of one natural cure for overpopulation. The tourist's experience is more than usually schizoid, his attention is directed entirely towards the animals and not to the men who live among them: ecology without sociology. Plessix Gray suggests that this 'segregation of nature from man' may be 'more harmful than the much deplored estrangement of man from nature, because it is more sentimental and based on false illusions of innocence which are always sure paths to brutality' – to the brutality of tourist vehicles that chase animals, to the immorality of a tourism that disregards the material and psychological needs of both animals and Africans in order to indulge its fantasies of atavism.

SECTION THREE: POLITICS

10 Sunbelt Politics

A holiday is a political action. The tourist is politically neutered, while the host country is subject to social strains which make its future peaceful evolution increasingly unlikely. The tourist unwittingly leaves the world's social fabric more fragile than he finds it.

Holidays are the ultimate products of our advanced consumer society, which can only survive by finding fresh incentives to motivate the labour force into further bursts of production. As the car becomes merely a utilitarian object, tourism is becoming the chief 'carrot' of our whole industrial structure, because it is almost infinitely expandable as a product. The amount we are willing to pay for a car is now limited by congested roads, petrol shortages and social pressures against conspicuous consumption, but the tourist operators can always find another twist to holidays to justify further expenditure. Tourists do not just pay according to the distance they travel, but according to degrees of privacy, atmosphere, culture, or chances of rubbing shoulders with people of similar tastes and wealth. Above all, extravagant expenditure on holidays impresses one's peers without offending those less fortunate than oneself. One can own a Cadillac or Lamborghini, but the disgruntled will vandalise, steal or openly resent it. A £30,000 round-the-world cruise, however, is a piece of conspicuous consumption (in Veblen's terms) which is significantly inconspicuous in crucial ways. The worker who returns from a week in Bermuda or Majorca somehow thinks that his experience is similar to yours. You, alone, know better.

Psychologically, then, tourism is an opiate, dulling the social awareness of the tourist. The act of buying an experience deliberately chosen to contrast with one's work situation serves as a safety-valve which previous generations never had. The overall work situation may remain as dull and as exploitative as ever, but the workers accept it quietly. Strikes might jeopardise the wage packets which allow welcome release in holidays. Where strikes take place, it is sometimes difficult to distinguish them from holidays. Observers in Spain in mid-1973 found British Chrysler workers reading British newspapers in the sun, to keep track of the strike they were supposed to be on back in Britain.[1]

But tourism is also part of a wider process which has led to what appears to be a general decline in class consciousness within most of the advanced industrialised societies. This is not because inequality has actually declined. Most studies show that inequalities in wealth and opportunity have not been significantly reduced over the years. Few people, though, would suggest that we can today find class conflict as naked as it was in Britain during the 1926 General Strike, Germany after the 1914–18 war, or in the USA during the Great Slump.

So, what has happened? Why do not European workers rise up and storm the gilded retreats of the jet-set like Gstaad, Marbella, the Costa Smeralda or St Moritz? Why do not American radicals assault opulent enclaves like Acapulco, Nassau or exclusive islands in the Bahamas' archipelago, like Lyford Cay, where the Firestones, Heinzes and Mellons play, or Eleuthera, the brainchild of ex-Pan Am Chairman, Juan Trippe?[2] To ask such questions is to answer them. These citadels of the rich are safe because they are physically far removed from the agitators and their audiences. It is exceptionally difficult for someone who can just afford a holiday in Atlantic City to imagine what the inner sanctums of St Moritz are really like. He merely reads about the vacationing stars of stage and screen, but misses the anonymous legions of those who have made their fortunes in business, or have inherited them. This latter group is often far richer and of more political importance than their more glamorous neighbours on the ski slopes, but they are not noticed. It is the growing invisibility of this group which is the key deradicalising force in tourist-generating countries like the USA and Northern Europe. Tourism has ushered in the era of politically inconspicuous consumption.

What we are seeing is the latest step in the long retreat of the rich from the poor, whose pockets ultimately provide the former's wealth. In the early days of the Industrial Revolution the mill owner would normally live in the same community as his employees. Proximity bred a form of paternalism but, also, increasing bitterness amongst the poor, who could see at first hand the extremes of wealth that our capitalist system produces. Gradually, though, increasing wealth and improved transportation systems allowed the rich to protect their consciences by moving away from poverty. They moved into suburbia and, sometimes, into private enclaves for the super rich like Tuxedo Park, which was designed to keep all but the socially acceptable beyond the perimeter fence. That canny observer, de Tocqueville, had this phenomenon well summed up when he wrote: 'The aristocracy created by business rarely settles in the midst of the manufacturing population which it directs: the object is not to govern that population but to use it.'[3]

However affluent the suburbs might be, there would still be inadvertent contact with the poor, clustered into their slums and ghettos. There would thus still be some inhibitions about displaying one's full opulence. The coming of motorways and airports helped the rich by further estranging them from the unpleasantnesses of everyday society, thus wrapping them ever more firmly in their cocoon of self-delusion that poverty is either deserved or non-existent; that privilege is part of the natural order, or else does not exist; that they and their ilk owe no favours to the less fortunate of society.

Tourism fits neatly into this pattern of self-distancing from all the evils of the world. When lying on some idyllic beach in the Caribbean or East Africa, how hard it is to believe in the ghettos of Philadelphia, or the crumbling slums of Glasgow. The sun shines and there is no bleakness in the world.

Richard Nixon is the first major political leader springing from this constituency. It is no accident that the sites of his two mini-White Houses, in San Clemente and Key Biscayne, are at either end of the American southern rim – the 'sunbelt' running from Southern California, through Arizona and Texas down to the Florida Keys. Commentators like Kirkpatrick Sale point to the fact that the bulk of his key pre-Watergate advisers and friends (and much of his campaign financing) came from the ranks of those Carl Oglesby has called 'the cowboys' (in contrast to 'the yankees' ' old eastern money). Virtually only Henry Kissinger amongst his major colleagues came from traditional yankee areas. John Erlichman, Bob Haldeman and Robert Abplanalp come from California; Bebe Rebozo from Florida; John Connally from Texas. Sale argues it is no accident that Watergate sprang from such a culture. He describes their political philosophy – and he sums up the conservative ambience of the Pleasure Periphery in general. 'These men,' he writes,

> tend to a notable degree to be politically conservative, even retrograde, usually antiunion, antiblack, anticonsumer and antiregulation, and quite often associated with professional 'anticommunist' organisations. Whether because of the newness of their position, their frontier heritage, or their lack of old-school ties,

they tend to be without particular concern about the niceties of
business ethics and morals, and therefore to be connected more
than earlier money would have thought wise with shady specula-
tions, political influence-peddling, corrupt unions, and even orga-
nized crime.[4]

He goes further and points to the way Nixon friends like Connally,
Abplanalp, Rebozo, the Murchisons, etc., have been investing
heavily in the Caribbean – a sign that the u.s. sunbelt is really part
of the global Pleasure Periphery.

So the political scene in the tourist-generating countries becomes
poorer as the paternalistic tycoons and patrician statesmen are
replaced by hard-nosed, abrasive politicians; the Kennedys, Roose-
velts, and Rockefellers give way to the Nixons of the world. The
same pattern appears in Britain, with true paternalist Conservative
prime ministers like Harold Macmillan and Sir Alec Douglas-Home
being succeeded by the abrasive Edward Heath. Not only was he
born in a seaside town, but his most publicised hobby is yachting.
It is admittedly hard, given British weather, to think of Broadstairs
and Cowes as being part of a British 'sunbelt', but Heath's upbring-
ing and leisure activities place his roots firmly in Britain's domestic
holiday scene. Even Heath's Labour successor as Prime Minister,
Harold Wilson, is as much known for his holiday home in the Scilly
Isles as for his geographical links with his industrialised birthplace
in northern England.

   The rich and the politicians are thus being gradually seduced by
the reassuring ambience of the Pleasure Periphery. Simultaneously
though, the poor of the tourist-generating countries is losing its
sense of grievance, as the wealthy increasingly lead geographically
distinct lives. This is because perception of relative poverty is always
easiest when the rich live and work near to the poor, thus aiding the
comparison of life-styles. The unequal distribution of wealth is
there for all to see. However, the Lord of the Manor no longer lives
at the edge of the village, nor does the industrialist live next door to
his factory. After withdrawing to the suburbs, they are settling on a
semi-permanent basis in the wealthier enclaves of the tourist belt.
They start to become shadowy figures, and the myth that disparities
in wealth are disappearing grows in the absence of easily perceived
contrasts in affluence. The anger needed to sustain significant radical
movements dies down as the targets sun themselves in resorts which
the average citizen (and author) is never going to be able to afford.[5]

Tourism's impact on host countries is complex and dire. The élites are corrupted – their eyes turned ever more firmly toward the delights of the industrialised, consumer-oriented world. The masses see the tourist as both a hated foreigner and a powerful symbol of the inequalities of our contemporary world. The results are societies split ever more deeply between conservative, self-seeking élites and ever more desperate masses – the kind of social structure which has produced dictatorships in countries like Brazil, Chile and Spain. The radicals do sometimes win as in that former tourist playground, Cuba, but normally the foreign exchange provided by tourism ensures that the élites are capable of hanging on to their privileges.

The reactions of the host élites are actually more equivocal than the above argument suggests for, despite the appeal of the tourists, the latter compete directly with the élites for the best beaches, food and women. Acapulco, for instance, was a Mexican resort before the foreigners moved in, and it is the wealthier, holiday-taking Mexican who is affected as tourist-inspired inflation pushes prices beyond his reach. Again, though there is little question but that tourists have been an important factor in improving the financial health of the London theatre, this is little consolation to Kenya, the Bahamas, and Puerto Rico.

There is, in fact, a fair degree of symbiosis between tourism and dictatorships – particularly right-wing ones. In the first place, the average tourist, being relatively affluent, is a natural conservative, and this is even truer of the permanent tourists who have made their home within the Pleasure Periphery. From our experience, the latter tend to exude the kind of anachronistic reaction which is found amongst ex-colonials, many of whom chose to settle in the authoritarian régimes of Franco and Salazar after the empires were dissolved. Again, the tourist industry looks for 'Order', since it needs not only to guarantee the physical safety of the tourists, but also the financial safety of its investments. Thus the European industry never had particularly strong qualms about building up trade with the 'Orderly' régimes of Spain and Portugal, nor did the Americans when opening up Cuba and then the Bahamas when it was under White control.

At its worst, the industry will enter the political arena by defending the régimes with whom it does business. As Roland Barthes points out in *Mythologies*, the *Blue Guide to Spain* openly endorsed Franco: 'The serious and patient effort of this people has also included the reform of its political system in order to achieve regeneration through the loyal application of sound principles of order and hierarchy.' More recently, the trade press is more concerned with assuring potential travellers that military coups are in fact harmless to travellers. An example is *The Travel Trade Gazette*[6] writing on tourism in the Philippines where martial law had been imposed a short while before: 'Since President Marcos imposed martial law . . . the tourism industry . . . has undergone a great change. It has become purposeful. It has received government support.' The author admits that from several thousand miles away, martial law 'might sound like a barrier to the enjoyment of a pleasant holiday'. We are quickly reassured, however, that martial law is really a benign and improving institution: 'Trees are being planted everywhere. Private armies have been abolished.'

There is also a sense in which tourism has parallel interests to nationalists – both left and right. For instance, when Mussolini restored Italian ancient monuments which symbolised the ancient glories of Rome, he was also giving a boost to the tourist industry which could capitalise on his initiative. Similarly, in Eastern European countries like Romania, the governments devote some effort to increasing the sense of national awareness of their citizens. This is important in a geographical area (the Balkans) where national boundaries have been redrawn at regular intervals. To foster this sense of nationalism, there is a drive to encourage appreciation of traditional Romanian music and dancing. The price of records is kept low, and official occasions are often graced with extremely colourful and professional folk-dancing. Yet, this is the kind of exotic tradition which interests the tourists as well, so that tourism and nationalism can here exist side by side.

Tourism corrupts such frail élites by dangling a model of advanced western consumer society before their eyes. They get the encouragement they scarcely need to forget the investments required to improve the education and health of the bottom third of their societies. Instead they prefer to spend the country's resources in more foreign travel for themselves, the erection of car assembly plants, or the importation of luxury consumer-durables, attempting to ape the touristic life-styles. How can one convince officials that air-conditioning in their offices is a waste of valuable foreign exchange, when the Hilton down the road has it in every room? Public buildings and the clothes and life-styles of officials become more extravagant in case the nation loses face before the tourists. Foreign travel increases so the tourists can see the wonders of Europe and America from which the tourists came. This sometimes reaches levels, as in Cyprus or pre-revolutionary Cuba, where the élite spends more money in such travel than the country is taking in through the tourist industry.

Obviously, in the case of countries as poor as the Ivory Coast, such behaviour verges on the criminal (though, would we be any more saintly?) The sensitive tourist, however, should be fully aware of the damage he is inadvertently causing by the mere act of travelling. This awareness should be disturbing. For instance, one has found oneself talking to genuinely idealistic local officials and intellectuals and, inevitably, the conversation slides round toward money, relative incomes and the values of one's possessions. Inexorably, a certain amount of material envy is aroused. One thus leaves, reflecting that the foreign exchange one has contributed to such countries must at least be partly offset by the fact that the people one has met have become more acquisitive in their thinking, and a little more aware of what they are personally losing by tying their fortunes to the development of a relatively poor nation. Of course, not all locals are idealistic in the first place, but every tourist either directly or indirectly contributes to the gradual loss of altruism on the part of those Third World élites involved in tourism. Frantz Fanon summed the whole process up when he wrote in *The Wretched of the Earth*: 'The national bourgeoisie will be greatly helped on its way toward decadence by the western bourgeoisies which come to it as tourists avid for the exotic, for big game-hunting, for casinos. . . .

'If proof is needed of the eventual transformation of certain elements of the ex-native bourgeoisie into the organisers of parties for their western opposite numbers, it is worth having a look at what happened in Latin America. The casinos of Havana and Mexico, the beaches of Rio, the little Brazilian and Mexican girls, the half-breed thirteen-year-olds, the ports of Acapulco and Copacabana – all these are the stigma of the deprivation of the national middle class.'[7] Anyone who still doubts the long-term social impact of tourism should ponder the hill-stations of India. These resorts were developed by the British empire-builders as places to which they could retire when the summer heat of the Indian plains became too much for them. The only British still remaining are a handful of tea-planters, but the traditions remain. It is Indians who now holiday there. The exclusive clubs, hunting and horse racing survive for an Indian clientèle. The imperial dream has been extinguished, but India is still affected by its leisure patterns.

Not only property owners have a vested interest in the industry. A range of other roles are created by it, such as taxi-drivers, waiters, guides, shop assistants and interpreters. All of these have some form of tie with the industry, though some are more strategically placed than most. Taxi-drivers, for instance, are the particular bane of tourist authorities round the world. In parts of the Caribbean, white tourists will find it difficult to get drivers to use the official taxi-meters; each journey thus ends in a haggling session which the tourist inevitably loses. The driver is also able to steer befuddled foreigners to hotels and clubs which give him the biggest cut. In the Mexican boys' town studied by Roebuck and McNamara, the bigger clubs gave taxi-drivers 40 per cent of each trick's expenditure, including both the cost of drinks and action with the club's prostitutes. Drivers in Beirut are legendary for their predatoriness. They openly take bribes from hotels and, in the late 1960s, it was common for passengers to be told that the hotel in which they had booked had been destroyed by fire, visited by the plague or closed on prostitution charges. 'What it means,' said one hotelier, 'is some 170 taxi-drivers are controlling a business worth 100 million pounds.'[8] Politically, these drivers possess what is probably the most powerful union in the country.[9]

Many of the locals employed at the more menial levels of the industry undoubtedly detest the tourist, while respecting the money he brings with him. However, the industry exerts a strong pull on the more escapist members of the host society, who drift to the resort areas searching for easy sex, the latest western fashions or, even, potential escape from poverty to the wealth of the tourist's home countries.

One anthropologist, Erik Cohen, studied this phenomenon in a mixed Arab-Israeli town in Israel. Many of the Arabs obviously felt themselves to be thoroughly trapped, both within a small-town puritanical, Islamic society, and within a wider Israeli society where career opportunities for Arabs are inevitably limited. The local Arab youths felt particularly frustrated, building up the incoming female tourists into fantasy answers to all their problems. This was not just a case of sex for, one senses, they were not particularly successful in this area. However, any kind of acceptance by foreign girls (particularly Scandinavian) gave them status within their local peer group. But the key to the whole relationship was the swopping of addresses. To the tourist girls, this was normally an action of little significance. The youths, however, avidly sought and cherished these mementoes, seeing ones from preferred destinations as Canada or Scandinavia as signs that the girls in question might some day help them escape their frustrations. Sadly, few actually did receive such invitations to leave, but the three who had done so within living memory were warmly recollected, particularly on those long, off-season evenings, when next summer's prospects were discussed.[10]

This specific form of escapism may only be a product of the particular situation studied: the local Israelis, coming from a more libertarian culture, had fewer sexual or career hang-ups, and were thus not as motivated to fantasise about the tourists as these Arabs. A Greek informant suggests that Cohen's picture is only partially true for the Greek islands. The local youths there certainly spend the spring building their muscles and perfecting their tans for the tourists' benefit, but there is little sign that they are dreaming of escaping Greece via the foreigners in the way Cohen's Arabs did – though Athens could be different. Cohen does, however, make the point that this fascination with tourists is only one way out of a particularly frustrating situation. Some Arabs coped by dropping out into drugs; others turned to radical politics. Significantly he found few extreme nationalists among the girl chasers, whose answer would seem to be emigration. Tourism thus becomes a force rendering at least part of the local community less likely to seek remedies for problems through sustained political action. Instead they seem to forget their problems through sexual fantasies about tourists – who thus become a conservative force.

11 Paradise Rejected

In the 1973 Monte Carlo elections the first communist candidate was returned, and a new radical party was formed as well. This was despite the fact that Monegasques, thanks to tourism and gambling, pay no taxes. The overriding issue, however, was property speculation, which is 'the most concentrated and most glaring . . . of all the real estate promotion scandals which disfigure large tracts of Europe'.[1] All this has been at the expense of local citizens who are starting to fight back through the ballot box – perhaps too late. The Irish, coming from a somewhat more militant tradition, faced similar problems by firebombing West Germans who came in buying up their land.

The real test has come in Switzerland, which is the one nation above all others which has built prosperity on being hotel-keepers to the world. They accepted the Grand Tourists on their way to and from Italy. They welcomed the nineteenth-century alpinists. The winter sports industry reached its culmination there. The legend of their hospitality has been boosted by their diplomatic neutrality which attracted bodies like the League of Nations, the International Labour Office and the Red Cross. Most of this development has been based in Geneva, which has become probably the most cosmopolitan city in Europe. So if world travel really is going to lead to world peace, Switzerland should be the country in which intolerance is hardest to find. The optimists would be wrong.

Firstly, as the Swiss grew rich, they decided that working in hotels was beneath their dignity. The hours are bad, and the job satisfaction of being a chambermaid or kitchen assistant is low. So they became bankers and office workers, importing Italians and Spaniards to do the menial work they refused to do themselves. Gradually, however, they realised that these exuberant, Catholic Latins really rather offended their more sedate, Calvinist souls. A backlash grew, centring round a parliamentarian named James Schwarzenbach. This culminated in a couple of referenda aimed at radically reducing the migrant population, even if this meant destroying the hotel industry. In both cases the forces of xenophobia came close to winning a majority, so the government has introduced strict quotas on foreign labour, much to the distress of the domestic tourist industry, which is having to close hotels down due to staff shortages.

There are even some signs of discontent in Spain, which has become the world's leading host nation. The press in Madrid is starting to carry stories about the difficulties facing ordinary Spaniards who want to have a holiday of their own. They will be forced to eat their lunch at the (to them) unearthly hour of 12.30 (instead of 2–3 p.m.). Waiters address them in German, English or Dutch. They moan at the way quick-buck showmen are degrading the bullfight by concentrating on all the superficial aspects which appeal to uninitiated foreigners. As yet, such self-questioning has not gone as far as in the Swiss case, but there is now serious debate about the way in which the quality of incoming tourists might be raised. Indications of deeper malaise are the ways in which movements to defend Spanish culture have become more noticeable in recent years. Partly these are reactions to the slow political liberalisation which has been taking place recently. Some observers, however, feel that the fact that traditional bullfight festivals in places like Seville are becoming focal points for such campaigns, indicates a resistance to the tawdry impact of the foreigners. Given the importance of conservative forces within the Spanish power structure, one suspects that such manifestations are the start of serious reaction against the impact of tourism – perhaps even leading to a decision to slow or stop the growth of the tourist inflows.

The social tensions created by tourism within Europe are slight when compared with those found in other parts of the world, where the tourist industry is imposed on societies where racial suspicions run deep. The Caribbean, for instance, is the home of vivid memories of the old, unlamented days of slavery. Most of today's West Indian citizens are descended in part from slaves who left the plantations to escape the slave–master relationship. Yet the tourist industry asks them to accept a relationship with the tourist which is very close to that found in the old days of slavery. Admittedly, the new relationship is based on cash, not overt force, but West Indians see the old servile bonds reasserting themselves in the tourist resorts. They even see their women being lured toward these enclaves, bringing back memories of the days when white masters could take their pick of the female slaves.

Racial memories do not explain all such tensions, since there is some evidence that Black Americans may be even less popular tourists than the Whites. This has disappointed the tourist industry which has looked upon this 'Black market' as a promising growth sector of the market. After all, there are 23 million Black Americans whom the industry believes '. . . if properly developed . . . would probably prefer travel in the Caribbean than any other place in the world. He spends $600 million a year on travel. All he needs is an invitation.'[2] The Trinidadian Tourist Board tried acting on this idea, and its experience was summed up by the board chairman. 'We thought this would be a marvellous idea, because it was opening up a whole new market. But we've found that our hotel staff hate waiting on them. Partly it's because they aren't too polite: if they want a drink, they don't say "please" very often. They're more inclined to shout "Hye, boy, get off your ass!" But the real trouble is that they're black – and our fellows would far rather wait on whites.'[3]

Undoubtedly there is some truth in such charges of reverse racism, but apologists for tourism should not take too much heart. Most Caribbean societies are powder-kegs, with high unemployment, extremely complicated racial cross-currents, made worse by the frightful slums produced by over-rapid urbanisation. Everyone is extremely conscious of the late 1960s which saw major riots in Jamaica (1968), Bermuda (1968), Curacao (1969), and Trinidad and Tobago (1970). All old-timers (including returning migrants) comment on how these societies are becoming more tense. This shows through the murder of Whites in the Virgin Islands, the assassinations in Bermuda, the widespread banning of Black Power literature, the rapid expulsion of expatriates employed in the Bahamian tourist industry, and the widespread complaints against the surliness of local Blacks employed in the industry.

Such tensions are even found in Hawaii, which is normally seen as the perfectly Americanised, deodorised, tourist destination. The original inhabitants discovered by Captain Cook have shrunk to a mere 100,000 (if one counts those of mixed blood). They are right at the bottom of the social pack, having been swamped by successive waves of migrants – the Japanese, Chinese, Filipinos and mainland Americans. Over the last few years, this deprived minority (so reminiscent of American Indians) has thrown up its own nationalist movement called Kokua Hawaii (Help Hawaii), which has organised civil disobedience against property developments threatening to raze Hawaiian homes. Concessions have been slow to come, so frustration has been building up, coming to the surface through drunkenness and

TRAVELLING LIGHT
John and Ada Galsworthy in the Egyptian desert, 1914 (above)
The hippie trail to Katmandu (below)

FOLKLORE FAKELORE;
War dance, New Zealand (above)
Limbo, Trinidad (below)

forays by street gangs. These tend to concentrate their attention on the more isolated hippie communes, and rumour has it that local businessmen have been known to encourage such activities by supplying these 'Primo warriors' (Primo is a local beer) with free alcohol.[4]

A reputation for such surliness and violence is commercially dangerous, and some governments react strongly. For instance, in 1972, Jamaica's Minister of Tourism even went as far as to claim that his country's industry was in 'a state of imminent crisis'. Despite the fact that outside observers did not generally feel that Jamaican problems were particularly bad by Caribbean standards, he claimed that his country's tourist industry was suffering because of increase in crime, racial abuse of visitors, and poor hotel service. As well as closing down the local Holiday Inn until its standards improved, he set up a large-scale training programme and decided to copy the 'Be Nice' campaigns which destinations like the Bahamas had used in similar crises. Speakers would go round meetings in places like schools and trade union branches, stressing how essential tourists are to the national economy, and how they must not be antagonised by surliness or outright hostility. Criticism has come from many directions – most vociferously from Caribbean political activists who simply dismiss their region's tourism as 'whorism'. Unlike the southern Pacific archipelagos, the Caribbean islands are close to metropolitan America – geographically and culturally. Since the Second World War the political theory of America's Black leaders has spread rapidly – assisted by the growing numbers of politically conscious American Blacks who are visiting the area. The result has been an upsurge of support for the ideas of militant nationalism, Black Power and Third World solidarity. At the 1972 San Juan Seminar of the Caribbean Travel Association, Neville Linton and Rex Nettleford (university lecturers from Jamaica and Trinidad respectively) argued that tourism had substituted a new colonialism for the plantation system. It was still a question of White masters, exploiting the area for their own benefit – taking over the best beaches and employing the cheapest labour: 'Owners and operators send their profits abroad; workers remain servants, and tourists, mainly white and wealthy, are viewed as symbols of the imperialism of the eighteenth and nineteenth centuries.'[5] Linton and Nettleford also attacked the CTA's symbol and slogan; in 1972 this consisted of the image of an island woman with a market basket balanced on her head and the words '8th Continent of the World'. They remarked: 'There is an ever widening gap growing between the rhetoric and the reality of the Caribbean. We can no longer caricature the Caribbean woman as a market girl. . . . And to use the imagery of a continent is to disregard the diversity of the region.' This is a singularly pertinent criticism since the Caribbean contains an enormous cultural diversity comprised of African, French, English, Spanish and Asian elements. This is particularly evident in its religious sects (for example, Jamaican Rastafarianism and Haitian voodoo) and its musical styles (Bluebeat, Reggae, Calypso).

The social problems that tourism has created – or exacerbated – in the Caribbean have forced its tourist industry to develop a new self-awareness, and even considerable powers of self-criticism. Herbert Hiller, the executive director of the government sponsored CTA, has said of the Caribbean in the early 'seventies: '. . . we began to face riots, insurrection and crimes of personal violence from the West Indian community where the outrage was felt most deeply. In the name of development our cultures were being disintegrated. Ways of life that can prevail even in the face of economic deprivation, because of strong cultural bonds were becoming unravelled because of the impact of television and tourism on the region.' Carleen O'Loughlin remarked: 'The more objective and unprejudiced observer can see definite dangers in the invasion of a foreign, although related, culture on such a scale and with such well-lined pockets. On smaller islands the start of the tourist season is nothing less than an invasion – not just a "foot in the door" but a hurricane blowing through the house that cannot fail to ruffle every aspect of domestic life.' Hiller cites the example of a tourism development scheme (which he does not name), which includes a waterway that 'severs a small village from its cemetery. Simultaneously, plans for the development of a nearby off-shore island go ahead with a causeway from the mainland island. The causeway . . . disturbs the fishing grounds that support the economy of the village. The people of the village are cut off from their past and from their present. It happens in the name of tourism development for their future.'

Until recently governments have welcomed tourism – largely uncritically – as a ready source of foreign exchange without paying sufficient attention to its sociology or psychology; the result has been 'domestic chaos, ambiguity, disorientation and incivility'. The violent protests against tourism of the early 'seventies were countered by the infamous 'smile campaigns' – 'rictus campaigns' might be a more appropriate description. These were a gross attempt to avoid facing the problem and they display an astonishing ignorance of the most basic human psychology. In Barbados a 'Pride and Industry Association' was created – among its catch-phrases were 'You need Tourism, Tourism needs you', and 'Island Beautification'. This is indeed cosmetics in place of the surgery required. The neglected substance becomes in Hiller's memorable phrase: 'a haunting stalking of our consciousness'.

Such campaigns are grotesque. Why should whole nations be brainwashed into living a lie? Coffee-growers are not expected to smile as they work. Sri Lanka tea plantation workers would kill anyone seriously asking them to feel perpetually grateful to the British housewives who keep them from starving (just). No, it is one more victory for The Smile – that forced, tired, strained, purely commercial grimace which has become the meaningless symbol of service industries the world over. However, there is something vitally different between, say, Avis instructing its employees to smile at clients, and a national policy by which governments in countries like Jamaica, the Bahamas, Fiji and Barbados instruct their citizens to 'appreciate' the symbols of their poverty. Both are pure commercially inspired actions – but the governments are graphically enmeshed in a neo-colonial situation. Despite their formal political independence, they still cannot actually do without their former masters. In 'Be Nice' campaigns, they are convincing themselves to grin and bear it.

However, the inadequacy and hypocrisy of the 'smile campaigns' is being registered and at the CTA's 1972 Haiti meeting, Premier James Mitchell, of St Vincent, uttered the now famous words 'To Hell with paradise'. This paradise, he insisted, 'has never existed, neither here nor in the Pacific. Having been led to expect paradise many visitors are disappointed when they discover that the Caribbean natives have problems, too, which may not be like those of the highly industrialised homelands of the visitors and hence may be difficult for the visitors to recognise. . . .' Eric Bergstrom, the CTA director, spoke on the same theme: 'We can no longer afford the irrational indulgence that, as we build and pollute according to the standards of modern technology, that we are still, somehow, island paradises, safely hidden, surrounded by seas so isolated that tortured souls from frantic worlds are automatically transformed just by travelling to us.

We have long since lost the innocence of paradise and we shall not find our answers in reminiscence of what might have been. Today it is a challenge to maintain our *relative* tranquillity and charm.' At the same conference, Hiller pointed out that there was a 'high rate of dissatisfaction and boredom' in Caribbean tourism – and that it should not be assumed that all visitors were unable to distinguish between fact and fantasy.

These are all laudable sentiments, but judging from recent evidence they have not yet had much effect on promotional language and photography. *The Sunday Times* colour supplement[6] carried a lavish Air Jamaica advertising feature – which declared, without any sign of embarrassment: '. . . Jamaica is above all a colourful island. Everything is colourful.' Jamaica is further described as: 'The Island of Dunn's River Falls and Ocho Rios and Rose Hall Great House and Banana Upside-Down Cake and Rum Bamboozles and Reggae and Yellow-Faced Grass-quits and a bus called "Romance" and a fascinating airline with "Love-Birds" and beautiful girls . . .'; not of course the island of racial tension and the Kingston ghettos – not the island of widespread unemployment, poverty, and economic exploitation. The accompanying photographs show, among other things, a pair of (white) lovers, drinks in hands, posed against a white balustrade, palm fronds above them, an evening seascape beyond, and, in the foreground, a terrace with immaculate dining tables bearing wine glasses and floral decorations. In another photograph, another pair of lovers embrace, hip high in a sea turned sulphurous yellow by a sunset. Native Jamaicans are represented by a group of suitably 'colourful' straw-hatted musicians and a girl posed so as to resemble, as closely as possible, an Air Jamaica plane – 'Love Bird' ear-ring much in evidence.

The emphasis on the 'Love Bird' suggests that literal dimension of tourism as whorism. The idea of the superior sexuality of Blacks is, implicitly, an important element in the touristic mythology of the Caribbean. West Indians undoubtedly take advantage of this but they also suffer from it. The myth is not wholly complimentary since the idea that black West Indians are superior in the realm of the physical carries with it the strong implication that the physical is the Negro's proper sphere – whether this be cutting sugar cane or serving the sexual needs of the white man or woman; culture and progress are the preserve of the white races. The *sensuality* of West Indian Negroes probably is superior to that of white tourists; since many of those tourists are middle-aged American east coasters, it would hardly be surprising. In general it may be said that West Indian culture is not yet much infected with the sexual neuroses of the western metropoles: the 'virile' Negro is not afraid to appear gracefully languid and is, given the chance, a natural dandy. White visitors do not come to learn from black sensuality but, in so far as they perceive it at all, to exploit it or simply indulge in voyeurism. The West Indian, like the Tahitian or Fijian, soon comes to value her/his sexuality in money terms, hence prostitution and the 'gigolo' soon appear in tourist-intruded communities, even where they had not existed before. The first white reaction to black sexuality was fear and suspicion, this has been sublimated into a factitious appreciation of 'these simply sensual people' (see Chapter 5). West Indians collude in the perpetuation of this image of themselves because it is profitable, but they are also motivated by more complex cultural factors. Black sexuality is an integral part of Black Pride which, in the West Indies, is massively influenced by Black American imports; especially the 'Shaft/Superfly' image of the super-sharp, super-cool, *super stud*. This violent and slick imagery provides a whole series of false aspirations and goals for young, rootless Blacks, especially those who have been attracted to the neon-meccas of the major tourist resorts, only to find that they cannot offer them fulfilment or even job security, but a life of frustrated lethargy and bitterness.

Tourism is, everywhere, the enemy of authenticity and cultural identity – and the chief weapon of this attack is the much-discussed 'demonstration effect'. To the indigenous population of a Third World state a tourist of only average affluence will seem to represent a life-style of unimaginable ease and irresponsibility. Tourists in the Caribbean tend to be more than usually affluent, since its tourist industry had concentrated on high-cost luxury tourism. Tourism apologists argue that the tourist's 'demonstration' of his superior standard of living has a beneficial, energising effect on local populations; they will work harder and show increased initiative, in pursuit of the material signs of affluence. This is a profoundly specious argument. Patrick Rivers has described the workings of the 'demonstration effect' in radically different terms:

> The community strives to adopt the obvious marks of affluence: transistors, sunglasses, pop, imported food and drink. In Dominica . . . the status climb begins by switching from the excellent local rum to higher-priced Barbados or Trinidad imports and from there

to still more costly Scotch. At many a modest hotel in the Leeward Islands the menu will offer hamburger, chips and imported frozen vegetables. This is not from a shortage of local breadfruit, avocado, plantain, yam, tomato, or pimento but because *such a menu is foreign and therefore desirable.*

Until tourists parade the symbols of affluence there had been little desire for them. Because, for most of the indigenous population, they remain tantalisingly beyond reach, the people's discontent grows accordingly.[7]

The 'demonstration effect' becomes an instrument of slow torture. In an attempt to get ahead and pull themselves up to the level of the tourists, growing numbers of the indigenous population will take jobs in tourist service industries, since these seem to offer a better chance of advancement than traditional agriculture. Consequently agriculture is neglected and the tourist-intruded society becomes increasingly dependent on imported foods (Hawaii imports, of all things, pineapples), and therefore increasingly tied to international cycles of inflation. Should the tourist industry, for any reason, decline, they would no longer be able to fall back on their own resources. Those individuals who are drawn into the service industry may make a temporary financial gain, but it is arguable that they will lose in cultural and psychological terms whatever they may gain financially. It is necessarily difficult for a nation of waiters, barmen, guides, hustlers and prostitutes to retain any sense of dignity or identity.

In aspiring to the material standards and adopting the values of the West, the more upwardly-mobile members of the indigenous population are, in Fanon's words, following 'the western bourgeoisie along its paths of negation and decadence'. The national bourgeoisie of the Third World country will already have attained these material standards; it is they who drink Scotch and eat imported, frozen vegetables in imitation of the tourists: 'In its beginnings the national bourgeoisie of the colonial countries identifies itself with the decadence of the bourgeoisie of the West. We need not think it is jumping ahead, it is, in fact, beginning at the end.'[8] Tourism is exporting to the Third World a style of life, the wisdom of which is being questioned increasingly in its countries of origin. It is not an exaggeration to see tourism in the Third World as a disseminator of metropolitan decadence. It is an important feature of contemporary class ritual, that is a display and consumption of wealth which has as its immediate audience some of the most desperate peoples of the world. It presents to them 'the norm as dreamed'. It is by means of such class ritual that the 'bourgeoisie is constantly absorbing into its ideology a whole section of humanity which does not have its basic status and cannot live up to it except in imagination, that is, at the cost of an immobilisation and an impoverishment of consciousness'.' Tourism is the exemplary global agent of this process of absorption and immobilisation.

Since the early 'sixties the Caribbean tourist industry has concerned itself largely with the creation of luxurious 'pleasure reserves'. As Fanon suggests, we should 'keep before us the example of certain Latin American Republics. The banking magnates, the technocrats, and the big businessmen of the US have only to step on to a plane and they are wafted into sub-tropical climes, there, for the space of a week or ten days, to luxuriate in the delicious depravities' – many of them simply wish to give their ulcers a rest – nevertheless, there are clear signs that such a market does exist and that it is being lavishly catered for. One of the most promising areas for future tourism development in the Caribbean is Haiti – where the Habitation Leclerc is to be found.

In the last decade and a half Haiti's Duvalieriste régime has rivalled Batista's in terms of corruption and repressive brutality. The atrocities of Papa Doc Duvalier are notorious, and too numerous to catalogue here. Papa Doc's reputation was so sinister and his government so proverbially inefficient that outside business interests were discouraged from investing in Haiti. Tourists expected to find corpses in their hotel swimming-pools (*vide* Graham Greene's *The Comedians*). Since Papa Doc's death in 1972, the Duvalieriste régime (now with his obese son, Jean Claude – or Baby Doc – as President) has liberalised its façade to the extent of disbanding the Tonton Macoutes,* and showering foreign investors with tax exemptions and long-term leases of land. Haiti remains a land of 3 to 5 million people (exact statistics are not available) – 90 per cent illiterate, 50 per cent unemployed and many of them living at starvation level. They have no trade unions and no political rights.

According to Greg Chamberlain of *The Guardian*, most of Haiti's coastline has been leased to foreign companies on the understanding that they will build hotels. The two most interesting and revealing of Haiti's recent tourism developments are the Tortuga development

---

* Papa Doc's private army, cum secret service, cum bogy-men.

and the Habitation Leclerc. The first involves the leasing of the entire off-shore island of Tortuga for ninety-nine years to the Texan group, Dupont Caribbean Inc. The island, which is twenty-four miles long and four miles wide, is at present inhabited by 5,000 desperately poor peasants. It is to be developed along the lines of Freeport, Grand Bahama, as a tax-free holiday haven for the very rich. Papa Doc's ruthless suppression of the Haitian labour movement made it possible for Dupont Caribbean to dismiss, summarily, 200 workers who had attempted to gain a pay increase by strike action. Such circumstances obviously make Haiti an extremely attractive proposition for outside business interests. Dupont Caribbean's vice-president remarked: 'One dollar a day is already too much for a Haitian worker.' The firm is now, in all but name, ruler of Tortuga and its 5,000 inhabitants, and a clause in the firm's contract with the Haitian government clearly shows that they have undertaken to maintain strict Duvalieriste standards: 'No concession or agreement shall be granted or made with a communist government or with a firm controlled by one, and no subversive activity shall be permitted on the island.'

Like Tortuga the Habitation Leclerc is designed as an exclusive 'pleasure reserve' for the very rich. It consists of a loving restoration of a palace built by Napoleon for his sister Pauline – standing in extensive grounds which also contain thirty-eight chalets. Each chalet is equipped with a private swimming-pool, three Haitian servants and gold-plated toilet fittings. A day's lodging in these surroundings costs $150; it would take the average Haitian living beyond the walls two years to earn this much. A photograph in a 1973 issue of *Time Magazine*, of a Habitation interior, displayed a beautiful creole girl reclining on a divan against a luxuriant backdrop of palm fronds. Clearly the girl is to be regarded as another luxury fixture, like the gold-plated taps – and object for the delectation and amusement of wealthy foreigners. The kind of wealthy foreigners who are interested in the Habitation is indicated by its list of financial backers. These include, 'Jean-Paul Belmondo, Mick Jagger, Alain Delon, the Duke of Bedford, Giovanni Agnelli, the Italian car magnate, Roger Vadim, Prince Egon von Furstenburg, Aristotle Onassis, Baron Edmund de Rothschild and other multinational business tycoons'.[10] The man who described the Habitation as the 'most extraordinarily lascivious and decadent place on earth' is its promoter Olivier Coquelin – who also owns the fashionable Hippopotamus discothèque in New York. Evidently the Habitation is planned as an extension (in a tropical setting) of 'seventies metropolitan decadence – of which New York is the undisputed capital. To most readers the mere existence of 'lascivious decadence' at $150 a day, in one of the most wretched places of the earth, must seem morally abhorrent. It is therefore necessary to consider in some detail what it is that makes this prospect attractive to the Jaggers, Vadims and Rothschilds.

Extreme contrast is indispensable to a genuinely decadent ambience – contrasts of refinement and vulgarity, sophistication and naïveté, abundance and scarcity. The resulting clash produces a kind of vicarious excitement that is never more than one step removed from the sexual. There are those for whom the enjoyment of excess and voluptuousness is heightened by its juxtaposition to poverty, starvation and disease. The road to the Habitation passes through some of Port-au-Prince's worst slums where one can literally see people dying from unchecked diseases; of this George Bebe, of *The Miami Herald*, remarked: 'The approach to the hotel may be distasteful to some guests – perhaps an exciting aspect to others.' Even when it is being consciously exploited, as at the Habitation, this element of social and cultural clash in the tourist situation must be controlled, otherwise poverty, starvation and disease might interfere with the enjoyment of a pleasant holiday. Against this, tourism has a number of defences, the most obvious of which is the isolation of the tourist in 'pleasure reserves'. The Habitation itself is surrounded by a high wall; tourists are free to intrude on the host society whenever they wish, but the intrusions of the indigenous population into the tourist's expensive fantasy world can be strictly controlled. More subtly, tourism has its psychological defence mechanisms – namely the conversion of social realities into the decorative elements of the picturesque and the exotic. Haitian life with its 'charming and friendly natives' and its fascinating hybrid of diverse French and African cultural elements, becomes a pageant; one enjoys its exoticism and primitivism, much as one admires the products of the famous Haitian 'primitive' school of painting. The natives, of course, would not be so picturesque if they were prosperous and educated, being picturesque is very much a question of *knowing your place*.

The presence of Mick Jagger in the Habitation's list of backers seems inevitable in retrospect. In recent years white rock stars have displayed a growing fascination with Caribbean culture, particularly reggae music. Paul Simon, Cat Stevens and the Rolling Stones have all recorded in Kingston; they claim to like the 'feel' of the place; its simplicity (the *funky* technical crudity of its recording facilities) and the spontaneity of its musicians. Occasionally they adopt diluted versions of reggae rhythm for their songs. Musical tourism has been gaining in impetus since the later 'sixties; popular music in the West is now almost entirely taken up with a nostalgic pillaging of its own past and a frenziedly eclectic borrowing of Third World ethnic modes (as well as Caribbean, Indian, Latin American, North African and West African). Apparently Jamaicans have not uniformly appreciated these stellar visitations. Their own musicians have for long been ruthlessly exploited by the Jamaican record industry, and, in consequence, our grossly overpaid popular musicians have been greeted with threats and verbal abuse; some have even been mugged (as also happened to Paul McCartney in Nigeria). Nevertheless, Bianca Jagger is said to be involved in opening a boutique in Jamaica.

For prototypical decadents of the 'seventies and like-minded members of our heterogeneous 'international aristocracy', Haiti offers the allure of a new and stronger *frisson*, something more than the discothèque décor of metropolitan decadence. The luxury of the Habitation, set against a tragic historical backdrop of oppression, vice and corruption, is the *real thing*, the veritable *fleur du mal*.

This has been recognised by Olivier Coquelin and intelligently exploited. In doing so he has taken a bold step forward for luxury tourism in the 'seventies; there will no longer be any need to rehearse the tired apologias concerning economic benefit to the host country ('tourism in support of development'), or increases in international understanding. Haiti and other oppressed Third World states will be viewed frankly as palliatives for the *ennui* of industrial magnates, financiers, film stars and directors, and rock stars. Such a development will find enthusiastic collaborators among the ruling élites of Third World states. They will in effect set up their countries as the brothels of Europe and America. In doing so they will also strengthen class divisions within their countries. The existence of exclusive 'pleasure reserves' – like Tortuga and the Habitation Leclerc or simply a Hilton (or Hilton-style) hotel increases the national bourgeoisie's sense of identification with the western bourgeoisie, and correspondingly reinforces its alienation from the oppressed majority of their fellow countrymen. Class distinction is now graphically expressed as the distinction between those who can enter the hotel as guests and those who can only enter it as servants (see also *Deep-Frozen Folklore*). It is necessary at this stage to make brief mention of the 'myth-alibi' of tourism as a means to general prosperity. The statistics that reveal this admirable prosperity to us do not take into account the fact that it is usually distributed in a strictly hierarchic manner. Any profits that stay in the country (discounting temporarily the high proportion that returns to foreign investors) will frequently accrue to an oligarchic business community which will regard the idea of *shared* wealth as, at best, a sentimental fallacy. It may be taken as a general rule that any economic boom (resulting from the rapid development of tourism and other industries) occurring within unjust social and political structures can only serve to increase the injustice of those structures. The kind of piecemeal and superficial economic development that tourism provides for the Third World is also a means of infinitely delaying necessary radical change. Tourism cannot provide the massive increase in employment that is needed and it will pay those it does employ at 'the going oppressive rate'. At the same time it subjugates Third World states to the requirements of international business. Inevitably the requirements of national development will take second place. In the smaller island states of the Caribbean this produces a radical distortion of previously agricultural economies that is virtually incurable. A cure would involve the kind of absolute reform which, since the Cuban revolution, has been so inimical to the tourist industry. If tourism has become central to the economy, such reform cannot be contemplated by government and business. Thus tourism contributes towards a general paralysis. It provides maximum social and cultural disruption with minimal economic benefit to the population as a whole.

When Fanon spoke of the conversion of countries into brothels, he was not resorting to mere rhetorical exaggeration; we have only to think of the Mexican border towns or Cuba under Batista to see the truth of his assertion. In Haiti poor families often sell their daughters to the brothels of Port-au-Prince – not because they are unscrupulous, but because this is the only way they can be sure their daughters will not starve. According to Jane Richardson of *The Guardian*,[11] exquisitely dressed male prostitutes frequent the verandahs of Port-au-Prince hotels in the evenings 'sweating with sincerity as they make conversational murmurs around their male and female targets'. One factor which may well impede the advertised 'lascivious decadence' of Haitian tourism is, predictably, the appallingly high venereal disease rate. In a more general sense Haitian culture is in danger of being prostituted as tourism prospers; it is already falling victim to the 'deep-frozen folklore' syndrome. The 'primitive' paintings are already being mass-produced for tourist consumption, and voodoo ceremonies are staged purely for the benefit of tourists. The Habitation Leclerc, for example, was 'consecrated' by a voodoo ceremony – a kind of pre-packed *Heart of Darkness*.

Hilton's Hyatt House, Playboy and American Airlines' Flagship hotel chain are all examining Haiti with a view to tourism development. Haiti's good tourism prospects are confirmed by the fact that Andrew Targalos, the retiring commercial attaché of the US embassy in Port-au-Prince, has obtained a fifteen-year personal concession to build a casino. For the tourist industry, Haiti has one signal advantage over the more highly developed Caribbean islands; there is, as yet, no racial hatred of Whites. Indeed, whiteness is frankly envied and one astonished tourist was told by a black Haitian that he was 'as beautiful as lemonade'. Unlike the Jamaican or the Virgin Islander, the Haitian is unspoilt – which means he has not been contaminated by radical political theory. This is to be expected since his ignorance has been scrupulously maintained by the Duvalieriste régime, and all political opposition within Haiti has been effectively suppressed. *The Economist* of 24th July 1971, while admitting that conditions in Haiti might not be ideal, cheerfully observed that: 'There is law and order compared with Guatemala; there are no mass slaughters as there were of students in Mexico before the Olympic Games. The streets are safe to walk about in, the people are charming and friendly.' Law and order are necessarily vital to the prosperity of a tourism industry: the question we should ask is – law and order for whose benefit? It is ironic, in these circumstances, that Haiti is becoming fashionable as a destination for colour-proud American Blacks, who see it primarily as the land of Toussaint L'Ouverture and Dessalines – the Black revolutionary leaders of the Napoleonic era. For them it is the land where, in Aime Césaire's words, 'négritude rose to its feet for the first time and said it believed in its own humanity'. It would seem that most of us see only what we want to see.

The reader will recall the enlightened opinions of the members of the CTA. It comes as something of a jolt when we remember that many of these opinions were expressed at a general meeting in Haiti. The speakers seem to have expressed no disapproval of the direction tourism was taking in Haiti – yet the Habitation and the Tortuga project surely represent a kind of *ancien régime* tourism that is entirely opposed to the avowed policies of the CTA. These policies centre on the rather ill-defined (and neologistic) concepts of 'Caribbeanisation' and 'indigenisation', and the complementary idea of 'alternative tourism'. They seek to 'rediscover the West Indian perspective' (assuming it had ever been found), to develop a tourism that is not 'the creature of the industrialised nations'. This is motivated by a genuine desire to make tourism serve the interests of West Indians, and by the uncomfortable fact that the Caribbean has the world's highest priced hotel industry and yet shows the lowest net return. Since the late 'sixties Caribbean tourism has been losing a substantial percentage of its market to Europe. Thus, from every point of view (both philanthropic and self-interested) a new tourism is required.

The chief instrument of 'Caribbeanisation' would be the small hotel. This would be locally owned, and its smallness and its setting *within* the community would lead to a more genuine interaction between tourists and local people. These ideas represent a conscious rejection of foreign-owned 'pleasure reserve' tourism – catering largely for the rich, middle-aged, middle-class tourist (i.e. the tourism of imperialist values). It is argued that the small hotel run by local people, serving local food, would attract a different kind of tourist – younger, less conservative, and less grossly affluent – hence, alternative tourism (i.e. the tourism of alternative value systems). The new Caribbean tourist would be more aware of Caribbean problems, more inclined to experiment and less interested in buying a glossy package. It would almost seem that the CTA is looking for a new élite – comprised of the politically and ecologically aware, the sons and daughters of the liberal bourgeoisie. At the San Juan seminar of 1972 Jean François Revel, the author of *Without Marx or Jesus*, suggested that tourism should no longer be directed principally at the 'tired businessman, the giddy honeymooners or the bored divorcee', but should take into account such varied groups as 'nature lovers, homosexual couples, Woodstock hippies, respectable "hardhats", sensuous secretaries, women's libbers and senior citizens'.[12]

The question of 'Caribbeanisation' and 'indigenisation' is ambiguous. So far we have seen tourism as always essentially *inauthentic*. Is there not some danger of an official programme of indigenisation tending to convert the Caribbean into a massive pseudo-event?

Could it lead to an institutionalisation of *suitable* elements of local culture – an insertion of local dishes into tourist menus, recalling the Hilton attitude to indigenous cultures? Is there any evidence that ordinary West Indians relish the idea of closer interaction with tourists? Would the dispersal of large numbers of visitors into the heart of local communities simply produce a more rapid disruption of 'ways of life that have prevailed even in the face of economic deprivation'?

The CTA's solutions do not, finally, encompass the full complexity of the situation. It is all very well to say that as the Caribbean is no paradise for its inhabitants it should not be sold as such to tourists, and that tourism, consequently, must relate more closely to 'Caribbean realities', but this would involve the complete revolutionisation of an industry that is everywhere based on illusion. The Caribbean appeals to the North American middle classes (whatever their age or opinions in politics and ecology), because it seems to approximate to the romantic myth of the paradise isle or the tropical Eden. The younger, more fashion-conscious tourists may add freely available dope, reggae music and a touch of Rastafarian mysticism to the basic idyllic ingredients, but their attitude remains equally 'mystified'. Since the mythology of escape is indispensible to tourism, it is not easy to reject the paradisal imagery. When tourists visit the Caribbean to forget the anxieties, frustrations and social responsibilities of the metropoles they can hardly be expected to take a serious interest in the problems of the society they are visiting. They come in search of a world of pleasure, an island of lotus-eaters (unless they are members of that exclusive avant-garde which prefers the Habitation orchid to the lotus). As we have seen in *Lido Libido*, the tourist's desires are largely regressive, hedonistic and selfish. He expects the beach to be clean and the natives to be friendly – if they are not he may be angry, he will feel cheated and confused, but he is unlikely to make much attempt to understand the root causes behind polluted beaches or local hostility. As Hiller has observed: 'People do not come here because their presence and their spending boosts our economies, they come for what they can't have at home.' A radical change in the nature of Caribbean tourism would have to be preceded by a radical change in the attitudes of affluent North Americans and West Europeans – and ultimately by the eradication of the neuroses that motivate their tourism. But this would also lead to the disappearance of tourism as an industry.

However, even if there is no change in tourists' motivation, there is still a strong element of self-destruction in an industry which cannot be saved by campaigns like the Jamaican 'Be Nice' programme, or the Tanzanian attempts to persuade visitors to call 'Rafiki' (Swahili for 'Friend'), instead of the dismissive ex-colonial 'Boy!' Firstly, the whole structure rests on the existence of people willing to serve the tourists. Throughout the world, however, there is a pervasive belief that serving one's fellows at leisure is demeaning and not a proper job. Also, the hours involved are extremely unsocial, since someone has to get up before the tourists, or go to bed later, or eat meals at off-peak times – anything which will allow the desires of the quest to be immediately satisfied. The lesson from Switzerland seems clear that, given economic growth, there will come a point where hotel workers will opt for 9–5 office jobs. In France, one finds that one out of every two students leaving French hotel technical schools switches to more attractive professions. The result is that the global tourism boom has led to a massive shortage of trained hotel staff. This can only be met by importing large numbers of migrant workers from lands where jobs are still rare and underpaid. However, it would be a brave man who argued that the Swiss reaction to the social implications of this policy is going to be atypical of the reactions of the majority of countries round the world. There comes a time when the tensions outweigh the economic benefits brought by the industry.

One solution is to automate. Morning maids are replaced by clock radios: breakfasts and nightcaps come from vending-machines placed in the hotel room. Even checking in and checking out becomes automatic, so that hotels become soulless institutions with all the atmosphere of a well-run morgue. Gone is the element of cosseting – the feeding of vanity which is so much part of the tourist experience. All that is left is a bleak reminder that we live in a machine-dominated age – and we do not need to go on holiday to become aware of that.

The only other solution is to take the tourists to the service. This means enticing them to the Third World where poverty ought to guarantee an adequate supply of servility. As we have seen, this will probably not be a long-term solution either. Most of such countries are still politically young and finding their identities in the first decade or so since Independence. As they mature and grow in self-confidence, some will decide to reject an industry demanding so much subservience. In others, grass-roots resistance will grow. The problems arising in the Caribbean are just the beginning of a process which will render large parts of the world positively hostile to tourism as an industry, and to tourists as individuals.

Ultimately tourism will only survive if it helps create societies which are less divided than they are at the moment. Instinctively everything one knows about this industry tells one it is the most socially disruptive one there is. As we have argued, a large tourist industry almost ensures a corrupted, selfish élite, which will try to forget the needs of its country's dispossessed. Already we can see in Latin America what happens when societies are run by élites with their eyes turned firmly toward the rich world beyond their borders. They become like Chile or Uruguay; social democracies drifting into dictatorships. They start to resemble Brazil or Argentina: volcanoes which alternate between forms of anarchy and brutal dictatorships. As the disaffected find reforms increasingly resisted, they turn to terrorism, looking particularly for symbols of foreign imperialism as their targets. At the moment, urban guerillas in countries like Argentina and Uruguay pick the managers of foreign multinational companies like Ford and General Motors as their victims. Tomorrow, we shall see such terrorism spreading to many of the Third World's leading tourist destinations, only the hotels and the tourists will be targets; and no one can afford to give all tourists the protection that a firm like Ford can give to its overseas managers.

It thus looks as if the tourist dream will be destroyed even in the world's poor countries. No one wants knowingly to spend their holiday in armed camps. Obviously there will be attempts to create the illusion that the tourist is still free to go where he wants, to do what he chooses. This will increasingly depend on the success governments have in suppressing the dissidents in their societies. However, if tourism is as socially disruptive as we suggest, then even the most efficient dictatorships will be unable to protect tourists all the time. No part of the tourist dream includes the chance of being assassinated.

12 A Kind of Solution

Agricultural and fishing rhythms were replaced by the incredible sleepless frenzy of July and August, followed by ten months of gradual preparation for the reappearance of the tourists.

D. J. Greenwood

And what shall become of us without the Barbarians,
They were a kind of solution.

C. P. Cavafy

So far we have concerned ourselves largely with the social impact of tourism in the Third World. In considering Haiti, Bali and Kenya we have referred to a kind of experience that may seem utterly remote from that of the vast majority of tourists. The tourist in Switzerland or Spain does not come into contact with the extremes of affluence and deprivation we have described – he does not see himself as playing a role in the creation of 'abrasive social situations'. Despite this, the impact of tourism can be highly destructive even in the relatively prosperous communities of northern Spain and the Swiss Alps. Nowhere can tourism be guaranteed harmless.

It is our intention to examine closely two case studies: one conducted in the Swiss alpine village of Kippel by J. Friedl, and the other in the Spanish Basque town of Fuenterrabia, by Dafydd Greenwood. Greenwood's analysis of tourism development is considered more extensively than Friedl's study which is not wholly concerned with tourism.[1]

In both Kippel and Fuenterrabia mass tourism has given rise to major economic growth: '. . . it has stimulated the commercialisation of agriculture and the creation of service industries and has ultimately led to the decline of agriculture and the development of a variety of specialised problems'. Both communities were predominantly or exclusively agricultural before the arrival of mass tourism in the late 1950s. It should not be forgotten, in this context, that tourism is a form of *industrialisation* even if, outwardly, it is not immediately recognisable as such. Too rapid, or ill-considered industrialisation in 'less-developed' communities and nations is widely accepted as having a destructive social impact. Tourism is an unusually rapid and unstable form of industrialisation which differs from the traditional forms in that it is superimposed directly on pre-existing social and economic patterns – without any migration from country to city.

The arrival of large numbers of tourists brings a new demand for agricultural produce, but at the same time agriculture declines – as Greenwood observes of Fuenterrabia: '. . . while farm profits are at an all time high, rural depopulation is increasing at a runaway pace. The profits are not translated into greater production and the market system of incentives does not seem to apply.' This seems paradoxical but 'culprits' are easily located. In the district of Fuenterrabia a new 'exclusive country club' development has 'closed out' more than fifteen farms in under a year. The number of farms in the whole district has declined from 256 in 1920 to an 'informally estimated' 120 in 1972. Tourism is evidently only one factor in this long process but it has unquestionably contributed significantly. J. W. Cole describes a similar development (or underdevelopment) in the eastern Alps: '. . . both winter and summer recreation centres have been established on land formerly used by alpine peasants. In a few extreme cases whole village populations have turned to catering to tourists and farming has been abandoned.' The younger generation in tourist-intruded, rural communities are naturally attracted to the service industries which offer shorter hours and fewer responsibilities: 'Of 169 farms in 1969 only 8 had heirs committed to carrying on the farm into the next generation, and even in these cases the chance of finding a spouse willing to farm is remote.'[2]

Already it is possible to gain some ideas of the ways in which tourism strikes at the heart of these communities – invading and shattering even the most intimate areas of life. Friedl's observations of post-touristic agriculture in Kippel reinforce this impression: 'The decline in agriculture has caused severe problems for those who have remained in it for they can no longer rely upon the communal efforts to help them through as in previous years. The burden has shifted from the community to the individual for the labour force has been removed from the village, and the agricultural economy which depended so heavily on co-operation is unable to continue at the same level.' What we seem to be observing is a specific fragmentation of the 'organic community'; this destruction of communal values, of mutual aid and co-operation, is a subject to which we will soon return.

One of the most immediate effects of tourism is to alter entirely the value of land, and to transform the peasant into a wage labourer. Gerald Berthoud suggests that the changes brought about by 'industry, tourism and trade' in the circum-Alpine region, render land 'almost useless'. But, despite this, 'in the case of an effective or prospective touristic development, the villagers are legally deprived of their landed property by national or international capital whose only objective is speculation and profit. This very capital will then be able to buy the labour force of landless villagers to perform menial jobs in the newly created resort.' Friedl records a massive inflation of land values in Kippel since the start of major tourism development, with a British owned development company planning to build a multi-million dollar tourist resort close to the village. In 1972 land was selling at $186,000 per acre (that is, 200 Swiss francs per square metre). This is an externally imposed valuation which makes little sense to the villagers as much of the land being sold is relatively unproductive. Few, if any, of the local inhabitants can afford to purchase much land at this price. In Kippel there are few land parcels large enough for a house, but the man who has to add only a few square metres to land already in his possession in order to build a house is now discouraged from building. The growth of the tourist trade has coincided with a 'natural (but indigenous) expansion of the village'. Friedl concludes that the chief victim of inflated land values is the younger generation of villagers, which 'includes those newly-married or newly-employed men who for the first time want to and are able to build a house'. Some individuals are virtually driven out of the village by inflation. In his study, F. Greenwood concludes that the lower-income groups are inevitably the principal victims of inflation, they are simply unable to buy land on which to build. Even when government steps in to control development, the results can still be problematic: '. . . the building regulations introduced with the intention of controlling residential development and hotels tend to affect lower-income groups adversely, both because of their complexity and also because the traditional way of building houses, perhaps over a period of time with the help of family and friends, is not catered for by such legislation . . .'.

Although we have restricted our attention to questions of agricultural and economic change, there are already clear signs of serious social disruption at all levels of life in the communities under consideration. This impression is corroborated in detail by Greenwood's accounts of Fuenterrabia's development as a resort. In the history of this development we can discern the familiar process by which aristocratic privileges and modes of leisure have been extended to the mass of the middle class. In the late nineteenth and early twentieth centuries Fuenterrabia became fashionable as a minor aristocratic resort – at the time nearby San Sebastian was the favourite summer resort of Spanish royalty. In 1918 there were thirty summer residences. Of the eighteen motor vehicles in the town seventeen were owned by the visitors who did not mix with the local people but rather, 'shrouded their lives with an air of conspicuous privacy'. Their influence on the life of the town was minimal in economic and social terms. Middle-class tourism began in the early 1930s but its development was interrupted by the Civil War and the Second World War. The real expansion began after 1950. By 1963 there were 30,000 visiting the town each summer; by 1969 this had risen to 40,000 and the number of elegant summer residences had exceeded 200.

Mass tourism's physical impact on the town was immediate and dramatic. Streets were cleaned out, the city walls were reconstructed, festivals and exhibitions were organised in the restored castle of Charles V. Fuenterrabia's beauty was advertised by the circulation of old prints, while at the same time its 'historic charm' was seriously impaired by the construction of a number of 'architectural monstrosities'. It was only in 1965 that the town was declared a national, artistic and historical monument, and that new, more stringent, building regulations were introduced.

In the surrounding rural area roads were improved and new villas were built 'often tearing down farmhouses to make room'. Cars and farm machinery multiplied. Craftsmen profited from the construction boom, farmers and fishermen found a new and expanding market in hotels and restaurants, but: 'As a consequence of this commercialisation and dependence on tourism the municipal economy became far more dependent on national and international business cycles than had previously been the case. Balance of payments problems and policies, inflation and exchange restrictions came to affect the people of Fuenterrabia immediately and directly.' Since agriculture was also declining steadily, it is clear from this that the community has entirely lost its former self-sufficiency; it can no longer turn in upon itself during times of crisis, as happened during the Civil War and the Second World War.

With its self-sufficiency it has also lost its social cohesion. Referring to the 'demonstration effect' Greenwood suggests that tourism might be viewed as 'a vast school for the modernisation of values'. The results of the rapid increase in material affluence and job opportunities are immediately apparent at a domestic level: family size has decreased, couples marry earlier, and a greater degree of mobility and independence is available for the young (especially for younger sons). There has also been a marked increase in generation conflict and since the value of family businesses has soared there has been violent 'sibling conflict' over inheritance (a phenomenon found also by Friedl in Kippel). Until recently Fuenterrabia had maintained its own tradition of inheritance in defiance of Spanish civil law. Parents would select a single heir to whom the property was passed on intact; all other children would then have to leave – the daughters with dowries, the sons with an education or money to get them started. This could be a ruthless system since 'any sibling who chose to stay must not marry and must subordinate himself to the chosen heir'. Spanish civil law requires equal inheritance but customarily families would make private arrangements to avoid this. Now, many younger sons and daughters refuse to accept the traditional system and force division of the property. This often results in long, destructive court fights. The eventual outcome may be liberative for the younger members of families but is frequently prejudicial to the aged: in previous generations ageing Basques could expect to live with their chosen heir and enjoy a few years of semi-retirement before death. Now social mobility usually implies residential mobility as well and there is an increased tendency for the aged to be left alone or uncared for. . . .'

Conflict and alienation *within* domestic groups is paralleled by new tensions *between* domestic groups. Affluence has brought with it the labour-saving appliances and cash reserves that allow families 'to disengage themselves from ties of mutual dependence and reciprocity. This allows them a much greater degree of privacy . . . and this privacy is highly valued.' The other side of this new independence and privacy is isolation: 'Domestic groups are more socially isolated now than at any time in the recent past. Without the mutual aid obligations of the past, they interact only infrequently or on a superficial level.' This decline in the idea of *vecindad* (neighbourhood) has made it possible for new kinds of class distinction to develop within specific occupational categories: there are now middle-class and lower-class fishermen, craftsmen and shopkeepers. The newly prosperous members of these occupational groups, now considering themselves middle class, will naturally indulge in competitive consumption patterns to demonstrate this to the community as a whole.

Such competitive patterns had existed before the arrival of mass tourism, but they are now carried to extremes, coming to dominate the community's internal relationships. In the rural area the adoption of these patterns of consumption 'has led to acquisition of many more reaping machines and power tillers than are needed' in local farming operations.

In Fuenterrabia the 'modernisation of values' seems to consist of the outright destruction of traditional communal values (especially the ties of *vecindad*) and their replacement by the most rabidly competitive values of alienated metropolitan suburbs. But to see the situation in such exclusively black-and-white terms would constitute a mystification. It is easy to fall prey to facile sentiment concerning the lost 'organic community' – whether this be located in rural villages or now demolished North of England slums. This attitude often amounts to little more than a sociological rephrasing of pastoral convention. In the hands of some erstwhile social critics the idealised image of non-bourgeois past is often used as a convenient stick with which to beat the present. Whatever its harmonious virtues the 'organic community' is also likely to have been poor, claustrophobic, inbred, and restrictive for individuals within the tightly-knit family groups. Farming may seem to have more dignity than a job in the tourist service industry – the first is 'natural', the second 'parasitical'. There is considerable truth in this, but it is also true that farming can be back-breakingly hard and is often unreliably profitable. If we reject the diffuse nostalgia which so often clouds these issues: it seems possible to argue that tourism is to some degree a benefactor, since its influence can lead to the abandonment of archaic and repressive customs – for example, arranged marriages or inheritance traditions like those of Fuenterrabia. We may regard with pleasure the increased self-respect and independence of behaviour of the young. Prosperity is apparent in new washing machines, mopeds, transistor radios and farm machinery, but to dismiss the harmful effects of social change as the inevitable minor casualties attendant on Modern Progress would be dangerously superficial. A serious disquiet concerning tourism as an agent of change need not be based on nostalgic sentiment or dogmatic hostility to the values of affluence.

In Fuenterrabia, class distinction shows signs of developing into an open class conflict – with the country club as its focus. The club has already contributed to the decline in agriculture (by 'closing out' farms) and the inflation of land values (by encouraging speculation throughout Fuenterrabia's rural district), but, most importantly, it has now become a focus of economic and political power:

> The advent of the country club signalises the local emergence of a non-aristocratic, upper middle-class as representatives of the good life of which cars, money, fine clothes and gentlemanly recreation are a part. Membership covers a wide range of occupations: store owners, doctors, notaries, lawyers, journalists, owners of construction businesses, artists, writers and so on. Political power in the municipality is increasingly becoming centred in this group and their ties with outside investors. The battle over plans for the future of the municipality is now being fought between this faction on one side and the farmers and fishermen on the other, with an outcome in favour of the former being in little doubt.

The circumstances of Fuenterrabia's country club are less dramatic than those of the Third World 'pleasure reserves' we have elsewhere described – contrasts of privilege and deprivation are much less extreme. What is surprising is that in a relatively prosperous area like the Fuenterrabia municipality – the similarities should still be so striking. In the exclusive environment of the club, the indigenous élite cements its links with foreign business interests and indulges in *haut-bourgeois* modes of leisure that are largely alien to the region and its traditions. Unlike the non-bourgeois groups in communities where an élite having ties with outside interests pre-existed the arrival of mass tourism, the majority of Fuenterrabia's inhabitants have not been decisively excluded from participation in the tourism boom. Instead the 'non-aristocratic upper middle-class' has *emerged* from this new prosperity. Yet the establishment of the country club has already indicated that this new class is consolidating its position by a process of exclusion; this means an exclusion of the middle and lower income groups from real economic power and from effective control over the future development of their community. This is in close accord with Berthoud's description of ownership dynamics in the circum-alpine region when he speaks of villagers deprived of their land 'by national and international capital whose only objective is speculation and profit'.

It can now be seen to what extent a community can become defenceless in the face of the growing exploitation of outside interests that characterise tourism's third developmental phase (as described in Greenwood's stage-three scenario of tourism development). The first phase is the period of aristocratic tourism with its minimal impact on economic growth and social structures: tourism and the local economy co-exist but are not mutually interdependent. The second phase (which in Fuenterrabia can be dated from 1950 to 1965) is the period of rapid expansion with 'response largely in terms of local initiative and investment, yielding substantial economic rewards for a large sector of the community'. This is also the period of increased social mobility in which new class divisions emerge, or in which pre-existing class divisions are exaggerated. As we have seen, this is accompanied by increased competition in patterns of consumption. In general it may be said that divisive elements now pervade the community at all levels, from the domestic outwards and upwards. The new prosperity is critically dependent on tourism and thus on economic cycles over which the local community has no control. The beginning of the third phase is marked by massive government intervention to improve transport and to install other necessary infrastructure – to preserve attractions and to promote arts festivals, sports, etc. Rather than controlling the process of change, this intervention accelerates it by bringing the community within the reach of a vast number of people – such as could not have been achieved by unassisted local initiative. The scale of tourism becomes so inflated that it passes beyond the scope of independent local control. The indigenous élite (whether newly emergent or long established) becomes increasingly entrenched in its dominant position and it will encourage the participation of powerful outside interests. Thus profits, as they get bigger, will move increasingly upwards and outwards. In Fuenterrabia it is this process that has been largely responsible for the decline of agriculture through rural depopulation and outside competition – and a similar decline of the fishing industry. It has also led to a 'deterioration in the situation of local artisans' through competition with large outside firms.

Greenwood proposes this model of tourism development in specific relation to his study of Fuenterrabia, but there would seem to be a significant correspondence between the Fuenterrabian experience and that of tourist-intruded communities in agrarian Europe and throughout the Third World. More detailed case studies would have to be undertaken before this could be considered a definitive analysis, however. For example, the three-stage model would have to be radically modified for it to be applicable to many Third World communities. In the Third World community the second phase simply does not occur in the same way. Tourism development occurs within the context of extreme social injustice and often rigidly hierarchic class structures which do not permit widespread participation and increased social mobility. Tourism moves directly from stage one to stage three and in consequence the process of change and adaptation to change is more violently disruptive.

In Fuenterrabia the threat posed by the encroachment of outside interests is 'clearly perceived by all', but the community is now so divided as to 'effectively keep people from banding together to procure legal aid, form co-operatives or lobby for their cause with outside authorities'. Friedl suggests co-operative arrangements as a means of protecting individuals from falling victim to inflated land values; the community (in Kippel) could make 'judicious use' of the land it already owns. In this way it could be ensured that 'enough building sites of suitable size and location remain available to villagers at a price they can afford'. Since it is precisely this co-operative outlook that tourism erodes, it would be surprising if this came about. After large-scale tourism development would there be anything remaining that we could call, with any degree of accuracy – 'a community'?

Fuenterrabia's reconstructed castle has been converted into one of a chain of government-owned historic hotels. Cleaned and refurbished – in a word, packaged – the town's 'culture and monuments have become centres of promotion, speculation and manipulation by outside investors. Fuenterrabia is more an enterprise than a town.' The whole town is a national monument with the inhabitants as living exhibits. Behind the monument's neo-Basque façade the people have either identified with the consumer values 'demonstrated' by tourism or they have retreated 'into ever more private cultural worlds, leaving only the outward forms of their life for touristic consumption'. Greenwood asserts that the Basques generally find the tourist trade 'unpleasant and conflictful'. The invasion of July and August is deeply resented despite the economic rewards it brings, and the retreat of September is greeted with manifestations of relief.

Fuenterrabia threatens to become indistinguishable from any other Spanish resort. If this comes about something irrecoverable will have been lost, something that we might describe as the sense of cultural identity. A once cohesive community has been fragmented into a number of alienated and competing groups. A community that was largely self-sufficient with a clearly defined sense of the limited way in which it related to the outside world is now exposed and vulnerable. It must now be related to an exploitative world system from which it can only disconnect by sacrificing its new prosperity. It must relate to this world system in an atmosphere 'suffused with anxiety and a general sense of frustration': what is required is nothing less than a revolution in outlook, in conditions of unprecedented stress and confusion. The affluence tourism provides is not accompanied by any sense of security since the industry is peculiarly susceptible to sudden and unpredictable changes of taste and direction. The fate of Fuenterrabia's economy is dependent on the fantasy life of an alien bourgeoisie:

> If the tourists should decide to move on to Asturias or Galicia, the entire pattern of growth would come to an end. The farmers are aware of this. Springtime is a period of worry and quiet conversation about the probabilities of the tourists' return. Every year there is a genuine doubt, despite the fact that thus far this has always been shortly converted into relief.

'And what shall become of us without the Barbarians?' – they may be offensive, vulgar, ignorant, but they are 'a kind of solution' – which provides an answer to the question of economic development, but in a way that discourages the creation of a more stable basis for development, which is suited to the cultural and psychological needs of local people. The tourists may continue to arrive each summer in the expected numbers, but the industry's machinery, having built on the initiative of the local people, now threatens to exclude the majority of them from the growing profits. Then, 'what will become of us?'

13 The Marketing of Moscow

Mobility and politics have always been linked to some extent. Thomas Cook, for instance, saw nothing wrong with taking over 1,500 travellers to a Paris working-men's demonstration in 1861. Many of the early rambling movements were linked with left of centre groups. The German *Naturfreunde* groups were originally formed in 1895 by the Social Democrats. In Britain, disputes over the rights of way over traditional paths could escalate into pitched battles between the employees of the landed aristocracy and left-wingers from nearby slums as late as the 1930s.[1]

Today, though, the prevailing ideology of tourism is neo-colonialist. The industry assumes that host countries should be moulded to the desires of the rich, tourist-generating super powers. There are some bizarre examples of this thinking. Anthony Haden-Guest, for instance, visited Edgar Rice Burroughs Inc., the empire built on the collected adventures of Tarzan. They unveiled plans to him for opening a series of Tarzan villages, with an African, back to nature theme – a sort of Club Méditerranée with leopard skins. Of course, they suggested, they would have to find some places with no law enforcement at all. A boggling Haden-Guest took up this theme. Why not, he suggested, a state of Tarzana with their own coinage and stamps? 'Don't laugh!' he was admonished: 'This is not just pie in the sky. We've been talking to the Rothschild Bank in Paris about this. There are a number of very, very small African countries which have absolutely nothing. No economy, no nothing . . . and the thought is to merchandise the whole country. . . . Take it over! Change the name and just take the resort ideas on a national scale, so the entire country is run as a . . . *beautiful place.*'[2] The spokesman went further: Gambia, the tiny West African state, was under active consideration. Should such a scheme come off, then they would form Air Tarzan, flying planes with zebra-striped tails, which would jet incoming adventurers to a land of 'beautiful girls in the various Lost, Hidden and Forbidden Cities . . . the barely attainable utopia once only reached by arduous swinging through the unspoilt jungle . . .'.[3] One imagines what Evelyn Waugh would have made of such a scheme.

Elsewhere, the ideology of the tourist empires is more overtly political. Haden-Guest went on to look at the American end of the Hilton empire. He came across the saying of Conrad Hilton himself. There was his prayer: '*America on its knees*, not beaten there by hammer and sickle, but *freely, intelligently, reasonably, confidently, powerfully.*' There was his belief that: 'As I see it, we are sharing the benefits of the American system abroad.' And that: 'Each of our hotels is a little America.'[4]

Hilton's successor, Curt Strand, has updated the gospel. He is less strong on the wonders of capitalism, instead stressing the psychological needs of Third World countries: 'Building a Hilton has an enormous effect, because it says to the local people and the world at large that we are now part of a world-wide picture . . . worthy of *Modern Times.*' Strand goes on to tell how he was once rebuked by a man from the Ford Foundation for advising a Third World government to build a costly hotel, instead of hospitals, schools or sewers. Strand argued they'd prefer the hotel, claiming: 'We are newly independent and we want some of the fruits of that now. It will take 100 years before we have enough sewers. And the hotel will bring in people and even some foreign exchange, won't it?'[5]

Many aspects of the international end of Hiltons (part of Trans World Airlines) remind one that one is dealing with an empire in its own political right. Its advertisements trumpet that 'The Nairobi Hilton is the tallest building in the country', implying 'Lucky Kenya'. A couple of years back, during a conference on Caribbean tourism, a Hilton manager was debating the issue of whether giant hotels actually benefit the local economy. Some speakers preferred small, locally-owned guest houses. Finally he could take it no longer. 'Without Hilton,' he claimed, 'most of these islands would just dry up and blow away.'

Such imperial assumptions are found elsewhere in the industry. Cruise companies tell their clients to come cruising in the Caribbean, which they imperiously call 'our sea'. Another cruise ad. listed an itinerary of Caribbean islands possessing some of the loveliest hotels in the area: 'Where we go,' it stated, 'the ship is the only place to stay.'[6] Again, the bland arrogance of such companies is caught in a quote from sex-magnate Bob Guccione (of *Penthouse* fame), who was called in to run a casino and advise on a tourist complex to be built on the Yugoslav island of Krk (after Hugh Hefner had decided against helping the Yugoslavs start up their own sex-magazine). Commenting on the problems of doing business with this reasonably relaxed communist state, he was quoted as saying: 'The workers' council is a joke. They've agreed to everything we want to do. They're really anxious to learn our business tactics. They bent the rules as much as they could to let us in. The Yugoslavs are really ideological soulmates.'[7] The days of the gun-boat are over. A phalanx of scantily clad 'bunnies' or 'pets' will now do the job just as well.

However pliant the host governments actually are, some form of coercion is still necessary. After all, a company can lose a lot of money if the host government cannot produce a relaxed atmosphere at its end. There is a crucial difference between a traditional firm exporting, say, a tractor and a tour operator. The former could not give a damn if the tractors it sells are left rusting in the fields because there are no skilled mechanics to maintain them. On the other hand, the tour operator loses valuable repeat business if his clients are bored to death through a general lack of night-life, or are delayed unnecessarily at badly equipped airports. To counter such problems, the industry has a tradition of putting political pressure on host governments, in a way which is much more organised than in most other industries.

They express their wishes through lobbies like IFTO (International Federation of Tour Operators), TOSG (Tour Operators Study Group), and LOCG (Long-haul Tour Operators Consultative Group). These trade bodies think nothing of flying a delegation to a host country to complain about its airports, tax structure or general inefficiency. LOGC, for instance, visited the Tanzanian tourist authorities to complain about the deterioration of that country's standards.[8] IFTO sent a delegation to Majorca to complain about the airport there, and the Spanish authorities promised immediate action.[9] Elsewhere, the pressure has been on taxes. TOSG succeeded in 1972 in getting the Greeks to delay tax increases on hotel bills. The previous year a TOSG delegation asked the Tunisians to end currency declaration restrictions, to improve airport facilities, to install an official classification system for hotels and to end overbooking. They returned the next year to find the authorities had given way on all counts.[10]

Of course, no country is forced to give in to such pressure, but they are faced with a flexible industry, which can easily divert its business to neighbouring countries. Even industrialised nations find themselves under such pressures. For instance, in 1973, the American charter airline Trans International Airlines was unhappy with the charter regulations found in Britain, Germany and other European countries. They decided to land their transatlantic customers in Brussels, since the Belgian regulations were much more relaxed. They were also considering whether to deal with equally flexible Spain. This is what commercial leverage is all about. Companies which do not like one country's regulations will base their activities where they do like them. No industry is more flexible than tourism.

Sometimes such leverage is applied for political ends. Some of Castro's most vocal and dangerous opponents were the hotel and gambling interests he displaced in his revolution. When Mexico expropriated foreign oil companies in the 1930s, Standard Oil of New Jersey (now Exxon/Esso) ran a campaign urging Americans not to holiday there. However, most tourist destinations are right-of-centre, so the political pressure comes from the Left. For a long time it was not respectable for left-wingers to holiday in Spain, scene of the dreadful civil war of the 1930s. The Greek military coup of 1967 created a similar backlash and, for two seasons, the number of incoming tourists actually fell below pre-coup levels. In part this merely reflected tourist worries about their safety, but it was noticeable that two other fascist countries, Spain and Portugal, were the only places which provided more tourists during the year of the coup. On the other hand, the Swedes and Norwegians observed Scandinavia's traditional liberal principles and boycotted the new régime in a major way. As late as 1970, only a third of the numbers of pre-coup days were going to Greece from these two countries. Travel from France and Italy, with two particularly strong communist parties, was also strongly affected.

Ultimately the average tourist is pretty apolitical concerning the countries he visits. This is mostly because tourists are relatively prosperous and, therefore, intrinsically conservative. Social issues do not worry them too much. All they generally want is a comfortable hotel, reasonable food, scenery and weather, and something to do at night. It is this latter requirement which is most likely to turn a tourist off left-wing destinations, like Eastern Europe, China and Tanzania, since such régimes find it hard to reconcile the more tawdry aspects of tourism with the goals of their government. The running of casinos, nightclubs or prostitution is not normally thought as fit for socialist planning. On the other hand, they do not want to let private entrepreneurs step in, as this would be a form of capitalism. Because of this, holidays in such left-wing countries are often relatively boring to the average tourist. However, despite this, there is a growing interest in communist destinations – Russia, in particular. The Soviet authorities are actively encouraging this. One wonders if they really know what they are doing.

No one has to teach East European governments about the political implications of unrestricted travel. The Berlin Wall stands as a monument to the suppressed travel urges of the East Germans. Those East Europeans who are allowed to travel to the West normally have to leave a spouse or child behind as a kind of hostage.

Even here, however, the desire for travel cannot be forever stifled. All East European countries have their own holiday areas: Lake Balaton in Hungary, the Black Sea resorts of Romania, Bulgaria, and Soviet Russia, the Carpathian mountains in Czechoslovakia, Yugoslavia's Dalmatian coast, Poland's Baltic resorts. The more privileged East Europeans will have visited many of these, since national boundaries within the region are being steadily lowered. Even so, the more orthodox communist governments of Romania and Bulgaria are still somewhat wary of letting their citizens holiday in the more ideologically relaxed Yugoslavia.

A fine example of the pent-up demand came in 1972 when the Poles and East Germans dropped all formalities for travel between the two nations. They devised an imaginative scheme which abolished the need for passports and visas between the two countries and allowed their citizens to buy what they wanted in the other country. The result was impressive. Nine million Poles crossed into East Germany within ten months, while 6·3 million East Germans went the other way. This was over a third of the latter's population and is the equivalent of some 20 million Britons going to France, or some 70 million Americans popping across the border into Mexico. The planners were taken aback, particularly when the heavy Polish purchases of goods from the more sophisticated East German stores threatened a balance of payments crisis. The East Germans, while glad of the increased chance of travel, started getting restive as the Poles bought up everything in sight (lack of consumer goods in Polish stores had been an important factor in the pre-Christmas Polish riots of 1970). Chronic Polish–German antagonisms started reviving with the Germans telling jokes like: 'Why do they play the Polish national anthem every two hours in East German department stores? – So that we can do our shopping while the Poles stand to attention.' The authorities hastily slapped currency quotas back on

the Poles, and everyone hoped that the breaking-down of international tensions via travel could continue. Whatever the problems,
the experiment showed that East Europeans respond even more
enthusiastically than westerners to the chance of foreign travel –
starting from a much more restricted base, admittedly.[11]

One sign of general East–West détente has been the increasing
enthusiasm with which various East European countries have been
encouraging western tourists. Yugoslavia is the prime such destination, though Romania and Bulgaria have also built large businesses
with the West on Black Sea resorts like Mamaia and Golden Sands.
Even secretive Albania allows in some thousand group tourists
annually, though the border guards zealously trim visitors' beards and
hair, while relieving them of most books and subversive fashions like
flared trousers and mini-skirts.[12] At one time, foreigners could only
come in as tourists if they were willing to spend part of their visit
working in the fields.

None of these governments is particularly happy with their
dependence on non-communist tourists, but they need the hard
currency these foreigners bring. This is of growing importance as the
Eastern bloc tries to increase its imports of advanced western technology. It is becoming embarrassingly clear how little it has got to
offer in exchange, so tourism has come as a god-send. One Soviet
study shows that the profit from one tourist is equivalent to that
from the export of nine tons of coal, fifteen tons of oil or two tons of
grain. If the tourist potential of Lake Baikal were exploited, it would
earn twice as much hard currency as the total export of oil from the
USSR – and tourist attractions are a non-depleting resource.[13]

A particularly ingenious source of hard currency is the emigré
community in western countries. Warsaw claims, for instance, that
there are 9 million people of Polish descent living in the capitalist
world: over half the 313,000 western visitors to Poland in 1971 were
of Polish origin. East European governments have therefore switched
policies. From the vicious attacks on emigrés made in the Cold War
period, the emphasis is now on the active support of organisations
aimed at identifying and wooing them. One goal in Poland is to
increase the repatriation of elderly emigrés. They are allowed to
remit their pension and earnings from the West, are given favourable
rates of exchange, are permitted to buy one-family houses in advance
of coming back, and can keep external accounts to which they can
transfer their assets, which can be used in any way they please. This

is a privilege offered no other category of private citizen in Eastern Europe. Apparently several thousand elderly people have shown interest in this scheme, which shows how far this government will go in its search for western currencies. Romania has a different scheme whereby emigrés can buy their Romanian relatives to the head of the housing queue by putting down deposits in precious hard currencies. Hungary has found its sons in the film industries of the West have been very useful in setting up profitable co-productions on Hungarian soil.[14]

The most fascinating tourist destination is Russia, which currently receives around 2·5 million tourists a year. Seventy per cent of these are from Eastern Europe, with the Finns, West Germans, Americans and Japanese leading the non-communists.[15] Growing numbers of westerners are starting to be brought in on package tours jointly organised by western operators and Intourist, the state-owned tourist organisation. The costs can be ridiculously low, like £32–£47 for three- and four-night trips to Moscow and Leningrad (1973 season). The operators have been having to turn clients away.

The strains are starting to show in Russia, which is trying to keep the industry under a control tight enough not to exacerbate the growing tensions in Soviet society. For instance, the Intourist machine is essential in keeping tourists in check, but this is extremely wasteful of scarce manpower. Even in 1972, Intourist needed 20,000 linguists to act as guides, a figure which has to increase to at least 30,000 by 1975. There is also obvious concern about how the expected 10 million tourists of 1980 can still be treated in the privileged way existing ones are. Intourist groups can jump the lengthy queue at Lenin's tomb: can get access to private beaches along the Black Sea: get special service at restaurants: can buy goods unavailable to domestic Russians at special 'foreign currency only' stores. Intourist now refers to these stores as 'temporary', but it is clear that Russian authorities have got some major ideological problems to handle in the future.

The bulk of this considerable number of tourists will still want to go primarily to Moscow and Leningrad, and the authorities will find it difficult to divert them to other parts of the country, where uncontrolled contacts with soviet citizens will be less easy to engineer. Currently, though, most visitors are satisfied with trips to the Bolshoi Ballet, the Moscow State Circus, the Moscow underground, and the Winter Palace in Leningrad, but it is clear that they are starting to demand more. For one thing, the Soviet authorities will have to get the general efficiency of hotels, restaurants and domestic transport closer to western standards of service and safety. This would strain the supply of experienced personnel, even without the massive hotel building campaign which is just starting to get off the ground. The West can help in the design of the necessary facilities, as in October 1973, when it was announced that Occidental Petroleum would help the Russians design and supervise a $125 million hotel, convention and trade centre in Moscow. The West could also help in training the hotel staff who will be needed, since it is clear that there are few Russian hoteliers with the kind of standards which come second nature to the Swiss. One answer would be to send batches of trainees to some of the better Swiss hotel schools, or else to set up their own training schools with the help of western-trained instructors.

More seriously, the Russians are going to have to come to terms with the increasing mobility of the tourists they are receiving. These tourists will want to break free of the limitations of the standard package holidays, by hiring cars and driving round the country by themselves. There are obvious limits to this development, since the language barriers are particularly serious, given the country's Cyrillic script. However, the numbers of tourists seeking independent holidays will increase, and one wonders just how ready the soviet system is to cope with this phenomenon.

We can already see from the treatment handed out to dissidents like Solzhenitzyn, Sakharov and Medvedev that the soviet authorities are having problems in handling internal critics. Tourism can only mean that these people will find it all the easier to meet sympathetic westerners, receive foreign publications, and get help and ideas from outside Russia. Even now, the Soviets are finding it difficult to stop people from smuggling controversial manuscripts out of the country for publication in the West. The growth of western tourism will help such tactics, and will increase the number of people in the West who will campaign on behalf of dissidents who fall foul of the Soviet authorities. As long as the USSR cares about western opinion, tourism will strengthen the hand of internal critics of the soviet system. There is, moreover, the further danger for the authorities, that the incoming tourists will trigger the demand within Russia for the reciprocal freedom to travel to the West – a demand which will be increasingly difficult to counter as the number of western tourists continues to grow. Unless the Russian government suddenly decides to liberalise, it is difficult to see how they can accept these demands. There is nothing more dangerous than to arouse expectations which one cannot fulfil.

Foreign critics of the soviet system will also find tourism a major aid. Muckraking journalists and television crews will find it much easier to report on the dark sides of soviet society. Already there are cases where tourism has helped investigators pierce the barriers of military dictatorships. The British documentary television programme *World in Action* has been involved with a continuing exposé of the use of torture in all parts of the world. Its crews have been banned from entering countries like Spain, Turkey and Chile, but they have got round this by entering as individual tourists. They have recorded their interviews on high-class tourist ciné cameras, which are even small enough for them to be smuggled into prisons for inmates to record statements. At some stage, foreign TV crews will start the same kind of investigations within Russia, and this will add a new channel by which internal protests will find a world audience.

There is evidence that East European governments are well aware of the tight-rope they are walking. There is normally a *de facto* segregation of tourist destinations by which different nationalities are put in different hotels or even resorts. To be fair, this is not always a formal policy: the westerners will tend to have more money, and can thus afford the most expensive hotels and resorts. One finds similar segregation amongst Spanish resorts, where the local Spaniards find the major towns too expensive in high season.

The Romanians have tightened up their legislation requiring local citizens to report conversations with foreigners (there is no particular evidence that this is strictly obeyed). Hungary is moving in the direction of actively restraining the expansion of foreign tourism, viewing it as a distinct ideological menace. Ultimately, though, these governments are trapped. It is virtually impossible to run an authoritarian society open to foreign travellers, unless one is in absolute control of one's citizens. The major explosions in Czechoslovakia (1968) and Hungary (1956), and the lesser one in Poland (1970), would suggest few East European governments can be confident that they have got the necessary solid, ideological backing throughout their societies. Foreign influence can thus be dangerous. Even the relaxation of tension between the two Germanies is posing problems for the East Germans: relaxation of *autobahn* travel has led to an increase of escape attempts to West Germany.

Domestic Soviet politics remain an enigma. One cannot prove that Solzhenitzyn and the other dissidents are representative of anything but a small minority, but even in this limited role, they are a severe embarrassment to Russia in the internal arena, and tourism can only strengthen their symbolic importance in world affairs. Since the Soviet Union seems convinced that it needs the foreign exchange from tourism, one would expect certain precautions to be taken to limit the industry's impact. If anything, though, it looks as though the authorities are building it up in exactly the wrong way. At the moment, the bulk of the tourists make for the big cities, which is exactly where they will meet lots of ordinary Soviet citizens. Rather, the government should, for self-preservation, be trying to build up an industry like Spain's, where the foreign tourists are packed into 'Golden Ghettos' well away from the main centres of population. They might find this difficult since their best beaches on the Black Sea are a long way from northern Europe, but their existing policy could be doomed for disaster. Unless they are exceptionally careful, tourism will bring them trouble both at home and abroad.

This may all seem to run contrary to the oft expressed platitude that international understanding will come through world travel. This assumes that the more a tourist gets to know a society, the more sympathetic he will grow to it: but this is a very dubious assumption. In the case of Russia, it is very difficult to see the authorities wanting to (or being able to) liberalise their society fast enough to impress western travellers. Non-Russian tourist managers also wonder if Soviet planners will be able to cut through the red tape fast enough to get standards of service and general entertainment nearer those found in western tourist destinations. As it is, the Russian authorities should take pause from the fact that many of the current group tours to Russia end with spontaneous cheers from the tourists as the aircraft finally take off from Moscow airport at the end of the holiday.

All the signs, therefore, are that tourism will be a major destabilising force within Eastern Europe.

14 Thirty-Year Vacations: Tourist as Victim

> We turned out beautiful ads because Portugal is a great place to do ads for. We were very careful not to mention Salazar or the fact that if you did something wrong in Portugal you could have the world's first thirty-year vacation.
>
> Jerry Femina, iconoclastic Madison Avenue executive[1]

Inevitably, some of the dreams turn sour, with tourists finding not relaxation and stimulation, but disease, prison, or even death. This is a logical by-product of an industry which meets people's desire for novelty and isolation by depositing them, overconfident, into the midst of some of the world's most fragile and intolerant societies. In most cases, nothing happens, and the tourist remains blissfully unaware of the tensions building up around him. For instance, few people staying at the Bali Beach Hotel at Denpasar in that 'Tourist Paradise', Bali, are aware that in 1966, at the time of the communal troubles in Indonesia, 300 out of the 1,000 then-employees disappeared and were presumed killed.[2]

Elsewhere, however, the tourist himself becomes a victim of such murderous impulses, like the twenty-two foreigners murdered in St Croix in the US Virgin Islands in the course of fourteen months during 1972 and 1973,[3] or the tourists gunned down in Tel Aviv's Lod airport in 1972, victims of general Middle Eastern divisions.

These cases are not merely sensational, but point to one of tourism's basic contradictions, which is that however much a tourist is willing to pay for a regression to a childlike summer (destroyed elsewhere), the industry cannot really deliver the goods. A belief that the sun always shines and that one's desires can be gratified is the stuff of daydreams, not the real world. There are few places left where money can still buy unquestioning servility, but the industry cannot admit this, preferring a conspiracy to maintain a cocoon of unreality round the tourists. In truth, though, this plot often fails, since however servile the waiters, and however hot the sun, the real world of hunger, envy and disease is extremely hard to blot out.

This need not entirely surprise us since leisure itself is generally dangerous. The French sociologist, Dumazedier, for instance, claims that there are twice as many accidents in July and August as there are in January and February.[4] What seems to be happening is that leisure increases our mobility, while decreasing our inhibitions and humility. Mountaineers have an ever wider choice of targets to climb, but fail to wear sturdy boots and clothes. Marinas multiply, but yachtsmen and swimmers forget that tides and storms can still kill. Car drivers push themselves to the limits of exhaustion and fall asleep at the wheel. A friend has even seen someone trampled to death trying to feed croissants to a wild elephant in East Africa. Leisure tempts one to lower one's guard. This can be fatal.

Sex, the fourth of tourism's '4 S's', can be dangerous, particularly to the large number of tourists who see a holiday as a way of getting away from puritanical pressure at home to destinations filled with sexual promise. People like the clients of Mexican brothels, or the girl student in a *Time* survey of teenage sex who told a sex-counsellor: 'My virginity was such a burden to me that I just went out to get rid of it. On a trip to Greece, I found any old Greek and did it so it wouldn't be an issue any more.'[5] However, greater variety of sexual experience means a higher chance of catching some form of venereal disease, and tourists are no more immune from this than all those other high-risk mobile groups like airline pilots and hostesses, commercial travellers, sailors and lorry drivers. A 1956 British study showed that of 6,000 men with gonorrhoea, nearly 40 per cent had 'itinerant occupations' and, though not yet an occupation, tourism is definitely itinerant.

It is difficult to say exactly how much of the current boom in sexually transmitted diseases relates to tourism itself, since the Pill and a general loosening of inhibitions are obviously other important factors. An official British study of the 1960s did, though, show that nearly 20 per cent of syphilis infections were contracted abroad – a proportion which was rising fast. A doctor at one clinic was quoted as saying: 'Modern holiday travel is having a big effect. A lot of young people go on holiday to some romantic Mediterranean place, meet someone, have a romantic situation, that ends with intercourse, and then come back infected.' Another doctor pointed out the difficulties in keeping track of such infections when you can have a patient contracting gonorrhoea in Fiji, noticing the symptoms at the airport in New York, then asking for treatment in London – all within 72 hours.[6]

Some tourist destinations go out of their way to minimise such dangers. A study of prostitute bars in a Mexican border town showed just how closely the Mexican authorities supervised them.

The prostitutes were not only registered but given a weekly medical examination and injection of penicillin. Those found infected are banned from working until cured. Each bar in the sector favoured by Americans has a prophylactic nurse who inspects customers for potential infection.[7] There are still, however, a number of destinations which are sold at least partly on their sexual reputations. We have already mentioned Air France's campaign for Tahiti, while the Seychelles islands go further by actively billing themselves as 'The islands of love', which is fair enough since their citizens do have a genuine tradition of guiltless promiscuity but, as a recent guide explains: 'The VD-rate in the Seychelles is high. It has been described as "rampant" and "ferocious". Which is not surprising in view of the promiscuity. One observer has quoted a medical services report as stating that nearly every male in the islands averages four to five gonorrhoea infections in a lifetime.'[8]

One can see this as justified retribution on us, the descendants of the classical explorers like Captain Cook whose crews left a trail of syphilis and gonorrhoea through the paradises they discovered. The Hawaiians, for instance, greeted Cook's expedition as friends. 'No women I ever met', wrote Cook, 'were less reserved, with no other view than to make a surrender of their persons.'[9] But this generosity was repaid with venereal diseases, measles and tuberculosis and the population which Cook estimated at 400,000 in the 1770s had shrunk to 56,897 in 1872.[10] Nothing likely to happen to contemporary tourists can be adequate recompense for the excesses of this era.

Holiday health problems do not stop with sex, since the industry progressively pushes its customers into some of the world's poorest and unhealthiest destinations. The tourist is immediately exposed to a range of diseases which have either been eradicated in his home country or else are new, exotic ones peculiar to tropical destinations. The results can be sometimes tragic and, in many cases, tour operators and host country authorities can be blamed for playing down the risks involved in order to protect their business. Author Patrick Rivers has listed some of the less expected health hazards facing the tourist, ranging from the stress linked to jet-lag, to diseases like typhoid, cholera, dysentery, brucellosis, hepatitis, worms, malaria, filaria and sleeping sickness.[11] This is a frightening list, but it is only too easy to find examples of tourists catching them. One thinks of the foreigners who caught cholera in the 1973 Naples epidemic; the Manchester lady who died of anthrax after a holiday in Tunisia; the elderly passenger travelling to Australia who died after a flight which merely stopped over in Bahrain, then a cholera-infested area. Even journalists are not exempt. Perrott Phillips of London's *Daily Mail* almost died of malignant tertiary malaria (the most virulent form of this disease) after a mini-safari holiday in Tanzania. In describing his frightening experience, he wrote of the unwillingness of the authorities to stress such dangers. The government rushes out warning leaflets when the hazards in certain areas get noticeably severe, but feels its responsibility ends there. Industry officials tend to say that such warnings are 'alarmism', claiming that 'emphasising health risks destroys the holiday atmosphere which brochures strive to create'.[12]

Quite so. This kind of reaction is found all round the world. The 1973 typhoid scare in Florida, for instance, resulted from the discovery that Miami Beach's public water supply contained a disturbing amount of *E. coli* bacteria, a sure sign that the water had been contaminated by human sewage. It was suggested that residents should boil all water, but the City Manager absolutely refused to have the word 'contaminated' used as a description of his water supplies.[13]

Such cover-ups can, though, take place on a much wider and more serious level. Cholera has, for instance, been moving westwards from Asia since the late 1960s and, by 1970, had officially hit crisis levels in Russia, Libya, Israel and the Lebanon. Officials at the World Health Organisation, however, claimed that a number of governments were not reporting that they, too, were suffering from this dread disease. Despite this, WHO was being asked for vaccine from Saudi Arabia, Congo Brazzaville, South Yemen, Sierra Leone, Algeria and Liberia. The following year the disease hit Spain, but the authorities dismissed it euphemistically as 'summer diarrhoea', as they innoculated 2 million Spaniards against cholera.[14]

Even the act of swimming can be dangerous where local authorities have neither the money nor power to enforce tight standards on local polluters. The main danger comes from the inadequate disposal of sewage (often the tourist's own), since most resorts have historically used the cheapest way of disposal – dumping it in the sea. Over recent years concern has been growing rapidly about this practice, particularly in those resorts where the sewage has visibly floated back on to the swimmers (the classic complaint came from the man who wrote to the tourist authorities in Spain claiming that the sewage off one beach was so bad 'that it is impossible to swim, one merely goes through the motions').[15] Even with full treatment in plants, millions of intestinal bacteria will be left in a pint of effluent, and Patrick Rivers cites a 1971 study suggesting that swimmers in the most polluted areas are three times more likely to catch a range of diseases than non-swimmers.[16] These need not be fatal, but enteritis and typhoid can be transmitted through such water. The death of one six-year-old girl who swam in polluted waters led to the formation of the Coastal Anti-Pollution League in Britain, which is dedicated to ending sewage pollution.

This problem is found all over the world. In Hawaii, for instance, the authorities have promised to build a £70 million sewage treatment plant near Honolulu. The danger, however, is highest in the Mediterranean which has virtually no tides and thus lacks the oceans' self-cleansing action. Italy is probably the worst offender on this inland sea, having a chaotic overlapping of official jurisdictions, which means that preventive action is often not taken until it is far too late. For instance, the Italian government knew that the Bay of Naples was a health hazard well before the 1973 cholera outbreak. Early in that year, it was calculated that the Bay was five times as polluted as the (high) national average. Virtually nothing, however, was done about this. As a result, people died of cholera.

It is no wonder, then, that Patrick Rivers suggests that future tourist brochures should bear the warning: 'Caution. Holidays abroad can damage your health.'[17] He would be supported by an investigation in the British consumer magazine *Which?* This found that only one in ten travel agents warned investigators to take precautions against typhoid, polio or malaria for holidays in Tunisia. An examination of the brochures of thirty-five travel firms, some offering exotic holidays in Africa and the Caribbean, showed that none suggested precautions should be taken against diseases like smallpox, cholera and yellow-fever, for which compulsory vaccinations are sometimes needed. Other less obvious, but equally real, health hazards were ignored. Facts about the real world are not allowed to intrude on the fantasies of the tourists.

Tourist operators also minimise the chances of accidents. These can, in fact, be high, whether one drives or flies. The more exotic or dreamlike the destination, the higher the risks are. This is not surprising since skills like disciplined driving take generations to diffuse through inexperienced societies, and travellers are not prepared for roads in countries where cars are still novelties. The Yugoslavs, for instance, claim that the Zagreb–Belgrade motorway is the most dangerous road in Europe. Whether that's true or not, it is still sobering to see burned out, wrecked cars all along it, with little crosses bearing witness to the dangers of mixing badly-lit local farm traffic, with trans-European juggernaut lorries, holiday-makers racing for Greece, and migrant workers returning to Turkey.

However, the cult of the touring holiday is strongly rooted, and holiday-makers press ever further into territories far less used to cars – and the legends abound. One hears of drivers running people down and then being lynched by local villagers (Turkey); of countries where one is advised by embassy officials to get over the border if one has a serious accident; even cases of armed ambush (Nigeria and Zaïre in the aftermath of their Civil Wars). On a less dramatic scale, automobile touring bodies cite the increased accident rates found the closer tourists get to ferries crossing stretches of water like the English Channel. Drivers are tired and in a hurry, thus taking that last fatal risk.

Flying is no more reassuring for airlines' safety records took a turn for the worse in 1971, after twenty years of steady improvement. 1972 saw a virtual doubling of the number of passengers killed (2,214 in the year), while 1973 was even worse. Obviously, one must be fair to the airline industry which does go to extraordinary lengths to discover the causes of accidents so as to eradicate them. This recent drop in standards, however, has been accompanied by expressions of worry from a number of people in the industry, particularly pilots and air-controllers. It looks as if the industry has moved too fast into countries which are not capable of running an airport or maintaining an airline to the standard that western tourists deem acceptable. This would not matter too much, but the tourist industry has a vested interest in developing holidays based on relatively inefficient airfields. Increasing protectionism by host countries means that greater proportions of tourists will be flown in locally controlled aircraft. The tourist is not informed that there is a greater risk involved.

The statistics are clear. *Flight International* studied the safety records of fifteen countries over ten years. The safest record was enjoyed by Dutch aircraft which had not had a single fatal casualty between 1963 and 1972, followed by Australia with two deaths. By flying with the eleventh safest country, Japan, the chance of violent death rose thirteen-fold over the Australian record: fifteen-fold for

France; twenty-five-fold for India; and an unnamed Middle Eastern country's aircraft raised one's chances seventy-nine-fold.[18]

However, with growing East–West travel, the most disturbing case is Russia, which has recently had a disastrous safety record, but is intensely secretive both about announcing accidents and publishing their causes. In the course of six months in 1972, Aeroflot, the state airline which claims to be the world's largest, had at least three (possibly four) major crashes, including what was then the world's worst, which killed 176 people. In addition, the record of Soviet-made planes was bad; the previous worst crash had involved an Ilyushin operated by the East Germans. The dire record continued in 1973 when, by July, Russian airlines and Soviet-manufactured planes had contributed over a fifth of the world's air accidents and deaths.

The Soviet record is symptomatic of the kind of safety problems we are now running up against. National pride is such that governments find it hard admitting accidents that western diplomats are sure have occurred. It is even harder trying to discuss the causes of such accidents. And yet if the relatively rich, sophisticated Soviet Union has such a dire record, what hope is there for the airlines of the Third World, which are already providing a disproportionate share of the accidents? Industry officials are profoundly worried about these new dangers.

Something over half of all today's air accidents occur in the approach and landing phases of flights, and pilots claim that the bulk of these stem from 'airfield deficiencies', caused by inadequate expenditure on landing aids in many parts of the world. Even within the USA, the US Airline Pilots Association claimed that in 1973 90 per cent of US airports did not have instrument landing systems and other aids for precision landings. Such shortages increase the chance of landing accidents by about ten, and the shortage of such aids in other parts of the world is far worse.[19]

The industry in Europe has, for instance, long been fighting to get the standard raised at various airports which are little more than death-traps; and these are normally in the heart of the tourist belt. The British Air Line Pilots Association set up an Airfield Deficiency Group in 1970 to campaign against totally inadequate airports at Gerona (on Spain's Costa Brava), Nicosia (Cyprus), Alghero (Sardinia) and Palermo (Sicily). More recently, the Italian pilots waged a boycott against sixteen Italian airports which they feel are dangerous. They want to close two of them permanently – Naples and Palermo.

Italian and British pilots are not alone in such protests. The International Federation of Air Line Pilots seriously considered a total ban on flights to and from India in 1973 after accidents and numerous near-misses at New Delhi and Calcutta airports. The problems were basically to do with the Indian navigational aids giving out the wrong information; one pilot claimed he had had fifteen or twenty experiences of Indian aids going wrong. More sinisterly, though, the pilots were also concerned with the working conditions of Indian air controllers. Local newspapers had reported cases of such officers having heart attacks because of stress and fatigue. This is a problem found nearer home.[20]

Air traffic controllers are the people most directly hit by the increasingly heavy demands of mass air travel. All round the world, their systems seem to be cracking under the strain. The West German controllers spent most of 1973 on a costly go-slow aimed at the government. Calling for a major reorganisation of the whole air-traffic control system, they carried out a survey which showed there had been at least 100 near-misses in German airspace in the course of two months in 1972.[21] Their British opposite numbers were also showing signs of strain, made worse by official blunders over the choice of computer systems to back them. A human relations study showed that in 1973 nearly 90 per cent of British controllers were dissatisfied with the equipment they were using and 50 per cent said their working conditions created severe fatigue and tension problems. The worst European air-traffic control disaster, however, took place in France (in March 1973) where the French controllers went on strike. The military authorities were called in only to steer two Spanish airliners into each other over Nantes.

These passengers were unlucky, but the French situation is an example of how the whole system can come to the verge of falling apart. The skies of that country are the crossroads of Europe's tourist traffic, as Scandinavians, Germans, Belgians, Dutch and British make for the sun of Spain, Portugal, Italy and North Africa. At least 60 per cent of the traffic passing across France will not land there, so the French authorities have had no great incentive to expand their facilities. Quite justifiably, they are now getting money from each over-flight to help expand the air-traffic control system but the expansion of the Spanish industry will continue to keep the

French system fully stretched. Problems are also caused by the fact that there is no one authority capable of revolutionising the whole European system, which is too heavily dominated by national air-traffic control systems jealously guarding their own interests. A body called Eurocontrol is trying to get control of all European airspace over 25,000 feet, but the authorities are hard pushed to keep up with the overall surge in air travel.

Such conventional dangers, though, are no longer all the traveller faces. To hazards like birds, military aircraft and mechanical failure should be added the risk of hijacking. This symbolises the tourist's growing vulnerability to strictly political hazards. Actually, not many people have died through such attempts, though one is obviously horrified to see official summaries of an accident putting it down to 'loss of control – crew shot by passenger'. On the whole, precautions seem to have paid off, though there was the Aeroflot crash of May 1973 which crashed during an onboard gunfight killing some hundred people. More sinisterly, there was the Israeli shooting down of the Libyan Boeing in February 1973, after it had strayed into Israeli airspace. Another 108 people died.[22] It is hard to decide whether one is more saddened by this destruction of an innocent aircraft or by the twenty-five tourists gunned down by the Japanese suicide team in Lod Airport. Travellers have become pawns in international disputes which have little to do with their making. In today's wars, though, pawns are expendable.

Finally, if you are killed, your relatives are likely to be cheated of adequate compensation by some of the most cynically composed small print to be found in commercial negotiations anywhere. In most activities where one is killed or injured through someone else's negligence, one can sue and have a chance of getting injury payments proportionate to one's status, potential loss of earnings, etc. Not so with the airlines. They saw early that the crash of a plane-load of wealthy passengers could bankrupt whole airlines, so way back in 1929, they clubbed together in an agreement known as the Warsaw Convention to limit the amount of their liability for deaths and injuries incurred on international flights. They settled on 125,000 French gold francs, doubled the figure in 1955, and have allowed inflation to eat into this figure since then. There has been an attempt to raise the limit to $120,000, a derisory figure when Americans and many Europeans or Japanese would value their lives in the millions of dollars, should they suffer accidents in their home countries. Of course, one can see the viewpoint of the airlines who shudder to think of what the cost of a fully laden Jumbo jet could be to them if it crashed. On the other hand, by making it impossible to take an international flight without first signing away one's rights to hold the company fully responsible for the negligence of its employees, is to deny the consumer a right of considerable importance.

Even if the tourist does not die in transit, he will be robbed and cheated upon arrival. The tourist is one of the world's natural victims.

His dangers start at the airports, which, all round the globe, attract some of the world's most daring criminals. In most of them, luggage loaders have found ways to plunder likely looking suitcases and packages. In London's Heathrow Airport, they look particularly for the luggage of Japanese travellers (packed with valuable photographic gear), or of Indians and New Zealanders, who may well be smuggling currency, and thus are unlikely to complain about their losses. The loaders will also generally loot the luggage being sent to expensive destinations like Cannes, Nice or Geneva – particularly the latter, if there is a currency scare on. In most cases the theft will go unpunished because, by the time it is discovered, the tourist is thousands of miles away, and how can one prove that the theft took place at any one part along that route? This mobility severely hampers detection, so organised crime has moved in on airports with a vengeance. The profit to be made from looting consignments of things like diamonds and gold bars is such that traditional raids on banks seem very risky and not particularly profitable.

Of course, not all tourists are victims. There are characters like the man who loaded four cases weighing 73 kilos on to a plane in Paris, carefully paying the excess baggage charges. In London, an accomplice removed them, so that he could use his baggage checks to sue BEA for £4,000, claiming that he'd lost a range of expensive possessions. One of the receipts he offered as proof of what he'd lost was fraudulent and his career was ended, but, before that, he had made similar, successful claims against seven other airlines.[23]

Arriving at one's destination can be just as traumatic. The tourist suddenly steps from a plane in which his every whim has been pampered, into an environment which is basically hostile. An American academic has even written a tongue-in-cheek description of this process called 'Why the American tourist abroad is cheated: a price-theoretical analysis'.[24] He suggests one can construct a

Befuddlement Index to measure the degree of confusion felt by a tourist, uncertain of language and exchange rates, when buying goods whose local price he may feel uncertain about too. Faced with such a victim, local vendors can always get the tourist to pay over the local odds. After all, tourists are usually relatively rich as well and hardly know the difference. Prices thus rise to levels approaching those paid by the tourists for equivalent goods back home.

This analysis is not just flippant, as anyone who has ever had to pay for a meal in a genuinely strange culture like, say, Eastern Europe will vouch. Any waiter worth his salt removes the menu, with its prices, as soon as the meal is ordered, writes the bill in his language (strange scripts like Cyrillic give an added advantage), refuses to recognise any convenient language like French, English or German, and, finally, gives inaccurate change. Against such concerted villainy, the average tourist has no chance. He will end up hopelessly over-tipping and prey to every trick of the local wide-boys. A powerful inflationary force is thus added to the local economy and the host society is taught that cheating can be very profitable. Those who learn to cheat the tourist will eventually turn on their fellow citizens and everybody ends up more cynical and suspicious.

The trouble with the tourist dream is that it blinds the tourist to the tensions bubbling round him in the host society. Sometimes, nothing happens, and he leaves for home with his illusions intact. On other occasions, though, the hatred felt against him is so great (perhaps even escalating into violence against him) that the cocoon in which he lives is shattered.

Anti-tourist resentment can be strong and serious. This has been particularly true of the Caribbean where the riots of the late 1960s were symptomatic of tensions running deep in these islands' social structure. No sane foreigners would enter the slums of Kingston, Jamaica, on foot. Foreigners have even been advised in Georgetown, Guyana's capital, not to venture on foot outside their hotels even by day, since attacks on Whites were growing.

By 1973, the worst of such troubles were over (at least for the moment), though the murders in St Croix were continuing. Travel operators and government tourist boards hasten to insist that such incidents are atypical of the 'real' Caribbean, and that tales of surly service and violence are vastly overstated. This could be so . . . but, as we have argued earlier, the social tensions of which these are symptoms run deep in most Caribbean societies.

Some tourists obviously ask for trouble. A good number of those going to the Mexico border towns or to Majorca are basically out for a good time which can easily turn to violence and gaol. The prime destinations soon get used to this. The Spanish police, for instance, used to spend time hauling indecently clad tourists off to prison, but they've now learned to leave foreigners pretty well alone. They concentrate instead on out-of-season raids on the bars and clubs where drug-dealing and fringe prostitution are likely to get established. In most cases they leave it to barmen to sort out the troublesome guests, and gaol is used sparingly for only the most glaring cases of drunkenness and assault. Even then, the temptation is just to put the offender on the next plane out of the country instead of getting involved in complicated cases which destroy the tourist image of the country. Every so often, though, the foreigners overstep the permitted mark. Possession of drugs is a case in point. The foreign ambassadors in Spain annually launch a campaign warning young tourists to Keep Off The Grass, but the message does not always get through. Those who are particularly vulnerable are people who've made the trip to Morocco where 'kif' (the Moroccan form of hashish) is on open sale. Serious traffickers fly back to their eventual destinations, but the amateurs and the foolhardy make the trip back to the north through Spain, where an arrest for possessing pot leads to a fairly automatic six years in gaol. There is evidence that Moroccan traffickers often inform on foreign purchasers to the Spanish authorities. There is considerable speculation about whether the confiscated drugs just get recycled back to Morocco. In late 1972, there were six British nationals in Spanish prisons for drug offences, with another twenty-one awaiting trial.

Sentences which seem disproportionate (in the eyes of the tourists) to the offence cause a great deal of international bitterness. Anglo-Turkish relations suffered this way in 1972 when the fifteen-year-old English boy, Timothy Davey, was arrested in Turkey on a drugs charge which, in Britain, would have resulted in a juvenile court care order. Under Turkish law he was tried and sentenced to six years in a Turkish gaol. He was lucky compared with the American girl who was sentenced to death on a drugs charge there in 1974.

Problems also arise with innocent activities like train and plane spotting in which enthusiasts are drawn, cameras to the fore, to level crossings and airports. They find it difficult to remember that the antique steam engine puffing down the line toward them may be the host country's 'military secret'. Photographing it may render them liable to a charge of espionage. 1973 saw two apparently genuine British plane enthusiasts being gaoled for four years by a Yugoslav military court. They were unfortunate enough to be caught taking down plane registration numbers in the midst of the Yom Kippur War when Yugoslavia was allowing its airspace to be used by other East European countries flying armaments to the Arabs. Such an incident is a possibility on most holidays in Eastern Europe and in tense areas like the Middle East. On the other hand, there is a ridiculous angle. Egypt, for instance, has produced a crop of stories about tourists arrested for photographing Cairo bridges which are on all the tourist postcards. Again, they are sensitive about possible attacks on the Aswan Dam and at one stage closed Aswan airport as a way of keeping track of aircraft in the vicinity. Tourists would be asked to leave their cameras behind them in their hotels when visiting this attraction, despite the fact that the lobbies were filled with brochures bursting with pictures of the dam. There were also the slot-machine telescopes on the top of the Cairo Tower to which the western military attachés used to repair at regular intervals with pockets bulging with piastres. They would gaze fondly through them at the progress the Russians were making with the SAM-3 missile sites on the far side of the Pyramids. Alas the day came when President Podgorny visited Cairo, and the offending telescopes were removed because, the officials said, 'there are not enough tourists these days'.[25]

Not all the stories are funny or trivial; not all the victims are people who could avoid trouble by knowing more about the culture they're visiting. Perhaps the most genuinely tragic cases are the 'Tug of Love' incidents. As people travel, some marry and have children by someone from a different nationality. Some of these marriages break down, the parents split up, and the fight starts for the children. In 1972 there was the case of a British wife and a French husband who fought for a child who was forcibly kept in France by the father despite judgements by the French courts. Commenting on this Desmarault case, British journalist Jill Tweedie wrote a powerful piece about how she had been involved in a similar case some years earlier, during which she had had to resign herself to never seeing her children again. The Hungarian father had abducted her daughter aged four and son aged three from Britain leaving little but a note saying they had gone to Europe. Being short of money, she was trapped in Britain, wondering how to kidnap them back. She did not know where they were, was frightened by the possessiveness of the father, and was daunted by the legal complications (the children's names were not on her passport). Eventually she learned where the children were and got the law grinding into action. The magistrate was a friend of her husband's and the translation was so bad that she missed every second sentence of the proceedings. She won the right to have the children for the summer holidays but, once she was back in Britain, her husband just refused to comply. After fruitless phone calls and long-distance legal battles, she finally just gave up and has not seen the children since.[26]

Admittedly this is an extreme case, but it is one of the kind of complications which are growing in numbers as an integral part of our increasingly mobile civilisation. This encapsulates all one's worries about tourism in its widest context. The dream-world of the brochures could only exist if one abolished poverty, ignorance, disease, xenophobia and cultural variations. It is fraudulent to depict the host citizens as universally friendly and welcoming, when there are nearly always significant currents of resentment swirling close to the surface. It is irresponsible to open up destinations in increasingly poverty-stricken countries, without making it thoroughly clear to the tourist that he is exposing himself to a range of health and safety risks which are well outside the normal range of experience. It is immoral to peddle the idea that being a tourist can sweep aside centuries of mistrust and isolation. The industry may kid itself that the sun shines from the hearts of the citizens of the host countries – but it just is not so. The victims are the tourists. Self-deceiving they may be, but that is no excuse for pandering to their blindness.

15 Travel without Vision

This section has been pessimistic. We have blamed tourists for corrupting whole societies and creating international discord. Surely tourism cannot be all bad? Surely there is some truth in the slogan 'World Peace through World Travel'?

Perhaps so, but no one has yet proved it. Basically, this is the old chicken-and-egg dilemma. We would probably agree that the world is moving into a more relaxed era in international affairs. Despite Vietnam and the Middle Eastern conflict, the danger of global holocaust along the lines of the two world wars seems to have retreated. Once-ravaged continents like Europe now bask in relative affluence (oil sheiks permitting). The Cold War and the omnipresent danger of nuclear destruction are slowly becoming memories. When disputes do arise, as between India and Pakistan, or Israel and the Arabs, the super powers move in forcing the combatants into wary truces.

But has this relaxation come about through the growth of world tourism? Or is tourism a product of growing world peace? On balance, one suspects the latter is the case. There is little evidence, for instance, that the architects of the European Common Market in the 1950s were particularly well travelled; on the whole they were idealists who were determined that Europe should never again see the fratricidal strife of another world war. Moreover, the bulk of their work was achieved by 1957 when the real tourist boom was still in its infancy. Again, the current East–West détente is taking place despite the fact that the last fifty years have seen minimal flows of tourists between Russia and the West. In the case of China, it was particularly clear that it was only after the political decision to relax relations with the West that the famous 'ping-pong diplomacy' started. Tours of sporting and cultural groups were important as symbols of an underlying diplomatic shift, not causes of it.

One can even search for counter-examples where eras of apparent cosmopolitanism have not been accompanied by international harmony. The two twentieth-century world wars, for instance, came after roughly a hundred years of virtually uninterrupted European peace.

The continent's royal families were heavily related; they saw each other frequently at family occasions like funerals and marriages; they tended to use the same spas, such as Baden-Baden and Marienbad. Even the activists of the fledgling socialist movements of Europe knew each other from a number of conferences. Yet in 1914 Queen Victoria's royal descendants led their nations against each other with only token regret, while at the other end of the political spectrum, the various socialist leaders waited to see who would be the first to renounce the reactionary nationalism that the war entailed. In practice, nothing happened. The vast majority of Europe's allegedly internationally-minded revolutionaries rallied to the appeals of their national governments. So, despite a century of ever-increasing mobility within Europe, two world wars saw intra-European slaughter on a scale and level of intensity never before experienced.

The point about tourism is that it is only one, fairly ineffective way of gaining insight into the workings of other societies. The attitudes expressed by governments and the mass media are of far more importance in shifting people's international attitudes than tourism. To take the US–China détente again, one thinks of the almost overnight switch in both official and private attitudes toward China by American citizens. This was a revolution in attitudes led from the White House, and picked up rapidly by the media. The stereotyped Red menace, from the East, was replaced by that of a vast, mysterious, relatively peaceful civilisation whose communist inheritors seemed to be considerably gentler and more tolerant than past propaganda had led the West to believe. Tourism played no part in either establishing or destroying these stereotypes, though the current restricted wave of approved tourists will doubtless lead to modifications of China's image as time goes by.

No one actually knows what goes on in tourists' minds. There seems to have been virtually no hard studies of how travel actually modifies their perception of the world and their fellow humans. One study did look at the apparent influence travel had on American businessmen. Significantly, it did not seem to render them more liberal. Certainly, they did become more aware of foreign attitudes, but the most travelled businessmen were mostly totally conventional Republicans, with views close to the national standard. Awareness of foreign attitudes was far from accepting them. As the authors explained: 'Like most of our colleagues, we expected that tourism would liberalise. . . . We were wrong.'[1]

Social psychology, however, should have made us wary about

expecting too much. In many ways, getting full, open understanding between tourists and their hosts is as difficult as getting tolerance within a racially prejudiced relationship. In both cases, one actor tends to be richer and more privileged than the other; in both cases, the perceptions of each other will be blatant stereotypes. So even if the literature is sparse on the psychology of tourists, we do have an understanding of how racial stereotypes are modified. The father of this work is Gordon Allport, who developed a 'contact theory' by which he tried to explain how prejudices could be broken down. He argued that they could be best removed when the majority and minority groups worked together toward common goals, sharing common status. This is particularly helped when local societies or laws emphasise such contact. So the key is that both sides should perceive common interests and be willing to admit their common humanity.

The trouble is that most tourists are not interested in that kind of contact. They are paying money in order to be waited upon; the vast majority do not really want to get to know their hosts, and when they do, they are hampered by the genuine problem that there is a limit to how much one can discover in a fortnight about someone speaking a different language. Their perception of local realities will therefore be superficial and prejudiced, just as the locals in return will view the tourists with suspicion. Psychologically the easiest way out for both sides is to give up attempts to understand each other, accepting the standard industry roles of 'tourist', 'local barmen', etc. One commentator sees this as an inevitable result of the commercialisation of the industry,[2] but really it is a defensive reaction, similar to those found in any society where people find themselves in a whole series of casual, random relationships. City-dwellers, for instance, have series of rituals for avoiding meaningful contact with people who may momentarily be travelling in the same lift or bus; the role of 'stranger' allows one to talk to each other about certain trivialities like the weather, but discourages any conversation which may result in one's privacy being really pierced. So, we find that, as we move from the individual to the mass tourist, we move from a situation where the tourist is treated as a genuine guest (thus having the chance of experiencing significant interaction with the local community), to one where he becomes a formal 'tourist', which precludes all but formal commercial relationships. Mutual understanding and the true interaction of cultures are lost.

Even an analysis of sixteenth-century travel literature confirms this pessimistic view of the understanding brought by tourism. One study looked at this first great age of travel – the era in which the successors of Marco Polo, Christopher Columbus and the Portuguese navigators roamed the world looking for sea routes to China. Accounts of their exploits sold well, and printers found that travel books were as popular as religious tracts. Almost uniformly, though, these accounts were filled with crude prejudice. The explorers viewed most of the natives they found as beneath contempt, portraying them as dark (already the mark of the slave), naked (sign of backwardness), and apparently anarchic (only Montaigne and the Franciscan missionaries saw that even apparent savages could have adequate social structures). What is fascinating is how these initial stereotypes came to dominate the ideas of succeeding centuries. One is almost left with the suspicion that the prejudices of the early travellers predetermined the expectations of their followers, perhaps even to the present day. As the author puts it: 'The striking fact remains that the European nations ultimately conquered or controlled many of the lands explored during the age of reconnaissance. The first impressions of a provincial Europe looking at an alien world were the lasting ones and became a permanent part of the ethos of western culture.'[3] Only a handful of travellers in those days ever bothered to identify with the local communities they discovered. One wonders if things have really changed. Where tourism does play a distinctive role in world affairs is when the destination is of symbolic importance to the tourist. One thinks at once of the 'ethnic market' – expatriates making sentimental trips back to the land of their fathers. In the section on Eastern Europe, we mentioned how its governments have been consciously strengthening their links with expatriate communities. One of their aims has been to persuade them to act as friendly pressure groups on their host governments where issues come up of concern to the homeland. The Israelis have been particularly aware of the importance of the Diaspora – particularly the Jewish community living in the USA. The more such Jewish expatriates are encouraged to visit Israel, the firmer, it is believed, they will support the Israelis with money and political backing. If one looks at the American policies toward Israel, one can appreciate the impact that the formidable cohesion of the Jewish community has had on Israeli-linked issues. Of course, tourism to Israel is partly a straight commercial enterprise, but it is also a political activity vital to the long-term security of the State of Israel.

However, the travel industry has also been strengthening the Moslem world. Islam is strangely under-reported in the West, but is spread more widely than most observers imagine, and is one of the very few world religions which is actually expanding its influence. In the Far East, both Indonesia and Malaysia are strongly Moslem; it is still a force in parts of the USSR: above all, its influence now extends well south of the Sahara into Black Africa, into countries like Nigeria, Uganda and Kenya. This is one factor which helps explain why the vast majority of African governments backed the Arab cause in the 1973 Arab–Israeli conflict.

One of the pillars of Islam is the Haj, the holy pilgrimage to Mecca, which every Moslem who is fit and can afford it is expected to perform at least once in his lifetime. The chief beneficiary of this pilgrimage is Saudi Arabia, and it has been estimated that the Haj which fell in January, 1974, was performed by at least 1·5 million people, 600,000 of whom came from outside Saudi Arabia and its immediate neighbours. The Saudi Government spends freely to encourage the inward flow and, with oil money pouring into the country, it can afford to do things in style. £20 million has been spent in expanding Jeddah airport to cope with the twenty aircraft an hour which land during the peak period. Millions have also been spent on accommodation and medical facilities.

The Haj is thus flourishing. The number of pilgrims expands rapidly each year. More and more young Moslems make the journey as affluence spreads through the Islamic world. In fact, the re-invigoration of the Haj is one of the great symbolic events of our time. The development of air travel has permitted the mass transportation of believers and, for the first time, significant numbers of pilgrims have had a chance to reach Mecca from the further flung Islamic posts like the Far East and West Africa. The Haj is thus becoming a major force for cohesion within Islam, at a time when the Arab–Israeli conflict has turned the spotlight on all factors which may influence the outcome of that struggle. At the very least, it means the Arabs are guaranteed firm diplomatic support for their case from a number of non-Arab, Islamic countries round the world. It may also be a unifying force which will keep the Arab oil-producers united in their dealings with the rest of the world, thus making the 'oil-weapon' a long-term political force on the international scene.

With a few exceptions, tourists are not yet true world citizens. Most of them stick to their own continent for holidays. If they do travel abroad they stay with fairly conventional destinations (i.e. the North Americans tend to make for Europe). This suggests a somewhat limited vision, and does not suggest that tourism is yet a major force for world integration. On the other hand, wherever tourists do travel, they seem to be effective in at least partially breaking down local national divisions. As they gain confidence, they want increased freedom to see more of a region. They learn how to use local trains and planes; they hire cars; they join tours taking in more than one destination. Above all, they refuse to be restricted by national boundaries. If they have spent a couple of hundred pounds flying the Atlantic to see Paris, they want to be able to cross the Channel to see London as well, with the minimum of fuss. Tourists visiting southern Spain suddenly find that Morocco is a short boat ride away, and they do not want official formalities to stop them crossing to see Tangiers or Marrakech.

This trend toward multiple destination holidays has forced governments to co-operate in order to maximise the flow of foreign exchange to them. Morocco and Spain, for instance, have been moving toward a joint plan for tourism. There would be collaboration over promotional literature, with brochures listing the festivals of both countries. Folk-lore companies would be swapped between them, and talk started about creating a joint transport company to link them both.[4] At the same time, the Moroccan Minister of Tourism also joined his counterparts from those other North African destinations, Tunisia and Algeria, to form a Maghreb tourism confederation.[5] In Asia there is a five-nation tourism promotion organisation which promotes Indonesia, Malaysia, the Philippines, Singapore, and Thailand.[6] In the Caribbean, there is a Caribbean Travel Association which helps sell the region as a whole – in the Pacific, the Pacific Area Travel Association. Scandinavian governments have set up a similar joint committee to deal with their region's problems. In France and Spain we find the Basque minority, which spills over both sides of the Pyrenees, sponsoring joint promotions of the Basque towns of San Sebastian in Spain and Biarritz in France. In East Africa, the governments of Kenya, Tanzania and Uganda developed a regional tourist circuit, though events in Uganda and Tanzania are now encouraging the Kenyans to go it alone. At their most ambitious, the implications of such events can be built up into visionary ideology. M. Robert Lonati, secretary-general of the industry's major world body, IUOTO, has made speeches in which he calls for the end of nationalist planning, demanding it be replaced by a 'geotourist' or regional outlook. He talks of the Mediterranean where he sees three different power blocs, Europe, Africa and the Middle East. 'Instead of considering it as three different areas, which is a political concept, we would like to think about it as one area, which is a geotourist concept.'[7]

Without question, then, the official ideology of tourism is internationalist, demanding that national borders be swept aside for the benefit of ubiquitous tourists. This can only be admired, particularly when we think of the misery that blind nationalism has caused in the past.

However, it is dangerous to push this argument too far. Tourism is only one way of breaking down national boundaries. For instance, one can argue that international trade links countries together far more firmly than tourist flows can ever hope to achieve. How could mere tourists have created the mutual interdependence which oil has woven between the Middle East and the industrialised world? One can also argue that international tensions can be broken down without any tourism at all. We are, after all, living in Marshall McLuhan's Global Village, and there is no reason why someone with access to good newspapers, books and radio and TV coverage of world affairs should not have a much clearer idea of what is going on round the world than the vast majority of tourists.

Indeed, we would go farther to argue that tourism is actually a malign force. For one thing, it is a new form of colonialism, in which the rich of the world fan out through the poorer countries looking for areas to colonise which are pleasanter than their existing homes. As George Young puts it: 'The spread of destination countries is much wider than that of the originating countries. The two most popular destination countries (Canada and Spain) account for about 25 per cent of the market, whereas the two most prolific suppliers of tourists account for about 40 per cent. International tourism therefore represents a dispersal, rather than concentration of people.'[8] Put slightly more concretely, tourism is the geographical dispersal of the rich of the world.

Since permanent settlers follow the tourists, we are describing a global search for attractive land, which is in no way different from the worldwide scramble for gold, uranium, oil or any other precious resource. In so far as such land is sought in Third World countries, we are dealing with a form of economic exploitation little different from that of previous decades. If past generations created oil-producing, mining, or rubber-growing enclaves, ours has produced tourist resorts which are, in many cases, just as irrelevant to the long-term development of the countries concerned.

Tourism is basically just another migration, and we remain supremely sceptical that the world is yet at the stage where tourists and locals can co-exist peaceably for any significant length of time. Mass tourism is still a new industry which is not yet fully understood by the host countries, but there is no reason why they should feel in the long run any happier about receiving hordes of rich, white foreigners than the Americans and Europeans feel about playing host to poor, non-white immigrants. Tourists may appear richer and less permanent, thus earning themselves an initially friendly reception, but one can see political pressures building up. The tourist industry requires a country's most attractive land, but how long can the hosts tolerate this? What civil rights will permanent settlers have? Can rich Whites really live peacefully in overcrowded societies dominated by poor non-Whites, as in the Caribbean? What sort of political concessions are host governments willing to make at the behest of the tourist industry? What happens to international understanding when tourists fall foul of strange local laws and customs? What happens when dissident groups choose tourists as victims?

At its best, tourism is but a minor factor in bringing about the relaxation of international tension. Most significant world events have been totally unaffected by its existence, though, in marginal cases, the existence of a tourist industry may gain a country a more sympathetic hearing in the world than its circumstances would otherwise demand. Tourism, perhaps, is more of an indicator of trends in international relationships. Thus America's heavy diplomatic involvement with Europe is paralleled by the annual trans-atlantic flow of North American tourists to the old world. However, there are distinct limits to how much one can read into such flows. If tourism was really so important, Spain would long ago have been a full member of the European Common Market, which supplies so many of the tourists to whom she plays host; instead, her northern neighbours find her a diplomatic embarrassment preferring to extend trade concessions to her, rather than the full diplomatic union which the tourist flows would suggest.

At its worst, though, tourism is a severely corrosive force. Admittedly, we should not get too concerned about the problems it creates in industrialised nations like Britain or France, whose governments should be strong enough to control tourism and its impact, should they so choose. The Third World, however, is another matter. Many of these countries are still struggling to overcome the class and racial problems left them by previous generations of imperialists, who swamped the original inhabitants with successive layers of African slaves, and then Indian and Chinese indentured labourers. Tourism will exacerbate this damage by adding yet another ethnic (and privileged) layer to these deeply divided societies. Whatever the immediate economic benefits, future generations will curse us soundly for this. Tourism may seem to be an innocent activity, but its impact is divisive, far-reaching and long-term. The tourist is involved in nothing less than the rewriting of the economic and political geography of the world.

SECTION FOUR: ALTERNATIVES

16 The Last Romantics

Mais les vrais voyageurs sont ceux-là seuls qui partent
Pour partir; . . .
Amer savoir, celui qu'on tire du voyage!
Le monde, monotone et petit, aujourd'hui,
Hier, demain, toujours, nous fait voir notre image . . .[1]
Baudelaire, *Le Voyage*

The development of the hippie trails presents tourism at its most paradoxical. As Jock Young has observed: 'The new bohemia remains a gigantic warehouse of contradictions and unexplored mystification.' When the members of this 'new bohemia' or 'international Underground' turn nomad the elements of contradiction and mystification are intensified. We are concerned with a specific and easily recognised form of tourism, but one that is hard to define or even *name* satisfactorily. These new, bohemian nomads are characterised by youth, long hair and an interest in drugs, but this statement must be immediately qualified, since they are not invariably under thirty, long hair does not necessarily entail regular drug use and is hardly a distinguishing characteristic in women. Their clothes are limited to variations on the international uniform of denim jeans and T-shirts. As they travel further into Asia or Africa they may adopt ethnic-exotic garb with more or less bizarre results, but in general they are, from the western standpoint, unexceptional young people. In the non-western countries they visit they are variously described as 'hippies' or 'beatniks', and often generally condemned as 'long-haired, promiscuous, work-shy, drug-taking degenerates'. For those inside the western counter-culture, however, 'hippie' is an inadequate term but for those outside it remains the most popular. This is especially true of officialdom in the Third World, for whom the term implies nothing more than a young, relatively impecunious traveller, with a presumed interest in drugs (principally marijuana/cannabis/hashish). Erik Cohen prefers to use the more neutral term 'drifter', and comments:

> The drug-oriented hippie is indeed the most conspicuous type of drifter, and there is a tendency in many countries to call all drifters indiscriminately 'hippies' or 'beatniks'. . . . One should take care however not to identify all drifters with the itinerant 'hippie';

though many drifters might occasionally engage in drug-taking, drugs are not for the most of them the purpose and the sole aim of the trip.[2]

Such a statement is a necessary corrective to the usual hysterical (and *histrionic*) statements about hippie depravity, however it is unlikely that any young person could make the trek from Europe to India, Nepal or Morocco without acquiring some taste for marijuana. Richard Neville[3] goes further and states that the 'flower children' are not dead but 'ghosts along the pot-trail, haunting hippie love-ins and tribal weddings'. At the same time he corrects an English journalist for describing the central square of Marrakech as full of 'rather unpopular English hippies looking for hash', with the words: 'They're neither necessarily English hippies, unpopular, or looking for hash (it looks for them). The travellers, of many nationalities, are of varying social persuasions: beats, bums, Boy Scouts, Maoists, mystics, or rather unpopular English journalists looking for some human interest.' Evidently we are dealing with a phenomenon of bewildering diversity, that probably deserves the ungainly and linguistically hybrid title of '*LumpenBohemia*'.

Erik Cohen defines the drifter as 'the most individualistic and least institutionalised type' of tourist, who is 'predominantly a child of affluence on a prolonged moratorium from adult middle-class responsibility, seeking spontaneous experiences in the excitement of complete strangeness'. From an objective standpoint this seems a reasonable if somewhat conservative definition, but from the standpoint of the confirmed 'drifter' it is virtually meaningless. For Cohen the 'drifting' of disenchanted youth is simply an extended version of the conventional holiday/leisure time in which 'subterranean values are allowed to emerge and take precedence'.[4] In place of a few weeks the offspring of the middle-class are allowed a few months, or even years, in which to live according to the subterranean values of hedonism and individual expressivity. The more ideologically conscious and *idealistic* members of the 'new bohemia' have attempted to make living according to subterranean values into a permanent way of life. Any assumption of 'adult, middle-class responsibility' is viewed as a defeat. They reject the pat, journalistic-sociological explanations of themselves: decay of the Protestant ethic, alienation, affluence and generation gap. To a large extent this new diaspora resists analysis – it is 'a way of life which rejects and despises, precisely, the language and act of interpretation'. One might, unkindly,

BROWN BECOMES BEAUTIFUL
*Bathing at Deauville, August
1927 (left)*
Vogue *acknowledges the
Riviera suntan cult, July 1929
(below)*

WHITE TOURIST, BLACK PROFIT?
A dress made in two hours, Jamaica

say that this is in part a defensive gesture since many of the assumptions on which this life-style is based cannot stand up to serious analysis. Nevertheless, many young travellers in North Africa, Afghanistan, or Nepal might well agree with Peter Levy, the hero of Mary McCarthy's *Birds of America*, when he reflects: 'It was funny how older people got excited by thinking about the Beats, as if they were some new form of pornography. . . .' The development of the hippie trails is, in historical and cultural terms, predictable, even inevitable; on its own terms, despite all the spiritual and intellectual confusion involved, it is an entirely logical development.

The two most immediately apparent characteristics of 'drifter-tourism' are its rejection of institutionalised mass tourism and the violent reaction it provokes in many of the countries on which it intrudes. As we have already observed no social group is more snobbish and dismissive about tourists than other tourists. The worst thing that can be said about a place is that it is 'too touristy'. Tourists thus express a 'blanket rejection that, if they sat down and analysed it, would have to include themselves'. This represents the emergence of that element of rejection of social class, which generally characterises 'bourgeois, post-romantic tourism' (see Chapter 2, 'Idylls of the Bourgeoisie'). To some extent the drifter avoids the problem altogether by simply avoiding the established tourist sights: 'You might miss the Topkapi Museum and the Taj Whateveritis, instead you can paddle your own canoe down the Mekong River, nibble aphrodisiac chocolate in a Thailand teenage brothel. . . . Drift with the current and end up in places you never knew existed.'[5] The 'fly-ways' of mass tourists and drifter-tourists inevitably meet on occasions. When this happens the two parties regard each other with mutual hostility and incomprehension. In *The Road to Katmandu* Patrick Marnham describes the situation with regard to Rat, a fellow overlander whom he meets in Istanbul:

> Tourists were frightened of Rat. They never knew when this private in the army of the unkempt was likely to spring up and do something that might focus the world's attention on them. That was what really worried the average tourist. The thought that he might have to draw attention to himself by reacting visibly to a situation was enough to paralyse him with fear. There was a possibility that he would have to leave the protective camouflage of his party and become just a person in the street. . . . It seemed to Rat that the average package tourist was already a very nervous man, and the possibility, in a city like Istanbul, was that he was also a guilty one. Everywhere he looked were the miserable poor.

In Neville's view the expansion of package tourism into more remote areas is always accompanied by persecution of 'longhairs'. He cites the example of Turkey where 'a fanatical boosting of the tourist industry' in the late 'sixties coincided with a systematic campaign against young European travellers, and the imposition of savage jail sentences for drug offences. (In 1968 Hans Der Aar was gaoled for thirty years for possession of 2 kilos of marijuana.) Since there is almost nowhere in the world where the drifter has not penetrated, examples of official victimisation can be cited from Argentina to Laos. The French seem to have been the pioneers in this systematic international persecution. In April 1966 French immigration officials were instructed to refuse entry to persons whose 'unkempt clothes, shaggy hair and evident uncleanliness might be thought to offer an undesirable spectacle'. Such a vaguely termed directive is an open invitation to the venting of personal prejudice. In 1967, after the military coup, Greece followed suit. In 1968 hippies in Rome were the victims of one of Italy's recurrent spasms of worry concerning 'public decency' – in the interests of which they were forcibly cleared from the Spanish Steps (see Fellini's film *Roma*). In the same year Yugoslavia 'declared war on hippies'. In the period 1967 to 1968 hippies were harassed and/or publicly criticised in Laos, Thailand, India, Mexico, Argentina, Spain and Singapore. In the early 'seventies a second wave began in Africa. In 1972 Tunisia, Libya, Uganda, Malawi and Kenya introduced restrictions directed against 'hippie-type' travellers. The Defence Council of the Republic of Uganda announced on 6 July that people wearing 'bushy beards and untrimmed hair' were given one week to change or, in the case of foreigners, to leave the country. The Moroccan authorities have been remarkably inconsistent. They have sponsored jazz festivals, they have refused entry to longhairs at some custom posts but not at others; the use of cannabis is indigenous to Moroccan culture yet young, foreign drug users have been horribly mistreated. Neville recounts the experience of a Scotsman arrested in 1969 for possessing 350 grams of kif (an especially potent variety of cannabis grown in Morocco). In order to get him to confess to 'pushing' he was 'tied to an iron pole like a butcher's carcass and left to hang. Police flayed the soles of his feet with a cowhide whip, wrapped his head and face in a wet towel and forced water into his nose and mouth'. Neville comments that Morocco is 'being cleaned up for tourists'. To a remarkable degree persecution of hippies in these countries *does* coincide with a government-promoted expansion in conventional mass tourism. But this does not explain the violence of the reaction, the note of panic and fear in public pronouncements against the 'hippies'. The hirsute invasion inspires the press to new heights of rhetorical excess; hippies are 'lice', 'ticks', 'parasites', 'degenerates', and – astonishingly – they are said to display 'an indifference to life'. In October 1968 *The Times of India* referred to a 'sinister pattern behind the hippie invasion of the capital'. In 1971 the Singapore government issued the following directive: 'To all Chambers of Commerce, Singapore Manufacturers Association, Singapore Employers Federation: Long, dirty, scruffy hair is coming back. It is easy to slide down the slippery slope – long hair, hippie clothes and medallions, pop music glorifying drugs and sex. Decisive action is therefore taken to curb the development of this unhealthy trend. . . .'

These disproportionate and paranoid reactions of 'guardians of public morality' throughout the world would be merely absurd, did they not lead to serious infringements of personal liberty, often brutally enforced. One might point out that most of the so-called 'hippies' are perfectly ordinary young people, that not all are regular drug users, that not all long hair is dirty, and so on. What is the sinister pattern behind a few extra inches of hair, a pair of denims and a medallion? Why do these trivial externals arouse superstitious dread in newspaper editors and heads of state? These questions cannot be answered quickly. Such over-reactions are the symptoms of a conflict of ideologies that has been endemic to western culture since, at least, the eighteenth century.

At the centre of this conflict is the idea of progress, that is a rational, scientific progress leading to the 'conquest of nature' by industry and high technology. The Romantic Movement was essentially a reaction against the over-mechanistic view of the world which grew from this idea of progress. In their debased and simplistic forms the romantic cult of nature and the irrational appear as a negation of the achievements of the eighteenth-century enlightenment, but the artists and the philosophers of the Romantic Movement also asserted the rights of the individual against the claims of society. As Edmund Wilson[6] says: 'The Romantic is nearly always a rebel', even if his rebellion is incoherent and seemingly 'without a cause'. The Romantic rebellion often includes a rejection of political commitment, often the result of a frustrated idealism. Mingled with this is a confused desire for 'revolution', conceived either as a bloody apocalypse or a new dawn of mankind. (Both views of revolution may be found in the work of Rimbaud.) In consequence the Romantic was often a compulsive wanderer in the manner of Byron's Childe Harold and Manfred – a self-made exile from his home society. These *insoluble* conflicts persisted throughout the nineteenth century and into the twentieth century. The 'beats', the 'hippies' and the drifters are the true 'last Romantics'. Disillusioned with the now all too apparent environmental and spiritual effects of 'scientific progress' (pollution and alienation) and tacitly challenging the hegemony of bourgeois values, they travel, they adopt distinctive styles of dress, they experiment with drugs. In this they follow a pattern set by the various bohemian groups of nineteenth-century Paris. Their travelling, their 'drifting' is, implicitly, a rejection of 'straight politics' of whatever colour. Theirs is a hedonistic, indeed an aesthetic response to life (presuming that we understand 'aesthetic' in its fullest sense of 'having to do with the senses'). In a frequently hostile world they attempt to live according to Pater's famous dictate: 'Not the fruit of experience, but experience itself is the end.'

If we return to Neville's *Playpower* with these ideas in mind we find a whole series of pronouncements that reveal a quintessentially Romantic philosophy, a philosophy also influenced by Norman O. Brown's idea that liberation can only be achieved by the rediscovery of 'the lost body of childhood'.

> Perhaps young Westerners realise that now is the last chance to see the world before it finally dwindles into comprehensibility when it will offer all the excitements and horizons of a baby's play-pen, unless, like babies, we relearn how to play.

The idea of a world 'dwindling into comprehensibility' reveals the Romantic fear of a world robbed of its diversity and mystery by an imperious and repressive rationality. The idea of 'relearning how to play' is taken from Brown whose *Life Against Death* Neville enthusiastically propagates. Quoting Brown, 'Children explore in indiscriminate and anarchistic fashion all the erotic potentialities of the human body', he comments (ungrammatically): 'Sounds like the sex habits of the Underground which is still, like children, narcissistic and guiltless.' Certainly the playful, childlike characteristics of the new-bohemian life-style are, at their best, qualitatively different from the infantilism of the packaged beach holiday. A return to infancy *within* repressive structures (in this case the three-week holiday in the working year) is inevitably neurotic and lacking in any creative possibilities. The hippies and related subcultural groups have attempted, in a diffuse and frequently incoherent manner, to re-evaluate the hedonistic and narcissistic models that our culture has too often slandered. They attempted to evolve a life-style based on the idea of 'conscious play', and 'conscious play' is, according to Brown, nothing less than 'the goal of humanity'. The hippie and Underground movements are, like all those movements which descend from the Romantics, 'divided movements'. The negative side of their rejection of formal analysis, and all other manifestations of repressive (scientific) rationality, is a theoretical inadequacy. Brown and Marcuse[7] support their statements with extended and subtle ratiocination: the hippies, having half-digested this 'new sensibility' theory, endeavoured to create 'paradise now', beginning with the consciousness of the individual. Consequently the hippie project for the transformation of life remained intellectually confused and they were ill-equipped to combat the hostility this project aroused. As Ernst Fischer says of German Romanticism and 'all later, similar movements':

> There is always the same conflict: on the one hand, a deeply felt protest against bourgeois values and the machinery of capitalism; on the other hand, fear of the consequences of revolution and escape into mystification which inevitably leads to reaction.

Reaction among the members of the Underground has most often taken the form of a retreat into the embrace of mystical proto-Fascist sects, with their simplistic formulae and their insistence on obedience, conformity and self-denial. In the tourism of the hippie trails we will find ample evidence of mystification. For all its virtues the Romantic stance is peculiarly vulnerable to subversion.

On page 174 of *Playpower* we find:

> . . . on a lonely treck from Marrakech to Agadir, in the Atlas Mountains, or 17,000 feet up the Himalayas, there is no-one but yourself to come face-to-face with. In a Greek or Spanish cave, not for three packaged weeks, – but for months, even years, the lost experience of solitude can be revived.

This last phrase recalls Byron's 'Here, to be lonely is not desolate'. 'Here', in solitude, in desolation, the traveller rediscovers a lost self, and loses his alienation, a process which between Marrakech and Agadir is likely to be assisted by generous quantities of kif This relates to a recurring motif in twentieth-century literature, that is: 'The motif of deserting a society which is felt to be catastrophic, in order to attain a supposed state of "pure" or "naked" being.' Ernst Fischer finds this motif in the highly influential fiction of Ernest Hemingway: 'He had made his camp. He was settled. Nothing could touch him. It was a good place to camp. He was here, in the good place. He was in his home where he had made it. . . . It was quite dark outside. It was lighter in the tent.'[8] Fischer comments:

> Hemingway's attitude is typical of a widespread longing in the late bourgeois world. Millions of people, particularly young people, seek to escape from unsatisfying jobs, from daily lives they feel to be empty, from a boredom prophetically analysed by Baudelaire, from all social obligations and ideologies, away, away, on roaring motor-cycles, intoxicated by a speed that consumes every feeling and thought, away from their own selves into a Sunday or holiday in which the whole meaning of life is somehow concentrated. As though driven by approaching disaster . . . whole generations in the capitalist world flee from themselves, to put up, somewhere in the midst of the unknown, a flimsy tent where it will be brighter inside than it is in the outer darkness.[9]

If we allow for the fact that 'roaring motorcycles' are not the drifters' preferred means of transport, drifter tourism in the 'seventies can be seen as the most extreme expression of this tendency.

In *Playpower*, 'the lost experience of solitude' is opposed to a statement of Billy Butlin's: 'The most important thing is that no one is left to himself even for a moment.' The experience of 'drifting with the current' is opposed to the regimented grossness and vulgarity of mass-democratic tourism. Such tourism, exemplified by the Butlin's holiday camps, is viewed as an instrument of ruthless social control.

Before Neville's hippies came the beats. 'The beat poets' response to Europe was unashamedly, naïvely Romantic. In the poetry of Gregory Corso this response is tied to the antiquity of Europe, particularly that of 'good, consoling Greece':

> Pressed face against a pillar I cried
> Cried for my shadow that dear faithful sentry
> Splashed across the world's loveliest floor.

This slightly too easy pathos, this avid relishing of sadness and ecstasy is typical of the beats. Their Romantic 'discovery' of Europe was preceded by the discovery of America, by means of a frenzied nomadism. Their Romanticism was of an aggressive and explosive kind, conscious of its bohemian antecedents. In Kerouac's *On the Road*, which remains a drifters' bible, we find the following central statement:

> . . . the only people for me are the mad ones, the ones who are mad to live, mad to talk, mad to be saved, desirous of everything at the same time, the ones who never yawn or say a commonplace thing but burn, burn, burn like fabulous yellow roman candles. . . . What did they call such young people in Goethe's Germany?

As we have already observed (in Chapter 2) travel had a symbolic value for Goethe. This was linked to the German-Romantic discovery of 'folk songs, folk art and folk-lore'. This rediscovery was an expression of the 'search for a lost unity, for a synthesis of the personality and the collective' that had been destroyed by capitalist alienation. These folk songs were 'very largely . . . a product of the highway, with its journeymen, runaway clerics, wandering students, apprentices, showmen and magicians of all kinds'. Music, folk and rock music, have always been central to the hippie-drifter experience. Frequently the drifter carries his own guitar or cassette player. Many modern folk-rock songs are directly 'products of the highway', chronicling the disillusionments of the foot-loose. This is so much the case that, in the early 'seventies, Carole King could sing with wistful world-weariness of 'one more song about moving along the highway', and ask, 'Doesn't anybody stay in one place anymore?' Many drifters on their way to Africa or India like to see themselves as wandering minstrels, troubadours, and even as 'showmen and musicians'. In this sense they are aware, however vaguely, that they are the end product of a long tradition.

The prototypes of Kerouac's cherishably 'mad' people who 'burn, burn, burn', are not to be found in Germany, however, but in nineteenth-century Paris. In *On The Road* we come across several characters who are reading Eugène Sue's *Mystères de Paris* – a novel which describes the low life of the Parisian Latin Quarter in the 1830s. Paris is, of course, the source of the bohemian tradition. This began in the 1830s with '*les bousingos*' a group to which Gérard de Nerval belonged. Like the bohemian groups that followed them *les bousingos* lived in a state of permanent revolt against the kind of self-seeking bourgeois society in which they found themselves. *Les bousingos* adopted exotic costumes and behaved in public with a studied outrageousness that foreshadows the Dadaists of the 1920s. Apart from the cultivation of bizarre modes of dress and behaviour the 'bohemians' of nineteenth-century Paris also placed a high value on the experiences of drugs and foreign travel. Hashish, opium and *voyages* to the Orient or Africa became the most favoured means of 'heightening' expérience.

Of all the artists who were attached to these bohemian groups, the poet Rimbaud was, for the beats, the most significant figure. He stood out as an exemplary figure whose life had about it a tragic completeness. His liaison with Verlaine, his anarchic and hallucinatory style and his compulsive travelling, all recommended him to the American bohemians of the 'fifties. Rimbaud was passionately concerned to escape Europe: '. . . he had always longed for some life that would take the place of the lost brutality and innocence of Europe, for the non-Christian, non-middle-class life of the Orient, of Africa. . . .'[10] This longing was shared in varying degrees by most of the significant poets of nineteenth-century France. Nerval travelled extensively throughout Europe before, in 1842, setting out for the Orient. In the course of his travels between Istanbul and Cairo he married the daughter of a Druse chieftain and enjoyed hashish idylls by the banks of the Nile. Early in his life, Baudelaire made a voyage to Mauritius and Réunion which left an indelible imprint on his imagination. The image of the voyage occurs frequently in his work. The tropical paradises of Réunion and Mauritius became identified with the lost paradise of childhood, '*L'innocent paradis, plein de plaisirs furtifs*'.[11] These 'green' paradises with their 'childish loves' can be identified, without distortion, as Norman O. Brown's world of anarchic infantile eroticism, or 'polymorphous perversity'. For the Romantics, the Symbolists, the beats, and the hippies, travelling is always seen, ideally, as a means of recovering something lost. Before embarking on his travels, Sal Paradise, the narrator of *On the Road*, reflects: '. . . somewhere along the line the pearl would be handed to me.'

Rimbaud's originality and his role of exemplar derive from the extremes to which he took this rejection of the West. In *Une saison en Enfer* he vilifies Europe: 'This people is inspired by fear and cancer. Invalids and old men are so respectable that they ought to be boiled. The wisest course is to quit this continent where madness prowls to provide these wretches with hostages.' His attempts to escape Europe and fulfil this savage dream of negation were repeatedly thwarted by his ill health. Nevertheless he reached Java, worked in Cyprus and Aden and lived for some years as a merchant

in Ethiopia. Even before leaving Europe he had led a life of vaga-
bondage with Verlaine. In these turbulent journeys through Belgium
and England he developed a prophetic 'philosophy of the road'. He
saw himself as Verlaine's liberator:

> I had, indeed, in all sincerity of spirit undertaken to restore him to
> his primitive condition of Child of the Sun. – and we wandered,
> fed with the wine of thieves' dens and the hardtack of the road, I
> eager to find the place and the formula.

In the light of this passage it is not surprising that one of the few
direct literary references in *On the Road* (apart from the references to
Mystères de Paris) should be to Rimbaud. Dean Moriarty, the
book's 'mad' travelling hero-saint, is described as a 'western kinsman
of the sun' and we are also told that he could become the greatest
poet since Rimbaud, 'if he wanted'. This Child of the Sun is easily
recognisable as the Noble Savage, specifically the primitive American.
An idealised version of the North American and Mexican Indian had
a special significance for Baudelaire. He saw the Indian as a sort of
'pristine dandy' and opposed his ideal life to that of civilised man
who has invented 'the philosophy of progress to console himself for
his abdication and his decadence'. In a curiously precise way this
anticipates the hippies who were to idealise the American Indian and
even adopt certain features of his 'pristine dandyism' – in the form
of head-bands, body-paint, ponchos, and so on. Unlike the Negro or
the chicano the Indian was a 'relatively remote actual presence in
American social life' and was thus a suitable figure around which to
build a new pastoral myth.

The sub-cultures of the American West Coast in the 1960s are
foreshadowed with even greater precision in a poem, *Albums* –
written in the 1880s by the French writer, Jules Laforgue. Here the
poet imagines an American West he had never visited. He will settle
down as a farmer with '*Une vache laitière et des petits enfants*'. But
even in these placid circumstances the 'flight of the Rocky Mountain
Condor' might disturb his repose by showing him a glimpse of the
infinite. If this should be the case:

> *Eh! bien, j'inventerais un culte d'Age d'or,*
> *Un code social, empirique et mystique,*
> *Pour les Peuples Pasteurs modernes et védiques!* . . .[12]

A social code that is empirical and mystic, pastoral people who are
modern and vedic, these formulations seem to sum up the tensions

and conflicts within the American and Western European 'Under-grounds'. These are, in Stuart Hall's view, the tensions between the expressive and activist roles. Hippies and other, largely apolitical, bohemian groups, represent the expressive pole. The hippie experiment might well be described as *'un culte d'Age d'or'*. At its heart is a pastoral-Arcadian philosophy, 'a view that life in its simpler forms and settings can be pared back to the bare essentials, and thus is counterposed to the frenzy, the stimulated wants and consumer anxieties of a modern, technological civilisation'.[13] This view of life comes to be applied generally to the primitive and traditional peoples of the non-metropolitan world. This is already fully apparent in *On the Road*. For Sal Paradise and Dean Moriarty the purpose of their trip to Mexico is 'to learn ourselves among the Fellahin Indians of the world, the essential strain of the basic primitive wailing humanity that stretches in a belt around the equatorial belly of the world from Malaya . . . to India the great subcontinent to Arabia to Morocco to the deserts and jungles of Mexico and over the waves to Polynesia to mystic Siam of the Yellow Robe and on around . . .'. These are the people and this is the life that will survive 'when destruction comes to the world of history'. In the late 'sixties and the early 'seventies this view of history was acted upon by some members of the Underground, who finding that 'capitalism could buy up any-thing and would contend with no opposition . . . retreated to the country or to the Bohemian colonies of Tangier and Nepal. Here a little money would go a long way and in the meantime they could wait for the inevitable collapse of the system.'[14] The meek and the mystic will inherit the earth!

Dean Moriarty's ecstatic reaction to Mexican life is particularly revealing:

> There is no *suspicion* here, nothing like that. Everybody's cool, everybody looks at you with such straight brown eyes, and they don't say anything, just *look* all of the human qualities are soft and subdued and still there. Dig all the foolish stories you read about Mexico and the sleeping gringo and all that crap, – and crap about greasers and so on – and all it is, people here are straight and kind and don't put down any bull. I'm so amazed by this. . . .

Here one system of mystification, that is based on a confidence in the superiority of the West, is swept aside to be replaced by another that is based on doubt, and results in a sentimental effusion that obscures social realities. In Kerouac's intoxicated vision, Mexico City, for all its filth and human suffering, becomes a kind of Holy City in a Promised Land: 'This was the great and final wild uninhibited Fellahin – childlike city that we knew we would find at the end of the road.' Mexico is 'one vast Bohemian camp'. Kerouac is, thus, in part responsible for the popularisation of a new distortion of pastoral myth: the life and culture of the poor people of the Third World are Natural and therefore Good; the rationale of western society is Repressive and Unnatural and therefore Bad. A strange misconception results from this simplistic thinking; this amounts to a view that ways of life governed by barbaric custom and restricted by a constant struggle to survive are somehow more 'liberated' than life in the affluent West. It is, of course, arguable that in spiritual terms the 'standard of living' in Katmandu or Marrakech is higher than that of most western cities. There is poverty and disease but there is not the same alienation and neurosis: the West has the material goods, but the 'Fellahin-Indian' has the spiritual knowledge. While subscribing to this general view Neville continues:

> This is not to underestimate the barbarities, injustices and un-pleasant superstitions which abound in primitive communities which are sometimes overlooked by myopic itinerants but it is to suggest, at the risk of being sentimental, that the new refugees from the West are profoundly and permanently affected by the fresh simplicity and sylvan logic of such a lifestyle.

What Neville risks is not simply sentimentality but the application of a western literary convention to an alien reality. Neville's hippie travellers would seem to regard the entire non-metropolitan world as their Arcadia. It was for much the same reasons that Corso found Greece 'consoling'. Greece contains the original Arcadia; it is a largely pastoral country, littered with the ruins of past grandeur, and so, to the sensitive wanderer, immediately conducive to philosophy and poetry.

The hippie experiment thus came to be dominated by an Arcadian-mystical ethos, and it is this that accounts for the striking difference between beat and hippie styles of travel. The beats devoured the road; the hippies 'drift with the current'. The beats avidly pursued 'experience'; the hippies emphasised receptivity, submergence in the stream of experience. Drugs (chiefly cannabis and LSD) and Oriental-ism play the most important role in the formation of their attitudes, which are perhaps most completely expressed in hippie-drifter travel. As we have seen, the connection between the experience of travelling and the experience of drugs had already been made in nineteenth-century France. The travelling was, ideally, travel to North Africa or the East, that is, to regions with traditional drug cultures. Drug-taking (hashish or opium) and travelling into *'une exotique nature'* were both means of escaping from western reality and at the same time of altering or 'expanding' consciousness. In certain important ways the aims of systematic experimentation with hallucinogens and those of the meditational disciplines of Oriental mysticism are the same. Both aim at transcendence by means of a dissolution of the ego. There are equally important differences of course, but for our present purposes we may take this to be sufficient explanation for that hectic mingling of Eastern mysticism and drug culture that reached its height in the so-called 'psychedelia' of the late 'sixties. One thinks of Leary's ritual LSD 'performances', Allen Ginsberg's Buddhist chants, and the Beatles' involvement with the Maharishi. 'Psychedelia' can be defined as a 'synesthetic aesthetic', and as such it is nothing new. It is foreshadowed in the work of the Romantics, and is already fully formed in the work of Rimbaud.

It can now be seen how completely drifter-travel is an expression of this sensibility. Any intensive experience comes to be referred to as a 'trip'. The exploration of the external world by 'drifting' parallels the exploration of 'inner space' by means of hallucinogens. A success-ful 'acid trip' requires the individual to allow himself to 'drift' on an altered stream of consciousness. All preconceptions must be jetti-soned and any attempt to continue to perceive things in terms of 'normal' consciousness must be abandoned. The principle of drifter-travel requires a similar willingness to submerge oneself in an 'alter-native reality', to diverge from any pre-planned route (throwing away the compass and the guidebook) and to allow preconceptions to be altered by experiences encountered on the road. Unlike the conventional tourist, the drifter is prepared to enter into the stream of a different way of life. This is the *ideal* drifter, and the reality is often very different. 'Drifting' seems very easy; travel to the East and you cannot fail to come across the Great Experience you have been waiting for. As it turns out 'the way' is full of pitfalls, and it is quite possible that the trek to Nepal will provide as little in the way of 'real' experience and personal fulfilment as a packaged holiday on the Costa Brava in August.

The road to Katmandu is the literal dimension of the new bohe-mia's identification with the East. The more self-conscious and literate young travellers on this road probably see themselves in the image of Herman Hesse's *Journey to the East*. For some time Hesse's philosophical novels have been widely read throughout the Underground. (A prominent American West Coast rock band even named itself after Hesse's most famous novel *Steppenwolf*.) Hesse is 'an artist of ideas' – unfortunately his ideas are invariably derivative and banal. In book after book 'the Great Ideas' pursue 'the Terrific Experiences, home to their all-too-obvious destinations'. That Hesse is something of an arrested adolescent only made him more attractive to the Underground. His most obsessive theme is homesickness ('*Heimweh*'): '. . . we have to stumble through so much dirt and humbug before we reach home. And we have no one to guide us. Our only guide is our homesickness.'[15] It is difficult to say exactly what constitutes 'home' for Hesse and his many young admirers, except that it has something to do with childhood. As we would expect, one of the chief means of assuaging this malaise is to travel, and most frequently travel to the East, since Oriental mysticism seems to offer one way of transcending the 'dirt and humbug' of the material world.

Hesse's eclectic orientalism has been generally adopted; the *Rig Veda*, the *Tao Te Ching* of Lao Tzu, the *Tibetan Book of the Dead*, the *I Ching* are all grist to the mill. Add to this list the quasi-autobiographical ramblings of western psychedelic gurus, and the result can only be the worst kind of intellectual confusion, what George Seferis has called (in a very different context): 'the little learning that distorts the mind and puts it to sleep. . . .' There is after all no short cut to 'revelation' or inner peace. And as Hesse himself was aware: '*Unser ewiges Heimweh auf* [Our homesickness lasts forever].'[16]

The attitudes we have been discussing follow naturally from the experience of affluence and alienation. In terms of 'metaphor, analogy, and symbol' they even have a certain cohesion. But they must also be judged in quite different terms.

As we have often had cause to note it is only possible to idealise 'the fresh simplicity and sylvan logic' of the rural poor from the vantage of comparative wealth and freedom. In the Third World scarcity and deprivation is real and apparently irreducible. In the late 'sixties the theoreticians of the counter-culture maintained that scarcity was a myth, claiming that any scarcity that did exist was the artificial product of a system based on waste: 'The abundance is so great that tremendous efforts, ingenuity and loss of life are going to create an unconvincing appearance of shortage.' As far as the West is concerned there is a good deal of truth in this, but since our advanced industrial societies have developed at the expense of the underdeveloped nations, this abundance that threatens to break through and transform western society could also only do so at their expense.

As Neville remarks: 'The desire of young expatriates to savour the "backwardness" of these communities, like anthropological gourmets is equalled only by the determination of the natives to catch up.' A disenchanted young American may well consider that life in Marrakech is richer than life in his home town but few of the inhabitants of Marrakech 'are in a position to evaluate his claims as most of them are denied equivalent freedom to travel'. It would also be wrong to assume that hippies and drifters are invariably appreciative in their attitudes and discreet in their behaviour toward Third World communities: 'When it comes to exploiting innocent primitives, hippie nomads can be as ruthless as governments.' In support of this statement Neville refers to the 'white pills racket' which is, apparently, common in Thailand:

> In Bangkok, many travellers keep alive by selling little white pills (probably aspirins) in a routine as bizarre as it is cynical: Thai employer introduces traveller to an unsuspecting, trusting village audience as, say, Dr Schweitzer from Harley Street. Traveller recites Shakespeare or dirty limericks to the crowd, while enthusiastically waving a little bottle of white tablets. Thai accomplice 'translates' this into an exciting sales blurb. The tablets sell swiftly and the traveller reaps a fat commission. Variations on this theme can be played to native communities throughout India and the Far East. . . .

It must be remembered that in a phenomenon which involves many thousands of young people this extreme cynicism is no more typical than pure idealism. On occasion hippie behaviour has caused genuine local outrage. In Bali a number of young travellers who had based themselves on Kuta Beach became involved in a series of lurid incidents, including naked dancing in a sacred monkey forest. On the island of Lamu, off the coast of Kenya, nude bathing caused predictable outrage among Moslem elders; one can imagine the reaction of a traditional Moslem male confronted by a naked Californian girl. As Kelvin Hall has observed,[17] young visitors 'are sentimental in expecting in Africa diminished inhibition and primitive harmony'. Lured by the Arcadian-mystical ideal of the tropical isle, hippies 'rush in where angels fear to tread'. '*Le vert paradis des amours enfantines*' turns out to be governed by a complex and highly sensitive culture, and in the case of Lamu, by a puritanical religious morality.

One might also question the morality of hippie begging in countries that are already overburdened with beggars. In many Third World countries the wealthier inhabitants traditionally distribute their small change to their less fortunate compatriots. The hippies are 'cashing in' on this tradition and at the same time they violate the sensibilities of the indigenous bourgeoisie; here are the products of the civilisation they envy 'begging, living in caves and dressing like madmen'. In general, it is not the poor of the Third World who are hostile to the hippie and the drifter but governments and the bourgeoisie. In this they are following the example set by many western countries in the late 'sixties. As we have seen, the new bohemians everywhere began to find themselves the victims of reaction:

> The reaction of powerful forces against bohemian subcultures occurs not because wider material interests are threatened but because the bohemian threatens the reality of the 'straight' world. By invoking a world of pleasure unrelated to productivity, of expressivity divorced from work roles he is a caustic to the moral legitimacy of the system . . . at the same time as threatening the affluent citizen's world of discipline and consumption he mocked the poverty of the working-class poor. . . .[18]

In the Third World this 'threat' assumes a crucial importance. For Third World governments that were desperately trying to attain some degree of economic self-sufficiency and stability in their countries, the arrival of the hippie travellers was deeply disconcerting. Committed to the ethics of work and productivity they discovered that the children of the affluence to which they aspired rejected both affluence and ethics. The young westerners were only interested in those elements of the indigenous culture that officialdom and the bourgeoisie regarded as 'backward'. This explains the hostility to drug use among hippies in countries where hashish has been accepted for centuries. Only ignorant peasants and tribesmen use hashish, the progressive (i.e. bourgeois) elements have switched to alcohol; the hippies who have had all the advantages of western education should know better than to imitate the habits of these recalcitrant 'primitives'. The hippie threat with its 'sinister pattern' was most often viewed as a threat to youth. In Morocco traditionalists complained that hippies were undermining Islamic culture; Moroccan teenagers looked up to them 'as a kind of cultural and social varsity', and imitated their styles of dress and behaviour. The fears this has aroused are not simply the product of bigoted and reactionary attitudes. In 1973 the Moroccan opposition newspaper *L'Opinion* called on the government to step up its 'quasi-campaign' against the drug culture. The cultivation of individual expressivity, and the determination to avoid ungratifying labour might have validity within the context of an affluent society, but, *L'Opinion* argued, these were inappropriate behavioural models for Moroccan youth. Morocco required 'dynamism and hard work' of its younger generation in order that they might help to rescue their country from its poverty and underdevelopment. In consequence hippies are seen as 'a dangerous phenomenon': 'In cafés one can find them engaged in destroying all that is good in our youth. They are teaching them a language which has nothing in common with our reality. They are popularising destructive ideas, propagating drugs – kif and hashish – in the midst of our youth for whom we are impatiently waiting to take in hand the destiny of this country.' It is probable that the Moroccan authorities would agree with much of this but an anti-drug campaign presents problems since some areas of the country are economically dependent on kif and hashish.

It is possible to argue that the hippie example has a liberative influence on Third World youth, who have a perfect right to indulge in the delights of kif, rock music, permissive sexuality, long hair and denims. But the charge of corruption cannot be so easily dismissed. The views expressed in *L'Opinion* echo those of Fanon:

> The young people of the towns, idle and often illiterate, are a prey to all sorts of disintegrating influences. It is to the youth of an underdeveloped country that the industrialised countries most often offer . . . their pastimes. Normally there is a certain homogeneity between the mental and material level of the members of any given society and the pleasures which that society creates for itself. But in underdeveloped countries, young people have at their disposal leisure occupations designed for the youth of capitalist countries. . . . In the West the family circle, the effects of education and the relatively high standard of living of the working classes, provide a more or less efficient protection against the harmful action of these pastimes. But in an African country, where mental development is uneven, where the violent collision of two worlds has considerably shaken old traditions and thrown the universe of the perceptions out of focus, the impressionability and sensibility of the young African are at the mercy of the various assaults made upon them by the very nature of Western culture. . . .

Fanon was not speaking of hippies since the phenomenon was unknown at the time he wrote *The Wretched of the Earth*, but if we accept his argument then surely hippies and drifters present an ostentatious display of 'inappropriate pastimes'. They become one more way in which the people of the Third World are diverted from the goals appropriate to development, only to follow the western bourgeoisie along its 'path of negation and decadence'. The violent rhetoric directed against the hippie example in the Third World would suggest that – to the establishment – it represents all the most degenerate aspects of western culture. It represents the 'permissiveness' and moral chaos that must be rejected, just as the progressive elements of modernisation and industrialisation must be emulated. As Erik Cohen observes: 'In a rather paradoxical manner, the very youths who in their way rebelled against their own culture and rejected it, come to be considered as the most fearsome representatives of its "negative" aspects.' The more articulate spokesmen among these 'youths' would probably reply that the developing nations are the victims of the progressive economic and industrial system they so admire. They reject the values of late capitalism and would argue that it is in the interests of the Third World to join them in this rejection. On a collective, national scale they must 'do their own thing', not accept a solution prescribed by their former colonial masters. We might also ask whether it is realistic, or even desirable, for any younger generation in any country to accept a scheme of 'dynamism and hard work' handed down by politicians, bureaucrats and intellectuals. It is in the nature of youth to reject whatever is considered suitable by its elders.

The 'moral panic' of officialdom and the press is largely self-defeating. This torrent of directives against long hair, mini-skirts, hot-pants and pop music, this outcry in the press has occurred in most of the Third World nations so far mentioned. In the West newspapers had already discovered that there was an avid public demand for tales of hippie depravities: 'The newspaper provides a myth which luridly describes the deviant, dwells on his hedonistic transgressions, teases out moral outrage and then plumps for the system by pointing to the disgrace, pain and suffering in which such behaviour *must necessarily* be seen to culminate.'[19] Thus hippie deviance from the norms of productivity and consumption acquires all the glamour of forbidden fruit. 'Disgrace, pain and suffering' even endow the hippie with a certain Romantic grandeur. Any

subject which at the same time attracts and repels is 'good copy'
Indeed the press might be said to have created hippies as a social
problem. The phenomenon became amplified out of all proportion
and, in Jock Young's words: 'The result was a forceful backlash of
social reaction and at the same time a widespread dissemination of
bohemian ideals amongst the young.' Neville quotes from a letter to
The Bangkok Post (1969) which complains that 'Parliament have
nothing to talk about except how to prevent long hair on men and
short skirts on women. . . . Anything they are not used to they con-
demn and try to stamp out.' What they are used to is vice, crime,
corruption, bureaucratic incompetence and 'numbered Swiss bank
accounts'. Outrage over the degeneracy of hippies thus becomes a
convenient way of avoiding discussion of the real problems of the
country, problems which, to a significant extent, are the fault of the
politicians, bureaucrats and intellectuals who preach hard work and
social responsibility to the young.

It would be entirely wrong to see the Third World hostility to
hippies as an expression of independence or a rejection of western
decadence. In reality it represents an inability to outgrow a state of
mind distorted by colonialism. This emerges most clearly in East
Africa. Reactionary colonial Europeans regarded all Africans as
shiftless and immoral; now bourgeois Africans apply the same epi-
thets to all hippie travellers. Outrage over nude bathing in Lamu is
paralleled by attempts to get the Masai and Karomojon tribesmen to
wear trousers. The use of hashish is traditional but again it becomes
an outrage when it is seen to be used by well-educated Whites who
have access to all the material benefits that upwardly mobile Africans
hope to gain by their adoption of the principles of 'modernisation'.
Su Walton has suggested[20] that in their attitude to the new breed of
disenchanted, nomadic Europeans, the East Africans are only
following the example of the old-style colonial Europeans who still
live in their midst. We have already encountered this unattractive
breed in our discussion of the safari holiday; they represent a kind
of white man 'popularly believed to be extinct outside South Africa,
Rhodesia and music hall comedy'. This embattled minority with its
contempt for everything African and its rabidly conservative attitudes is inevitably hostile to the hippie culture which is associated
with these things that have made Europe as foreign to them as
Africa: '. . . socialism, intellectuals, the permissive society, queers,
women's lib, drugs, groupies, 4-letter words'. These have dispossessed

them. According to Su Walton the Africans of Malawi follow suit:

> If the white man, who is powerful, rich and confident, hates hippies, then the African who wants to be powerful, rich and confident hates them too. But not as an expression of independence. He despises them as a servant in the deep south despised 'white trash' in imitation of his master.

The educated African's rejection of the hippie is based on his continuing sense of inferiority to the West. In contrast, the hippie relishes the 'otherness' of African life, its exotic diversity of tribal customs. For all its sentimentalism this attitude is based on genuine doubt:

> *Peuples nomades, pasteurs, chasseurs, agricoles et même anthropophagues, tous peuvent être supérieurs par l'énergie, par la dignité personelles, à nos races d'Occident.*
> *Celles-ci peut-être seront détruites.*[21]

The hippie is a convenient scapegoat, a colourful symbol of all that is equivocal about the western solution. Despite their enthusiasm for modernisation and industrialisation the leaders of developing countries are often ambivalent in their attitude toward western culture. The real question is not whether hippies will corrupt youth, but whether progress on the western model is appropriate to overpopulated agrarian countries. The drive for modern efficiency can cause widespread misery and hardship since: 'The people in the poor countries of the world are still generally attached to their trades and professions, their satisfaction is greatly decreased if they are forced to change from one type of employment to another.'[22] The energy which should be directed towards this vitally important question is instead dissipated in sterile rhetoric against long hair and the sexual content of rock music. The presence of hippies in the Third World countries means that it is impossible to ignore the problematic nature of late-capitalism. If they are not themselves degenerates their style of revolt points clearly to the decadence of the West. It is just possible that they could prove to be a useful catalyst by undermining the complacency of Third World élites. Just as in the West their style of life expresses 'the repressed potential of the present social order', so, in the Third World their 'anthropological gourmets' delight in native customs may jolt the educated into a sharper awareness of the creative potential of indigenous culture.

Against this radical potential we must set the tendency of drifter tourism to become increasingly institutionalised 'on a level completely segregated from but parallel to that of ordinary mass-tourism'. The mass expansion of drifter tourism only became possible when the established economic interests realised that it could be profitable. They provided cheap transport by air-charter and 'overland' minibus. The late 'sixties and early 'seventies saw the emergence of 'fixed travelling patterns, established routines and a system of tourism facilities'.[23] The young traveller can now purchase any number of pre-planned 'safaris' or 'treks'. TWA's 'Worldtrek' offers a series of 'action holidays' in Greece, North Africa, Turkey and Persia as well as 'long-haul expeditions' to India, South Africa and South America. Their 1973–74 brochure begins: 'JET TO ADVENTURE' and continues: 'This is "real" travel with a style and grandeur never before imagined.' This is, to say the least, an extravagant claim, and we doubt whether the 'trek' is any more 'real' than other forms of organised tourism. The 'Trekguide' map lends the whole brochure an air of curious unreality, presenting an eccentric version of Near Eastern geography. The Turkish Lake Van has moved south, coming to rest somewhere in Eastern Syria. The Persian cities Rezaiyeh, Hamadan and Kermanshah have all migrated into Iraq (Kermanshah has even reached the borders of Saudi Arabia), while Persepolis has merely shifted several hundred miles to the east. A tour which covers Morocco, Algeria and Tunisia in six weeks – whose organisers are under the impression that Djerba is 'The island home of Ulysses' – can hardly promise much in the way of 'real' experience. ('Worldtrek' might at least have remembered that Ulysses was a Greek, not a Tunisian.) Nevertheless the brochure diligently makes all the 'right' verbal gestures. It offers 'insight into every aspect of Moroccan life' and the anthropological delights of 'peasant villages as primitive as any in Africa'. It does not hesitate to rehearse the clichés of the counter-culture:

> To the average European, used to the clinical and air-conditioned nightmare of our Western society, the 'culture shock' of a first time contact with Africa can often be a staggering experience. He rarely returns unchanged.

Although it talks of 'social customs, religion, ways of thinking and reacting to things', the brochure can still describe the Greek 'national personality' in terms of 'happy, carefree, sunsoaked "joie de vivre" '. What kind of 'insight' does this suggest? 'Worldtrek' and similar businesses offer the appearance of adventure and 'real' travel, without the risks and discomfort involved in the real thing. Once industrialised, the tourism of the young assumes all the worst aspects of conventional mass tourism; one thinks of the girl, 'mini-trekking' to North Africa, who noted in her diary: 'Spain, passed thro' several villages.'

This is the case even among those drifters who still avoid the organised 'mini-trek'. As Cohen observes:

> The mass-drifter is not really motivated to seek adventure and mix with the people he visits. Rather he often prefers to be alone to 'do his own thing' or focuses his attention on the counter-culture represented by the other drifters whom he encounters on his trip. His social contacts, hence, become progressively narrowed to the company of other drifters. In its social dynamics, mass-drifter tourism develops a tendency parallel to that observed in ordinary mass-tourism: a loss of interest and involvement with the local people, customs and landscape and a growing orientation to the in-group. . . .

This is the negative aspect of the world viewed as 'one vast Bohemian camp'. A false uniformity is imposed on the world, a uniformity summed up in the words of one of Joni Mitchell's songs: 'Maybe I'll go to Amsterdam / Maybe I'll go to Rome . . . . I caught a plane to Spain / there were lots of pretty people there reading *Rolling Stone*.' Here the prized spontaneity of the drifter has become mere aimlessness and in every destination are the same 'pretty people', determinedly keeping in touch with the rock music scene.

The drifter's disdain for guide-book tourism and his avoidance of the conventional ('Taj Whateveritis') tourist sights, was, from the beginning, ambivalent. Hippies and drifters frequently display a complacent ignorance of the histories and cultures of the countries they are visiting. This is apparent in Patrick Marnham's generally intelligent and observant book *The Road to Katmandu*. In Turkey the author passes through Sivas, Erzurum and Trebizond, but the wealth of architectural remains from the Byzantine and Seljuk eras to be found in these places goes unmentioned. His eyes and those of his fellow travellers are focused entirely on the alluring East: Trebizond is just a place one passes through. Among overlanders on the India trail there seems to be a good deal of crass competitiveness and status-mongering; the burning question would seem to be: 'How far East can you get, and how quickly?' This suggests that, in general, the rejection of capitalist values is strictly superficial, an impression confirmed by the readiness of some to exploit the hospitality and gullibility of 'innocent primitives'.

After Istanbul the first place in which Marnham stops for any length of time is Herat. Herat is apparently very popular with over-landers who like its relaxed atmosphere. It appeals to Marnham in much the same way that Marrakech appeals to Richard Neville, or Mexico City to Kerouac. Marnham, and the other overlanders he meets there, seem entirely unaware of the history and cultural signi-ficance of this city. Founded by Alexander the Great, it reached its height as the capital of the Timurid Empire in the fifteenth century, at which time it was one of the world's leading centres of art and science. No mention is made in *The Road to Katmandu* of the surviv-ing monuments of Timurid Herat. No one should feel obliged to visit methodically all 'sights of historical interest', but there is something rather pointless about visiting an Islamic country and not bothering to look at its mosques and mausoleums. If the suppression of the present life of a country, in favour of its monuments reduces the reality of the past, then equally the suppression of the past reduces the reality of the present. To refer again to the analogy of the LSD trip, the best experiences are obtained by those who have taken the trouble to prepare themselves. The same can be said of travelling in Asia or Africa. If the amiable dope-dispensing natives whom Dean Moriarty found 'cool' and 'amazing' were seen in their historical and cultural context, the itinerant hippie might avoid committing those indiscretions which do genuinely offend local opinion.

Once drifter tourism becomes institutionalised it loses its validity as an alternative to conventional mass tourism. This has not pre-vented some people from seeing a modified form of counter-cultural tourism as a solution to the industry's problems. We refer, of course, to Herbert Hiller's theory of 'alternative tourism' (see 'Paradise Rejected'). Hiller envisions tourists who are 'antipathetic to the milieu of technology and to the leisure creations based on it'. Hiller's young, individualistic traveller, sensitive to local feelings and appreciative of local culture sounds very much like an idealised, 'hygienic' version of the drifter. Much the same is implied by the following observation of Patrick Rivers': 'Out there in the market place are many, many people who would like contact with the *real* world, away from the pools and boutiques, but they don't know how to do it and the travel industry has so far failed to reach them or satisfy them.' Hiller and Rivers refer specifically to the Caribbean, a region not much frequented by those 'alternative tourists' who exist already. Their principal destinations remain Europe, North Africa and India. In these areas the tourism industry has already learnt ways of reaching and satisfying them with organised 'minitreks' and 'overland' tourism. When Hiller asks: 'Why are we building merely for those trapped in fantasies?' he ignores the fact that his sensitive young tourists would be just as firmly 'trapped in fantasies' as the rich, middle-aged, middle-class tourists, who are at present the mainstay of the Caribbean tourist industry. No doubt they would be trapped in different fantasies – ones more appealing to a man of liberal conscience like Hiller, but they could not provide the basis for a tourism which was genuinely sensitive to Third World problems and supportive of 'development'. The Caribbean Islands would remain Paradises, Edens, Arcadias, places in which to assuage the incurable 'homesickness' that Hesse has described. Even for the ecologically aware and politically committed, tourism functions as a temporary escape, an escape perhaps made all the more necessary by reason of their awareness and commitment.

Compared to India or Nepal, the Caribbean lacks the necessary 'symbolic weight' to attract 'alternative tourists'. These tourists generally avoid regions already established as tourist resorts and it is more usual for conventional mass tourism to follow in the wake of the 'hippie-pioneer'. Would there have been a Katmandu Hilton if Nepal had not been 'discovered' by the hippies? Perhaps the hippies themselves are agents of that process which is 'reducing the world to comprehensibility' and deathly uniformity. As Edmund Wilson said in 1931, it is 'unsatisfactory' and 'impossible' to imitate the example of Rimbaud since: '. . . we carry within us, in our minds and habits, the civilisation of machinery, trade, democratic education and standardisation to the Africas and Asias to which we flee, even if we do not find them there before us'. On arriving in his imagined Arcadia of 'innocent primitives', 'diminished inhibition' and freely available dope, the idealistic young traveller finds that the inhabitants are anxious to leave by any means possible. He finds that they avidly covet the material benefits of the civilisation from which he is in flight, that their governments are bent on modernisation and increased efficiency, and he finds himself the object of violent and uncomprehending hostility. An appropriate epitaph for such a young traveller might be: 'ET IN ARCADIA EGO'.

17 The Future

In forecasting the future one should always err on the side of scepticism. Of course, we all have idealistic visions of what the world should be like, but the future is generally just like the past, only a bit larger or hungrier – or whatever the long-term trends would indicate. One has to assume that most things one personally wants will never happen, and one also assumes that any particularly extreme trends will gradually be moderated. This is probably just as well since, if tourism goes on growing at around 10 per cent per annum, the industry would be annually handling over 2,000 million people by the year 2000, or the combined current population of China, India, USSR, USA, Indonesia, Japan, Brazil and Bangladesh. However, even if one assumes the industry must slow down to perhaps an 8 per cent annual growth in the 1980s, and 6 per cent in the 1990s, then it will still be handling around 1,300 million people, which is the combined population of India and China. This would demand something like 200 major new resorts each year just to handle the extra growth. Something, we feel, must come along to put a stop to this explosion. Otherwise the world will turn into one great Florida-style, concrete, ribbon development.

We are stuck with the logic of these trends unless we can identify convincing 'system-breaks' – those revolutions or catastrophes which make futurologists look foolish by changing the forces which are behind the trend lines. Thus Castro's successful revolution in Cuba killed a booming tourist industry, and led to an unexpected boost in the role of Bahamian tourism. Are there any larger problems which could lead to the growth of international tourism being slowed down (or maybe reversed)?

The energy crisis could be one such break, even if, at the time we started writing this book, few people believed that international tourism was about to receive a blow as serious as the massive rise in fuel costs which followed the Yom Kippur war. There were a few sceptics like Patrick Rivers, author of *The Restless Generation*, who foresaw a serious world shortage of oil (though only within the next twenty-five years), and growing environmental resistance to the spread of airports. On both counts, he suggested that tourists would be faced with higher fares, and that the industry's growth rate might well be curtailed in favour of more essential activities.

Conventional wisdom, however, dismissed such arguments. The industry was felt to be too dynamic to slow down. Static or falling air fares meant that the real cost of travel was declining. The relaxation of the rules governing charter flights had led to a surge of transatlantic business. Proposals to extend this liberalisation to cover internal flights within Europe were expected to give an extra fillip to the European holiday trade.

The aftermath of Yom Kippur has changed all that, and, as we write, international tourism is seeing its first annual decline since the end of the Second World War. Partly, this has come because higher oil costs have led to a slow-down in the growth of the world economy, thus leaving less money for travel. Partly, higher fuel costs have increased the cost of travel, thus pricing tourism out of the reach of some potential travellers. Does this mean, however, that travel must now become so expensive as to slow down the growth of international tourism for good?

One doubts it. One suspects that all this current crisis means is that the cost of international travel has been given one hefty hike upwards, but, once stabilised at a new higher level, all the forces which were at work before will continue. People's incomes will continue to rise, and they will again start to spend on tourism, though for the initial years their money will buy them less.

The continued erosion of artificially high airfares will continue, thus charter flights will eat further into the market; higher fuel costs means that the price of such charter flights will be higher than originally foreseen, but they will still be well below the standard airfares existing before the crisis. There may well be a switch away from planes to more economical coaches and trains but, for all that, modern aircraft are not disproportionately prodigal with fuel, if they are run fully loaded (which is the whole point about charter flights). A fully loaded Boeing 747 can do something like 58 passenger-miles per gallon, which is certainly more economical than half-utilised cars, where the average passenger-mile per gallon averages somewhere between 20 and 50.[1] One would, however, expect to find a stubborn decline in the fortunes of the cruise liners which at 14 passenger-miles per gallon (fully loaded) are about the most wasteful form of transport outside spacecraft.

All told, then, one suspects the current energy crisis will slow international tourism down for a couple of years – but that is all.

The possibility that we may face over 1,000 million tourists by the year 2000 will most likely be confounded by the growing congestion of the world's destinations. Already major tourist attractions in the developed world are reaching their capacity limits. The British tourist authorities are now having to ration the number of coaches bringing tourists to the Changing of the Guard outside Buckingham Palace (the military authorities have refused to put this on twice a day, arguing that, Gad Sir, they're soldiers and not a bunch of circus performers!). Such problems are hardly surprising, since the density of tourists to the square mile in London is higher than that of most receiving countries other than Monaco, which is really just one big city, itself.

Perhaps it is unfair to compare a city with host countries, but it is still clear that many destinations are now receiving numbers of tourists which must be approaching the upper limits of tolerance. In peak months, there is roughly one tourist for every five residents in Bermuda and the Bahamas; one to ten for Monaco; one to twenty for London and Austria. Within the Caribbean, Antigua, Montserrat, the British Virgin Islands and the Cayman Islands have notably high tourist densities both in reference to population and land area. 'Four of the ten most dense countries by reference to land area, and five of the ten most dense countries by reference to population, are in the Caribbean region.'[2] What more compelling explanation can one give for this area's reputation for anti-tourist resentments? What stronger reason can one put forward for suggesting that the growth of tourism in this area must inevitably be stabilised?

We have already argued that Alternative Tourism will never be more than a fairly minor aspect of international tourism. The bulk of this industry will be made up of mass tourists who are not really interested in the countries in which they travel. For most people, a foreign holiday will be a socially acceptable device for filling some of the increasing amount of leisure time we will be faced with. One study suggests that by the year 2000 paid holidays should be around thirteen weeks a year in industrialised countries.[3] This is a great deal of unstructured time to be filled. A certain amount will be filled by expanding Christmas holidays and devoting more time to adult education and voluntary associations. Beyond this, the expansion of the foreign holiday seems one of the most promising strategies. On one level, it appeals to the materialist in us all as a piece of conspicuous consumption; at another, it is respectable because it still has the educational image given it by the days of the Grand Tour; it also can provide a wide range of experiences, thus providing the variety which we need in our everyday lives.

There are some who would disagree, claiming 'the day will come when there will be no more traffic at all and only newlyweds will travel',[4] and one can make out an argument to support this. We are, for instance, moving inexorably toward McLuhan's Global Village, in which information about the whole world will be at our fingertips. Why, then, travel to a country when one can read its newspapers, watch its TV programmes, talk to its citizens on the phone, listen to its music on records, read about its art, politics, social structure or whatever in lengthy, detailed books? Why should our more cultured brethren visit unpleasantly congested cities like Rome, London or Acapulco anymore? Why don't they merely rely on the media for their impressions?

The only trouble with this argument is that we have not yet bred people, other than Howard Hughes, who are willing to live vicariously through the media. We are moving into an age in which activity is seen as a key aspect of leisure, and the pressures against the passive bookworm or TV addict will increase. The impact of all that electronic gadgetry may actually have the effect of making people travel more. What is the point of having cameras or tape-recorders without doing something more than merely recording beach scenes? The feeling will grow that one must record the 'real' world beyond the tourist compounds. This will, though, not make many into true Alternative Tourists, since their prime motivation will be to find activities spectacular enough to be filmed or recorded. These do not often tell you much about the real world.

This is a point which Susan Sontag has similarly made in a series of articles on the art of photography,[5] which she also sees as being an essential part of the tourist experience. She has traced examples back to those nineteenth-century North Americans who used the newly built transcontinental railroads to complete the victories over the Indians through a brand of 'colonisation through photography'. She also stresses the role that photography plays in documenting consumption carried on outside the immediate view of one's intimates, and there is no reason why this aspect of human nature should change. In fact, photography is the technology which allows one to get the best of all worlds by turning tourism into a piece of selectively conspicuous consumption. The physical act of spending one's money is removed to places where one will not meet fellow-citizens who might feel resentful of the disparities in one's wealth. Upon returning home, however, one is bearing photographs which will be shown only to those that one positively wants to impress. The well-photographed holiday is thus highly attuned to the vulnerable psyches of the rich, which can be simultaneously protected from envious comparisons, and boosted by discriminating display.

A second reason why mass tourism will continue is that the industry can only grow on the first-time travels of citizens from those countries which will become 'affluent' over the next twenty years. Thus the Japanese have only just become significant forces in world tourism. Tomorrow we would expect increasing numbers of Spaniards, Mexicans, East Europeans (politics permitting), Brazilians, Arabs and Venezuelans. The speed with which these new travellers appear on the international scene depends on just how fast their countries grow economically, but their arrival as tourists means that there will still be a heavy base-load of tourists who are travelling for the first time. Still new to affluence, they will be imbued with all those psychological impulses which make mass tourists so unattractive. Holidays will be seen as status symbols rather than as chances to improve one's understanding of new cultures. They will still feel unsure of themselves and will thus play safe, sticking to established tourist centres, rather than spreading out into more adventuresome areas. As fast, then, as existing mass tourists convince themselves that the tourist rabbit-runs are pretty ghastly, they will be replaced by these new, first-time ones. No one should believe that the nature of the industry will change very much.

What will be new will be the emergence of a sizeable minority of experienced travellers, who have visited some ten or twenty countries and are getting somewhat jaded as a result. Hotel life becomes increasingly monotonous; trailing round St Peter's in Rome is little different from 'doing' the cathedral in Mexico City; everywhere there are tourists, guides, extortionate bars, tawdry mementoes, and yet more tourists. What new experiences can one possibly have?

New strands in mass tourism will thus be developed as the entrepreneurs strive desperately to create tourist environments which are noticeably different from other experiences. The industry has already exploited most of the cultural legacy of our major civilisations and is finding that tourists really get little in the way of new experiences, when traffic jams and pollution now go inevitably with major tourist attractions; they can get these anywhere in their daily life. So there will be a switch to the realm of Nature. The East African game reserves have already shown that people enjoy being confronted with the Wild, even if it is only from inside air-conditioned coaches. The demand, though, will be for greater active involvement with the elements. So, group tours will be disguised as expeditions and will press into the Antarctic, the Amazonian forests and other barely opened territories. Ocean yachting will become more popular, and the underwater fraternity will probe ever deeper with improved leisure-oriented diving equipment. Overland minibus trips will push south into the Sahara and Central America. Eventually, when space flights are commercially viable, tourists will move into the last great unknown.

These developments are a throwback to the days of the old Roman games. Then, the gladiatorial contests were a way of compensating for the restrictions which urbanisation had placed on the behaviour of the citizens of Rome. Today, in a world in which militancy, physical courage and stamina are virtues which have been processed out of most people's existence, we can start to pit ourselves against the vagaries of Nature. The world of the Frontier which was destroyed by the spread of urban, industrialised, bureaucratic societies, is being re-created in the Pleasure Periphery. The computer operator, assembly-line worker and middle manager can temporarily escape their restrictive work roles; whatever their occupational frustrations, they too can follow the trail of Livingstone, Cousteau, Sir Francis Chichester or Ernest Hemingway. No corporation can destroy their holiday achievements.

For some people, though, even Nature begins to pall. One lion looks much like another, and how many people can really wax enthusiastic for long about distinguishing a Grant's Gazelle from a Wildebeest or Uganda Kob? How many of us cosseted creatures truly relish the thought of being attacked by sharks, drowned off Cape Horn, or possibly catching malignant malaria, or worse?

These less adventurous souls will seek their novelty in twenty-first-century fantasy – in pleasure cities like Las Vegas and Disney World, where all our frustrations can be soothed away. Gambling provides the *ersatz* experience of being Man against Nature; unlike the mountaineer or ocean yachtsman, the only thing one can lose is one's money. The top entertainers allow one to identify with the only public figures whose haloes are never allowed to slip. The Hollywood settings of Las Vegas, Disneyland and Disney World are invitations to retreat into a world where nothing will surprise or upset one, unless it's the mechanical hippopotami in the Jungle River Cruise.

This search for pleasure (fantasy) domes is motivated by different drives from the search for simplicity which we have examined in much of this book. Disney World and its imitators have roots going back to the fantasy of children's fables, to the razzmatazz of urban pleasure gardens like Copenhagen's Tivoli and of P. T. Barnum's 'Greatest Show on Earth', and to the technological awe created by the great industrial exhibitions triggered off by the Crystal Palace show of 1851. Even at that time, Barnum, that 'prince of humbugs', had a clear idea of the public's desire for mystification and wonderment, but the Industrial Revolution which had produced the steel, guns and locomotives which were the stars of the Great Exhibition were not yet developed enough to allow Barnum to deliver more than a proportion of his claims. Thus his 'mermaid' was in fact a 'black-looking specimen of dried monkey and fish that a boy of a few years old could easily run away with under his arm'.[6] In contrast, Disney has been able not only to develop his own pantheon (carefully protected by the copyright lawyers), but he has been able to draw on the full range of technical skills developed in Hollywood where Walt laboured so long. So, instead of having to rely on unreliable actors and trained animals, the Magic Kingdom draws on 'audio animatronics' which turns the traditional wax figures of Madame Tussaud's into moving, talking, singing robots which do everything but walk (though that will doubtless come).

Disney World is the ultimate pseudo-event for a generation for which the electronic revolution has taken all the mystery out of nature and our industrialised society. Symbolically, Florida's Cape Kennedy has now merely become an incidental attraction which one visits after going to Disney World. Again, though it may be unfair to claim the latter's automated Jungle Ride makes the Everglades appear rather dull, they have become overshadowed by the capital-intensive leisure parks which have sprung up all round the State. Who wants to spend a day wandering about a swamp in the hope of seeing an alligator and various unidentified birds, when one can see the reptile along with performing dolphins and killer whales in the various Marinelands, Seaquariums and Sea Worlds? In an age which is blasé about technology, who needs serious exhibitions like the World Fairs, which were created in the days when the latest industrial processes were genuinely exciting? In this age which devours experiences through television, aren't Disney World and its imitators merely giving us back the Spectacular and Wonderment which have been in short supply as the world's belief in both religion and technical achievements has declined? Who wants to be reminded of the complexities of the real world when we can revisit our childhood cartoon friends, listen to a speech from an animated Abe Lincoln, and thrill to a simulated space flight – all in the course of a day.

One mentions the influence of Hollywood because in most of the latest resorts round the world, one senses that Hollywood is finding its final, permanent expression in late twentieth-century culture. The impact on classic developments like Las Vegas and the Disney projects is direct and clear. However, one can visit a new marina on Spain's Costa del Sol which, from the sea, is a miniature port surrounded by apartments in a heightened version of the blazing white Andalucian style; approach it from the land, and one realises that the buildings round the waterfront are exactly one building deep; what one sees from the sea is a stage setting; from the back, one could be in MGM's back lot. Or one can visit a Bulgarian Black Sea resort in which there is a nightclub influenced by the Hollywood Bowl and restaurants straight out of *Casablanca* or the Errol Flynn *oeuvres*; eating in a 'stranded' pirate's galleon, one reflects that the communist and Disney planners are really brothers under the skin; both realise that the future demands that they design pleasure cities as single entities, and that success comes as much from picking popular 'themes' as from conventional architectural skills.

Disneyland has spawned imitators, but these have mostly been in mainland USA. Elsewhere the emphasis on fantasy has been less; attention has been mostly paid to the improved planning of traditional resorts, which has meant increasing the size of the towns which are planned. Thus Mexico's Cancun and Ixtapa developments will cost $100 million; Portugal's Armacao de Pera, $250 million; France's Languedoc–Roussillon scheme will have had $500 million invested by 1975 and Hawaii's 'City of Flowers' project in Maui will cost £300 million.[7] Once planning is done on this scale, it should be easy to impose themes on new developments, though there are few European projects on the drawing-board which would rival Disney (one such, is a pleasure park designed for Britain, which would have a Merrie England theme).

The backwardness of Europe is surprising because commercial logic suggests that the Mediterranean area is ripe for the development of a Las Vegas. Monte Carlo has the potential but just is not brash enough, since it is still run by people who want to preserve its turn-of-the-century flavour. The Spanish resorts like Palma, Benidorm or Torremolinos just have not developed the kind of vast nightclubs-cum-hotels which can attract the Frank Sinatras of the world. Perhaps this is because most European governments view gambling equivocally, believing it should be controlled. Perhaps it is because there is no common European popular culture as there is in North America (certainly there are few European artists with a trans-European appeal such as Presley or Sinatra have in North America). Perhaps it is just that the European Pleasure Periphery has not yet spawned the crooks and impresarios with sufficient self-confidence both to gauge the tastes of the average European tourist (if such a creature exists), and to win *de facto* independence from the national governments round the Mediterranean.

So, the mass tourist industry will continue to grow, and there is little sign that anything is going to slow it down in any significant way. However, this fatalism does not mean that host countries have to lie back and be raped without a struggle.

Firstly, all tourist destinations should be led by governments aware that there is no rule which says they have to welcome tourists. If the rich countries can discriminate about the Third World immigrants they choose to accept, why should the Third World blindly accept tourists from the rich world?

Tourism is socially corrosive and should be controlled. The economic case is unclear and, very certainly, governments would be well advised to tax tourists to ensure that they pay for their full share of costs of the infrastructure they make necessary. There is absolutely no point in encouraging tourism if the money they bring is merely spent in improving life for future tourists. There is no earthly reason why the local community should subsidise tourists.

From the very start there should be a clear policy on the foreign ownership of land and businesses. In the long run, does one want a permanent foreign community? If so, how large should it be? To what extent should it be allowed to compete with local citizens for land and houses? Admittedly, there can be no clear answers to these

LEISUREDOME
Disneyworld © Walt Disney Productions

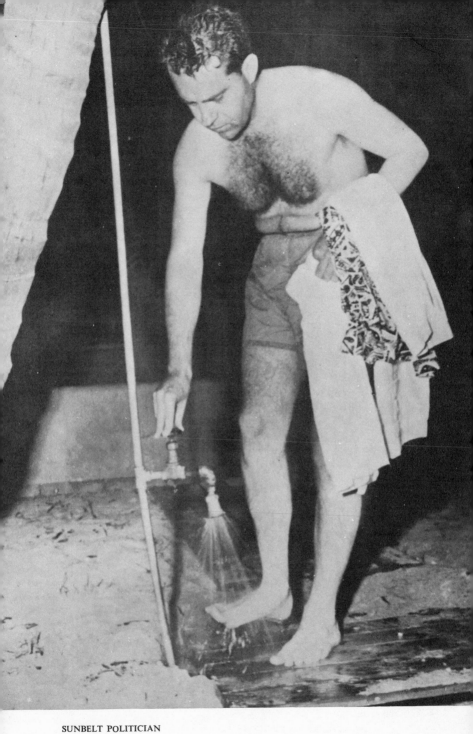

SUNBELT POLITICIAN
Richard M. Nixon

questions which would be valid everywhere, but from the start it should be remembered that permanent tourists will be relatively rich and thus of a political importance far greater than their numbers would suggest. It is therefore desirable to set an upper limit to the number of permanent tourists one is willing to allow one's country to receive. Lay down strict terms about the amount of money they must bring into the country with them. Specify the exact terms on which they can buy and dispose of property. Do not let them pull down old buildings to put up new ones. Resist the temptation to limit immigrants merely by their wealth. If one's country is popular enough, give first preference to people with skills which may be of use to it.

Wherever possible, ban cars. They are a nuisance, causing congestion and involving heavy investment in roads. Encourage tourists to ride bicycles (as in Bermuda) or even walk. If they have to ride in cars for their own safety, then one probably should not be in the tourist industry in the first place.

The poorer one's country, the more essential it is to keep tourism heavily localised. The aim in such circumstances is to get the maximum amount of money from the foreigners, while minimising the amount of social damage they can do. Bring your local arts and crafts to the tourists in the form of dance troupes, art shows, etc., rather than encouraging the tourists to leave their ghettos to disrupt your countryside.

Finally, there is a need for a world body to look after tourism. This does exist in the form of the World Tourism Organisation (formerly the International Union of Official Travel Organisations), which is an intergovernmental body with consultative status to United Nations. There is a lot of useful work to be done on standardising the incentives offered to tourist operators, so that countries do not over-compete in attracting them. There is also a need for a kind of touristic commodity agreement, which would aim to orchestrate the investment flows made by tourist destinations in the Third World. This WTO could also help sort out the new range of legal complications we examined in Chapter 14. Above all, this is the body which might look at tourism as a social phenomenon which requires extremely delicate handling.

The Golden Horde is, though, now virtually out of control. The problems of some countries are approaching their peak, like those of European cities such as London, Paris and Rome which make up the contemporary Grand Tour. They are actually pricing themselves out of the mass tourism market, since new hotel space in them is horrendously expensive. Unlike the USA where cheap hotel chains have spread as a result of low land prices and relatively lax planning controls, European hotels are faced with expensive land and tough authorities. Add on considerable shortages of cheap labour in the heart of large cities like London, and there is no way of reducing the cost of tourism to these countries.

The Horde will thus continue to move on to the cheaper destinations in the Pleasure Periphery – and here the problems of political control are grave. Tourism is too glamorous, and looks too easy. It also attracts some of the world's most ruthless businessmen and criminals. This surge to the sun can only end up with a number of virtual states-within-states, which bodes ill for the long-term political future of many of the world's poorest countries. Some of the micro-states of the Caribbean and the Pacific may well tear themselves apart as rich foreigners try to turn their more desolate islands into personal kingdoms.

Underneath everything, tourism is still basically a migration, in which people leave the cold and grime of the older industrial countries for the sun and environmental purity of the Pleasure Periphery. The numbers of permanent tourists are not yet significant, but the massive flows of conventional tourists will ensure that their number steadily increases. Many will work loosely within the tourist industry, but gradually conventional industries will move new plants down after them. The world's economic and political centre of gravity is moving slowly toward the equator. Industrialisation and a new form of colonisation are moving forward hand in hand. In a fit of absence of mind, we are redrawing the map of the world.

On a psychological level, the tourist industry in the Third World is concerned with the manipulation of divergent aspects of human experience, so it is not surprising that the individual tourist sometimes encounters the kind of alarming and disturbing experience that ruins a holiday; it is not a question of whether or not a tourist should be more effectively insulated from shock, but of whether we have the right to demand that we be able to enjoy a holiday in a world in which the circumstances of Cairo, Beirut, Port au Prince or, even, Hong Kong, are commonplace. This is, of course, the question which must never be asked if the tourist industry is to continue to prosper. A common reaction in the holiday-maker who encounters poverty and squalor in the country he is visiting is anger – not anger at social injustice, but anger that the host country should have the presumption to invite *respectable, civilised* people when it is not ready to receive them, when the sanitation is inadequate, the food is not up to international standards, the people have no conception of personal hygiene and there are beggars in the streets.

Our general impression is that average tourists in the Third World have a rigidly polarised view of the world. They cannot, or will not, see any causal link between the wealth of their class and the prevailing poverty of the countries they visit. For them the division of the world is complete and ineradicable; the wealth of the developed nations justified by virtue of their superior energy and organisation and made possible by their progressive innovations in technology and commerce. The 'backwardness' of the underdeveloped nations is not the result of poverty, but their poverty is a result of their *innate* 'backwardness'. Their governments are invariably corrupt and inefficient ('socialist incompetents'); their people lazy and ignorant. In fact tourists often propound a variant of the Victorian ethic of 'self-help'; in a world of free enterprise and unlimited opportunity – it is implied – it is open to any individual or nation to pull themselves up to the western level of prosperity. Any suggestion that the relation between the two poles of the human condition might be more complex and ambiguous, might be an *inter-relation*, a dependency of one on the other, is rejected. To suggest that a specific historical process might have played a part in establishing this opposition involves talking in terms of capitalism and imperialism and could, therefore, be dismissed by them as the clichés of communist doctrine. In fact, as Raymond Williams has pointed out in *The Country and the City*,[8] such a polarisation of human experience and cultural values is enshrined in the Communist Manifesto itself, which opposes the values of modernisation and urban civilisation to 'the idiocy of rural life' and 'the barbarism and semi-barbarism' of colonised, subject nations and races. The metropole is seen to have subjugated the periphery but metropolitan values are, at the same time, endorsed as the values of progress.

It is essential to tourism as mythology and as industry that the polar opposites are *not* seen in relation to each other. As Erik Cohen has observed, tourism does not destroy the misapprehensions of one country concerning another, it perpetuates and reinforces them:

I would hypothesise that the larger the flow of mass tourists becomes, the more institutionalised and standardised tourism becomes and consequently the stronger the barriers between the tourist and the life of the host country become. What were previously formal barriers between different countries become informal barriers *within* countries.

In relation to what we have already said, we can perhaps identify these barriers as the barriers between modern and antique, urban and pastoral, mechanical and natural. These divisions are found not only *within* countries but fixed in the mind of the tourist. They are paralleled on a global scale by the divisions between metropole and periphery, rich and poor – divisions that are real enough in political, historical and economic terms, but the effect of tourism's mythology is to dissuade us from seeing anything in these terms. This is the sense in which Roland Barthes defines bourgeois myth as 'depoliticised speech'. The mythology of tourism does not deny the existence of extremes of poverty and wealth. 'It purifies them, it makes them innocent, it gives them a natural and eternal justification.' Such a state of affairs is *immemorial*, it *goes without saying*; we feel no need to explain it, or to examine its causes, we are reassured. The myth 'abolishes the complexity of human acts, it gives them the simplicity of essences, *it does away with all dialectics*, with any going back beyond what is immediately visible, it organises a world which is *without contradictions* because it is without depth.'[9]

It is only in this way, and at this cost, that we can enjoy 'the best of both worlds'. The world of the Pleasure Periphery must remain outside our real experience literally *out there* and *back there*. Thomas Cook's philanthropic vision has not been fulfilled. In the latter half of the twentieth century it is no longer possible to see mass tourism as an agency for 'the advancement of human progress'; indeed, there is some reason to believe that it actively *impedes* development and progress. On the other hand, it is possible that the apprehension and pessimism of the Romantic will prove to be justified. In our search for the 'change that is as good as a rest', in our eagerness to savour 'local delicacies in perfect safety', we may succeed in making an objective reality of Baudelaire's 'desert of boredom' – a small, monotonous world that everywhere shows us our own image. The search for simplicity ends in technological complexity and accelerated social change; the pursuit of the exotic and diverse ends in uniformity.

Notes and References

Introduction

1. The statistics in this section have come from various issues of *International Tourism Quarterly*.
2. G. Young, *Tourism: Blessing or Blight* (1973), p. 93; Spain – *International Tourism Quarterly*, 3 (1973), p. 1; global figures – Young (1973), pp. 53, 93; USA – Middleton, 'Development and trends in travel to Britain' (1972) and *International Tourism Quarterly*, 3 (1973), p. 11; UK – *Financial Times* (4 May 1973).
3. G. Young (1973), pp. 30–41, summarises a lot of statistical material. See also Dumazedier, *Towards a Society of Leisure* (1967), pp. 129–31; Peaker, 'Holiday spending by the British at home and abroad' (1973).
4. Dumazedier (1967), p. 12, citing an 1869 definition. He also cites Huizinga, *Homo Ludens* (1949), on play (p. 21).

1. The Pre-history of Mass Tourism

1. 'The flesh is sad, alas! and I have read all the books / To escape! To escape far away. . . . I shall depart! Steamer with swaying masts, raise anchor for exotic landscapes!' Translation of 'Sea Breeze' from Stéphane Mallarmé, *Poems* (1965).
2. Brigid Brophy, *Don't Never Forget* (1966).
3. Horace, *Epistle 1*, to Maecenas.
4. Balsdon, *Life and Leisure in Ancient Rome* (1966).
5. Balsdon (1966); McKenna, 'Transport in the Roman Empire'; Marlowe, *The Golden Age of Alexandria* (1971).

2. The Grand Tour

1. R. Duchet, quoted in Sigaux, *History of Tourism* (1966).
2. Knebel, *Soziologische Strukturwandlungen im modernen Tourismus* (1960).

3. Trease, *The Grand Tour* (1967).
4. Byron, *Epistle to Augusta*.
5. Barthes, *Mythologies* (1973).
6. Barthes (1973).
7. R. Gray, *Goethe: A Critical Introduction* (1967).
8. Auden, *Lord Byron: Selected Poems*.
9. Barthes (1973).

3. Thomas Cook: Tourism and the advancement of human progress

1. Thomas Cook, *Letter to the American Press* (1866).
2. Knebel (1960).
3. De Nerval, *Selected Writings* (1973).
4. J. Pudney, *The Thomas Cook Story* (1953).

4. The World, the Flesh and the Devil

1. Bocca, *Bikini Beach* (1963).

5. Simplicity without Innocence

1. R. Graves and A. Hodge, *The Long Weekend* (1971).
2. E. M. Forster, *Where Angels Fear to Tread* (1947).
3. Frye, *The Stubborn Structure* (1970).
4. Ibid.
5. Jock Young, 'The Hippie Solution' (1973).

6. The Pleasure Periphery

1. Wright and Stopford, *Note on the Air Inclusive Tour Holiday Industry* (1972) – on Bermuda.
2. Hewins, *J. Paul Getty: The Richest American* (1961).
3. Peters, *International Tourism* (1969), p. 77, claims that Hawaii was receiving inclusive tours, as well, from cities like New York and Chicago.
4. The bulk of the statistics in this section come from *International Tourism Quarterly*, 'National report No. 2: Spain No. 2 (1971), pp. 8–29.

5. *Playboy* (May 1966).
6. For a brief social history of Torremolinos, see Turner and Ash, 'The Golden Hordes' (1973).
7. *Travel Trade Gazette* (9 February 1973).
8. 1972 figures are from *International Tourism Quarterly*, No. 3 (1973), p. 11.
9. *International Tourism Quarterly*, No. 2 (1972), pp. 52–68, and No. 3 (1973), pp. 10–14.
10. Hiller, 'The development of tourism in the Caribbean region' (1972). Hiller was then director of the CTA.
11. Thomas, *Cuba or the Pursuit of Freedom* (1971), p. 1098. Much of the information on Cuba comes from his massive work on Cuba, but even his description of the tourist industry is sketchy. See also Girth, 'Nixon and the Mafia' (1972), for much illuminating information about the links between Florida-based organised crime and the Caribbean. His attempts to link President Nixon with this process are, to say the least, interesting.
12. Much of this account comes from Barratt, *Grand Bahama* (1972). He was the town planner in charge of Freeport's development. The information on Lansky comes primarily from Girth (1972) who summarises the copious material about organised crime and the Bahamas.
13. *Life* magazine (1 May 1972), p. 38.
14. Read Divine, *Certain Islands* (1972), for the history of the pirates, and for interesting chapters on many of the world's most attractive islands.
15. We would recommend here Peters (1969), Burkart and Medlik, *Tourism: Past, present and future* (1974), and Chapter 5 of George Young (1973).
16. G. Young (1973), p. 78.
17. *Travel Trade Gazette* (10 November 1972).
18. *Financial Times* (16 March 1973); *Travel Trade Gazette* (20 November 1972).
19. *Sunday Mirror* (1 April 1973); *Business Week* (7 September 1974).

7. Dismal Science

1. This is a common, but erroneous, belief. The earliest we have traced this claim is to UN, *Recommendations on International*

Travel (1964), p. 21. However, we should note that official tourism statistics do not include the money spent travelling to and from the destination; if this were included, tourism's place in the world trade league would move up a couple of places.

2. *International Tourism Quarterly*, No. 2 (1973): tables between pp. 38–9; p. 55.

3. *International Tourism Quarterly*, No. 2 (1973), p. 56.

4. *International Tourism Quarterly*, No. 2 (1973), pp. 60–1; IUOTO, *Economic Review of World Tourism* (1972), pp. 25–7.

5. *Editor*, cited in IUOTO, *Monthly Press Summary*, PR/020/73.

6. O'Loughlin, 'Tourism in the tropics' (1970).

7. *The Times* (29 February 1972).

8. Both G. Young (1973), p. 145, and Bryden, *Tourism and Development* (1973), pp. 73–5, make major methodological criticisms of the influential early reports by Zinder, *The Future of Tourism in the Eastern Caribbean* (1969) and Checchi, *The Future of Tourism in the Far East* (1961). See Bryden's book for an extremely elaborate investigation into this issue.

9. World Bank, *World Bank Operations: Sectional programs and policies* (1972), p. 385.

10. O'Loughlin (1970), p. 105.

11. World Bank (1972), p. 385.

12. *The Guardian* (28 March 1973); *West Indies Chronicle* (February 1973).

13. Antigua, see O'Loughlin (1970); Kenya, Bahamas, see *International Tourism Quarterly*, No. 2 (1973), p. 61, and *Travel Trade Gazette International* (5 November 1973).

14. G. Young (1973), p. 151.

15. The growing literature on technology transfer suggests that all host governments should watch this area very closely. See Reuber, *Private Foreign Investment in Development* (1973), pp. 185–207.

16. Bryden (1973), pp. 139–143.

17. Antigua, see G. Young (1973), p. 86; Tanzania, see *African Development* (December 1971); Thailand, see *Business Week* (10 February 1973); Greece, see *Travel Trade Gazette International* (9 March 1973); West Germany, see *Travel Trade Gazette International* (7 September 1973); Spain, see *Lookout* (March 1972); Seychelles, see Alexander, *Holiday in the Seychelles* (1972).

18. G. Young (1973), pp. 116 and 126.
19. Lord Beeching, cited in G. Young (1973), p. 94.
20. Bryden (1973), p. 137; in the limited space of this chapter it has not been possible to do these issues full justice. Chapters 5 and 7 of G. Young (1973) are readable introductions; Chapter 8 of Bryden (1973) presents an economically sophisticated treatment of these issues in relationship to the Caribbean.
21. Greece, see G. Young (1973), p. 141; Belgium, see *Travel Trade Gazette* (10 November 1972); Sicily, see *Travel Trade Gazette International* (25 August 1974); Ivory Coast, see *ibid.* (12 January 1973).
22. World Bank (1972), pp. 397–8.
23. G. Young (1973), p. 138.
24. O'Loughlin (1970), pp. 106–7.
25. *Business Week* (10 March 1973).
26. Rudelius, et al., 'Analyzing state tourism' (1971), p. 250.
27. Cohen, 'Towards a sociology of international tourism' (1972) p. 179.
28. Cosgrove and Jackson, *The Geography of Recreation and Leisure* (1972), p. 59.
29. Medlik and Middleton (1973), pp. 34–6.
30. France, see Peters (1969), p. 163; hotels, see G. Young (1973), p. 75.
31. *International Tourism Quarterly*, No. 1 (1971).

8. The Barbarian and the Tourist

1. Lévi-Strauss, *Tristes Tropiques* (1961).
2. Barthes (1973).
3. *The Sunday Telegraph* (10 September 1972).
4. See Boorstin, *The Image* (1962), for analysis and examples of the pseudo-event. The term is his.
5. *Travel Trade Gazette* (26 January 1973).
6. Forster, 'The sociological consequences of tourism' (1964).
7. See G. Young (1973).
8. Haden-Guest, *Down the Programmed Rabbit Hole* (1972).
9. Milner, 'Samoan Lesson' (1972). These remarks were made about public utility buildings but they seem equally appropriate to hotels. Milner defines neo-colonialism as 'cultural arrogance'.

10. Quoted by Charles Jenks, *The Sunday Times*.
11. *The Sunday Telegraph* (27 August 1970).
12. *The Sunday Telegraph* (3 July 1973).

9. Lotus Eating

1. Brophy (1966).
2. *Ibid.*
3. Divine (1972).
4. Alexander (1972).
5. Geertz, 'Deep play' (1972).
6. *Ibid.*
7. World Bank (1972), p. 389.
8. *New Society* (1 February 1973).
9. *Travel Trade Gazette* (9 February 1973).
10. See Geertz (1972) for a fascinating account of this process.
11. *The Observer* (25 November 1973).
12. Foley in *ibid.*
13. Lind, *Hawaii* (1969), p. 37.
14. Foley in *The Observer* (25 November 1973).
15. Nigel Buxton in *The Sunday Telegraph* (1 February 1972).
16. *Business Week* (19 August 1972).
17. Roslyn Poingant in *The Observer* (1 November 1972).
18. Milner (1972).
19. *The Times* (7 July 1972).
20. *The Times* (14 July 1972).
21. F. de P. Gray, 'On safari' (1973).
22. *Ibid.*

10. Sunbelt Politics

1. Dumazedier (1967), pp. 31–2, has made this point about leisure in general. He wonders if the man of leisure will not become politically supine, 'ungrateful for any past, indifferent to any future'.
2. *Forbes* (1 May 1972).
3. Auden and Kronenberger, *The Faber Book of Aphorisms* (1964), p. 161.

4. Sale, 'The world behind Watergate' (1973).
5. This analysis owes a lot to Runciman's concept of Relative Deprivation.
6. *Travel Trade Gazette* (9 February 1973).
7. Fanon (1967), p. 123.
8. *Daily Star* (7 November 1969).
9. *International Tourism Quarterly*, No. 2 (1973), p. 6.
10. Cohen (1971).

11. Paradise Rejected

1. *Evening Standard* (16 November 1973).
2. *Washington Post* (16 January 1972).
3. *Sunday Telegraph* (19 March 1972).
4. *The Observer* magazine (25 November 1973).
5. *Washington Post* (16 January 1972).
6. *The Sunday Times* colour supplement (17 February 1974).
7. Rivers (1973).
8. Fanon (1963), p. 123.
9. Barthes (1973).
10. *The Guardian* (15 October 1973).
11. *The Guardian* (18 November 1972).
12. *Washington Post* (16 January 1972).

12. A Kind of Solution

1. We have also referred to Berthoud, 'Introduction: dynamics of ownership in the circum-Alpine area' (1972).
2. Greenwood, 'Tourism as an agent of change: a Spanish Basque case' (1972).

13. The Marketing of Moscow

1. Knebel (1960), pp. 32–3.
2. Haden-Guest (1972), p. 8.
3. *Ibid.*, p. 9.
4. *Ibid.*, pp. 125–34.
5. *Ibid.*, p. 140.

6. Hiller (1972).
7. *The Sunday Times* (12 March 1972).
8. *Travel Trade Gazette* (25 May 1973).
9. *Travel Trade Gazette* (9 February 1973).
10. *Travel Trade Gazette* (20 November 1972).
11. *The Guardian* (21 December 1972).
12. *The Guardian* (21 August 1973).
13. G. Young (1973), p. 133.
14. *The Financial Times* (23 March 1973).
15. *Travel Trade Gazette* (26 January 1973).

14. Thirty-Year Vacations : Tourist as Victim

1. Femina, *From Those Wonderful Folks Who Gave You Pearl Harbor* (1972), p. 31.
2. *Far Eastern Economic Review* (5 August 1972); Geertz (1972).
3. *Travel Trade Gazette International* (2 November 1973).
4. Dumazedier (1967), p. 128.
5. *Time* (21 August 1972).
6. *The Observer* (18 February 1968).
7. Roebuck and McNamara, 'Ficheras and free-lancers' (1973), pp. 242–3.
8. Alexander (1972), p. 41.
9. Davenport, *Fodor's Hawaii 1973* (1973), p. 45.
10. Divine (1972), p. 42.
11. Rivers (1972), p. 158.
12. *Daily Mail* (7 April 1973).
13. *The Guardian* (10 March 1973).
14. *The Guardian* (29 August 1970); *The Financial Times* (23 July 1971).
15. *The Financial Times* (22 August 1970).
16. Rivers (1972), p. 158.
17. *Ibid.*, p. 159.
18. *Flight International* (17 May 1973), pp. 737–46. They measured fatalities per million flights.
19. *The Financial Times* (13 August 1973).
20. *The Sunday Times* (22 July 1973).
21. *The Sunday Times* (27 August 1972).
22. For a good history of hijacking, see Arey (1972).

23. *The Sunday Times* (21 January 1973).
24. Adams, 'Why the American tourist abroad is cheated' (1972).
25. *The Guardian* (13 July 1971).
26. *The Guardian* (31 July 1972).

15. Travel without Vision

1. Bauer *et al.*, *American Business and Public Policy* (1963), p. 171; see also Pool *et al.*, 'The influence of foreign travel on political attitudes of American businessmen' (1956).
2. Bryden (1973), pp. 94–5.
3. R. G. Cole, 'Sixteenth-century travel books as a source of European attitudes toward non-white and non-western culture' (1972), p. 67.
4. *Le Matin* (5 August 1972).
5. *Daily Star* (28 July 1972).
6. *Travel Trade Gazette International* (17 January 1972).
7. *Travel Trade Gazette* (11 May 1973).
8. G. Young (1973), p. 54.

16. The Last Romantics

1. 'But the real travellers are those who only depart
   For the sake of departing. . . .
   It is a bitter knowledge one derives from travel!
   The world, monotonous and small, today
   Yesterday, tomorrow, always, shows us our own image. . . .
2. Cohen, 'Nomads from affluence' (1973).
3. Neville, *Playpower* (1970).
4. J. Young, 'The Hippie Solution' (1973).
5. Neville (1970), p. 168.
6. Wilson, *Axel's Castle* (1967).
7. Marcuse, *Eros and Civilisation* (1968).
8. Hemingway, *In our Time*.
9. Fischer, *The Necessity of Art: A Marxist approach* (1957).
10. Wilson (1967).
11. 'The innocent paradise, full of furtive pleasures . . .'
12. 'Ah well, I will invent a cult of the Golden Age,

A social code, empirical and mystic
For Pastoral Peoples, modern and vedic . . .'
13. Hall, 'Hippies: An American moment' (1969).
14. J. Young (1973).
15. Hesse, *Steppenwolf.*
16. Hesse, 'Ode to Hölderlin'.
17. Kelvin Hall in *New Society* (30 November 1972).
18. J. Young (1973).
19. *Ibid.*
20. Su Walton in *New Society* (21 December 1972).
21. 'Nomadic peoples, shepherds, hunters, farmers and even canni-
    bals, *all* may be superior in energy and personal dignity to our
    Western races. The latter will perhaps be destroyed.' Charles
    Baudelaire, 'Mon Coeur mis à nu'.
22. Theobald, *The Challenge of Abundance.*
23. Cohen (1973).

17. The Future

1. Connolly and Perlman, *The Politics of Scarcity* (1975).
2. Bryden (1973), p. 92. The peak month calculations were derived
   from tables in G. Young (1973), pp. 59–60, and a rough seasona-
   lity index from *International Tourism Quarterly*, No. 1 (1973),
   pp. 51–65.
3. *Le Matin* citing an unspecified IUOTO study.
4. Max Frisch, cited by Boorstin (1962), Chapter 3.
5. Sontag, 'Photography' (1963), 'Photo freaks' (1974) and 'Shooting America' (1974).
6. Barnum, quoted by Boorstin (1962).
7. Mexico, see *Business Week* (31 March 1973); Portugal, see
   Travel Trade Gazette International (30 November 1973); France,
   see Bryden (1973), p. 144; Hawaii, see *The Observer* colour
   supplement (25 November 1973).
8. Williams, *The Country and the City* (1973), p. 303.
9. Barthes (1973), p. 143. The italics are the authors'.

Bibliography

ADAMS, JOHN. 'Why the American tourist abroad is cheated: a price-theoretical analysis', *Journal of Political Economy* Vol. 18,1 (Jan./Feb. 1972) 203–7.

ADDISON, WILLIAM. *English Spas* (London: Batsford, 1951).

ALEXANDER, DOUGLAS. *Holiday in the Seychelles* (Cape Town/London/New York: Purnell, 1972).

ALLPORT, GORDON W. *The Nature of Prejudice* (Cambridge, Mass.: Addison-Wesley, 1954).

AMORY, CLEVELAND. *The Last Resorts* (New York: Harper & Bros., 1952).

AREY, JAMES A. *The Sky Pirates* (New York: Scribner's, 1972).

ASH, JOHN. 'To hell with paradise', *New Internationalist* (Feb. 1974) 10–13.

AUDEN, W. H. (Ed.) *Lord Byron: Selected Poems* (Signet Classics).

AUDEN, W. H. and KRONENBERGER, LOUIS. *The Faber Book of Aphorisms* (London: Faber & Faber, 1964).

BALL, D. A. 'Permanent tourism: a new export diversification for less developed countries', *International Development Review*, No. 4 (1971) 20–3.

BALSDON, J. P. V. D. *Life and Leisure in Ancient Rome* (London: Bodley Head, 1966).

BARRATT, P. J. H. *Grand Bahama* (Newton Abbot: David & Charles, 1972).

BARTHES, ROLAND. *Mythologies* (London: Paladin, 1973).

BAUER, RAYMOND A., DE SOLA POOL, ITHIEL, and DEXTER, LEWIS ANTHONY. *American Business and Public Policy: The politics of foreign trade* (New York: Atherton Press, 1963).

BERTHOUD, GERALD. 'Introduction: dynamics of ownership in the circum-Alpine area', *Anthropological Quarterly*. 45,3 (July 1972) 117–24.

BOCCA, GEOFFREY. *Bikini Beach* (London: W. H. Allen, 1963).

BOORSTIN, DANIEL J. *The Image: What happened to the American Dream* (London: Weidenfeld & Nicolson, 1962).

BROPHY, BRIGID. 'The Menace of Nature', in *Don't Never Forget* (London: Cape, 1966).

BROWN, N. O. *Life Against Death* (London: Routledge & Kegan Paul, 1959).

BRYDEN, JOHN. *Tourism and Development: A case study of the Commonwealth Caribbean* (Cambridge: Cambridge University Press, 1973).

BURKART, A. J. and MEDLIK, S. *Tourism: Past, present and future* (London: Heinemann, 1974).

CAVAFY, C. P. *Complete Poems of Cavafy* trans. Rae Dalven (London: Hogarth Press, 1961).

CHECCHI & CO. *The Future of Tourism in the Far East* (1961).

COHEN, ERIK. 'Arab boys and tourist girls in a mixed Jewish–Arab community', *International Journal of Comparative Sociology.* 12,4 (1971) 217–33.

COHEN, ERIK. 'Nomads from affluence: notes on the phenomenon of drifter-tourism', *International Journal of Comparative Sociology.* 14,1–2 (1973) 89–103.

COHEN, ERIK. 'Toward a sociology of international tourism', *Social Research.* 39,1 (1972) 164–82.

COLE, JOHN W. 'Cultural adaptation in the Eastern Alps', *Anthropological Quarterly.* 45,3 (July 1972) 158–76.

COLE, RICHARD G. 'Sixteenth-century travel books as a source of European attitudes toward non-white and non-western culture', *Proceedings of the American Philosophical Society.* 116,1 (Feb. 1972) 59–67.

CONNELLY, PHILIP and PERLMAN, ROBERT. *The Politics of Scarcity: Resource conflicts in international relations* (London: Oxford University Press, 1975).

COSGROVE, ISOBEL and JACKSON, R. *The Geography of Recreation and Leisure* (London: Hutchinson, 1972).

DAVENPORT, WILLIAM W. *Fodor's Hawaii 1973* (London: Hodder & Stoughton, 1973).

DE NERVAL, GÉRARD. *Selected Writings* (London: Panther, 1973).

DIVINE, DAVID. *Certain Islands* (London: Macdonald, 1972).

DOWER, M. 'Fourth wave: the challenge of leisure', *Architect's Journal* (20 Jan. 1965).

DUMAZEDIER, J. *Towards a Society of Leisure* (New York: Free Press, 1967).

FANON, FRANTZ. *The Wretched of the Earth* (New York/London: Grove Press/Penguin, 1963).

FEMINA, JERRY DELLA. *From Those Wonderful Folks Who Gave You Pearl Harbor* (London: Pan, 1972).

FIELD, JAMES A., JNR. 'Transnationalism and the new tribe', *International Organisation*. 25,3 (Summer 1971) 353–72.

FISCHER, ERNST. *The Necessity of Art: A Marxist approach* (Harmondsworth: Penguin, 1957).

FORSTER, J. 'The sociological consequences of tourism', *International Journal of Comparative Sociology*. 5,2 (1964) 217–27.

FRIEDL, JOHN. 'Changing economic emphasis in an Alpine village', *Anthropological Quarterly*. 45,2 (July 1972) 147–57.

FRYE, NORTHROP. *The Stubborn Structure* (London: Methuen, 1970).

GEERTZ, CLIFFORD. 'Deep play: notes on the Balinese cockfight', *Daedalus* (Winter 1972) 1–38.

GERASSI, JOHN. *The Great Fear: The reconquest of Latin America by Latin Americans* (London: Macmillan, 1963).

GIRTH, JEFF. 'Nixon and the Mafia', *Sundance*. 1,3 (November–December 1972) 30–42, 64–8.

GORDON, SHEILA. *Holidays* (London: Batsford, 1972).

GRAVES, CHARLES. *Royal Riviera* (London: Heinemann, 1957).

GRAVES, ROBERT and HODGES, ALAN. *The Long Weekend* (London: Penguin, 1973).

GRAY, FRANCINE DU PLESSIX. 'On safari', *New York Review of Books* (28 June 1973) 25–9.

GRAY, H. PETER. *International Travel – International Trade* (Lexington: Heath Lexington Books, 1970).

GRAY, RONALD DOUGLAS. *Goethe: A Critical Introduction* (London: Cambridge University Press, 1967).

GREENE, GRAHAM. *Our Man in Havana* (London: Heinemann, 1958).

GREENE, GRAHAM. *The Comedians* (London: Penguin, 1967).

GREENWOOD, DAVYDD J. 'Tourism as an agent of change: a Spanish Basque case', *Ethnology*. 11 (January 1972) 80–91.

HADEN-GUEST, ANTHONY. *Down the Programmed Rabbit Hole* (London: Hart-Davis, Macgibbon, 1972).

HALL, STUART. 'Hippies: An American moment', from *Student Power* Ed. Julian Nagel (London: Merlin, 1969).

HERN, A. *The Seaside Holiday* (London: Cresset Press, 1967).

HEWINS, RALPH. *J. Paul Getty: The richest American* (London: Sidgwick & Jackson, 1961).

HIBBERT, CHRISTOPHER. *The Grand Tour* (London: Weidenfeld & Nicolson, 1969).

HILLER, HERBERT L. 'An illustration of regional cooperation and an approach to West Indian integrity through tourism'. Submission to a conference on regional cooperation in tourism among the commonwealth Caribbean countries, 5 December 1972, Barbados.

HILLER, HERBERT L. 'Selling the idea and facts of small hotels in the Caribbean'. 21st annual general meeting of the Caribbean Travel Association, 1972.

HILLER, HERBERT L. 'Some observations, assumptions and hypotheses about Caribbean tourism'. Annual meeting of the St Thomas–St John Chamber of Commerce, 30 November 1972.

HILLER, HERBERT L. 'The development of tourism in the Caribbean region', *Air Travel and Tourism* (August 1972).

HUIZINGA, JOHAN. *Homo Ludens: A study of the play-element in culture* (London: Kegan Paul, 1949).

IUOTO (International Union of Official Travel Organisations). *Economic Review of World Tourism* (Geneva: IUOTO, 1972).

JORDAN, TERRY G. 'The origin and distribution of open-range cattle ranching', *Social Science Quarterly* (June 1972) 105–21.

KNEBEL, H. J. *Soziologische Strukturwandlungen im modernen Tourismus* (Stuttgart: F. Enke Verlag, 1960).

LÉVI-STRAUSS, CLAUDE. *Tristes Tropiques* transl. John Russell (New York: Criterion Books, 1961).

LICKORISH, L. J. and KERSHAW, A. G. *The Travel Trade* (London: Practical Press, 1958).

LIND, ANDREW W. *Hawaii: The last of the magic isles* (London: Oxford University Press, 1969).

LUNDBERG, DONALD. *The Tourist Business* (Chicago: Institution/VFM Books, 1972).

MCCARTHY, MARY. *Birds of America* (London: Penguin, 1972).

MACDONALD, JOHN D. *A Flash of Green* (Greenwich, Conn.: Fawcett, 1962).

MCKENNA, G. H. *Transport in the Roman Empire* (Unpublished PhD Thesis: Manchester University).

MADDEN, MURDAUGH STUART and COHN, SHERMAN L. 'The legal status and problems of the American abroad', *Annals of the American Academy of Political and Social Science*. 368 (1966) 119–31.

MALLARMÉ, STÉPHANE. *Poems* (London: Penguin, 1965).

MARCUSE, HERBERT. *Eros and Civilisation* (London: Sphere, 1968).

MARLOWE, J. *The Golden Age of Alexandria* (London: Gollancz, 1971).

MARNHAM, PATRICK. *The Road to Katmandu* (London: Macmillan, 1971).

MEDLIK, S. and MIDDLETON, V. T. C., 'The tourist product and its marketing implications', *International Tourism Quarterly.* 3 (1973) 28–35.

MICHENER, JAMES A. *The Drifters* (London: Corgi, 1973).

MIDDLETON, VICTOR. 'Development and trends in travel to Britain', *British Tourist Authority, Research Newsletter*, No. 5 (Summer 1972) pp. A–D.

MILNER, G. B. 'Samoan lesson', *New Society* 26 (6 July 1972).

MINISTRY OF OVERSEAS DEVELOPMENT. *Report of the Tripartite Economic Survey of the East Caribbean* (London: HMSO, 1967).

MITCHELL, FRANK. 'The value of tourism in East Africa', *East African Economic Review.* 2,1 (June 1970) 1–21.

MUIR, RICHARD. 'Booming Benidorm', *Geographical Magazine* (June 1973) 45.

NEVILLE, RICHARD. *Playpower* (London: Cape, 1970).

OGILVIE, F. W. *The Tourist Movement: An economic study* (London: P. S. King, 1933).

O'LOUGHLIN, CARLEEN. 'Tourism in the tropics: lessons from the West Indies', *Insight and Opinion.* 5,2 (1970) 105–10.

PEAKER, A. 'Holiday spending by the British at home and abroad', *National Westminster Bank Quarterly Review* (August 1973) 47–55.

PETERS, MICHAEL. *International Tourism: The economics and development of the international tourist trade* (London: Hutchinson, 1969).

POOL, ITHIEL DE SOLA, KELLER, SUZANNE, and BAUER, RAYMOND A. 'The influence of foreign travel on political attitudes of American businessmen', *Public Opinion Quarterly.* 20,1 (Spring 1956) 161–75.

PRITCHETT, V. S. *The Offensive Tourist* (New York: Alfred Knopf, 1964).

PUDNEY, JOHN. *The Thomas Cook Story* (London: Michael Joseph, 1953).

REUBER, GRANT L. *Private Foreign Investment in Development* (London: Oxford University Press, 1973).

RIVERS, PATRICK. *The Restless Generation: A crisis in mobility* (London: Davis-Poynter, 1972).

RIVERS, PATRICK. 'Where is tourism travelling?' Paper given to the Haiti Conference of the Caribbean Travel Association, 1972.

RIVERS, PATRICK. 'Tourist troubles', *New Society* (1 Feb. 1973) 539.

ROBINSON, G. W. S. 'The recreation geography of south Asia', *Geographical Review* (October 1972) 561–72.

ROEBUCK, JULIAN and MCNAMARA, PATRICK. 'Ficheras and freelancers: prostitution in a Mexican border city', *Archives of Sexual Behaviour*. 2,3 (1973) 231–44.

RUDELIUS, WILLIAM, PENNINGTON, ALLAN L., and ROSS, IVAN. 'Analyzing state tourism: a case study of the Midwest', *Journal of Leisure Research*. 3,4 (Fall 1971) 250–60.

RUNCIMAN, W. G. *Relative Deprivation and Social Justice* (London: Penguin, 1972).

SALE, KIRKPATRICK. 'The world behind Watergate', *New York Review of Books* (3 May 1973) 9–16.

SHIVJI, I. G. (Ed.) *Tourism and Socialist Development* (Dar es Salaam: Tanzania Publishing House, 1973).

SIGAUX, G. *History of Tourism* (London: Leisure Arts, 1966).

SONTAG, SUSAN. 'Photography', *New York Review of Books* (18 Nov. 1973) 59–63. Plus subsequent articles 'Photo Freaks' and 'Shooting America' in issues 15 January 1974 (13–19) and 18 April 1974 (17–24).

SUTTON, W. A. 'Travel and understanding: notes on the social structure of touring', *International Journal of Comparative Sociology*. 8,2 (1967) 218–23.

THEOBALD, ROBERT. *The Challenge of Abundance* (New York: Mentor Books).

THOMAS, HUGH. *Cuba or the Pursuit of Freedom* (London: Eyre & Spottiswoode, 1971).

TOMKINS, CALVIN. *Living Well is the Best Revenge* (London: André Deutsch, 1972).

TREASE, GEOFFREY. *The Grand Tour* (London: Heinemann, 1967).

TURNER, E. S. *Taking the Cure* (London: Michael Joseph, 1967).

TURNER, LOUIS. *Multinational Companies and the Third World* (London/New York: Allen Lane/Hill & Wang, 1974/1973).

TURNER, LOUIS and ASH, JOHN. 'The Golden Hordes', *New Society* (19 April 1973) 126–8.

UNITED NATIONS. *Recommendations on International Travel and Tourism* (New York: United Nations, Sales No. 64.I.6., 1964).

VON THUNEN, JOHANN HEINRICH. *Von Thunen's Isolated State* trans. Carla M. Wartenberg (Oxford: Pergamon, 1966).

WATERS, SOMERSET R. 'The American tourist', *Annals of the American Academy of Political and Social Science*. 388 (1966) 109–18.

WILCOX, RICHARD. 'Worldwide view of venereal disease', *British Journal of Venereal Disease* (June 1972).

WILLIAMS, RAYMOND. *The Country and the City* (London: Chatto & Windus, 1973).

WILSON, EDMUND. *Axel's Castle* (London: Fontana, 1967).

WORLD BANK. *World Bank Operations: Sectional programs and policies* (Baltimore: Johns Hopkins Press, 1972).

WRIGHT, DAVID L. and STOPFORD, JOHN. *Note on the Air Inclusive Tour Holiday Industry* (London: London Business School – mimeo, 1972).

YOUNG, GEORGE. *Tourism: Blessing or blight?* (London: Penguin, 1973).

YOUNG, JOCK. 'The Hippie solution: an essay in the politics of leisure', in *Politics and Deviance*, edited by Ian and Laurie Taylor (London: Penguin, 1973).

ZINDER AND ASSOCIATES. *The Future of Tourism in the Eastern Caribbean* (May 1969).

Index